HOW EAST ASIANS VIEW DEMOCRACY

HOW EAST ASIANS
VIEW DEMOCRACY

Edited by Yun-han Chu, Larry Diamond,
Andrew J. Nathan, *and* Doh Chull Shin

COLUMBIA UNIVERSITY PRESS   NEW YORK

COLUMBIA UNIVERSITY PRESS
Publishers Since 1893
New York   Chichester, West Sussex

Library of Congress Cataloging-in-Publication Data
How East Asians view democracy / edited by Yun-han Chu... [et al.].
    p. cm.
  Includes bibliographical references and index.
  ISBN 978-0-231-14534-3 (cloth : alk. paper : alk. paper) —
ISBN 978-0-231-51783-6 (e-book)
  1. Democracy—East Asia—Case studies. 2. Democracy—East Asia—
Public opinion. 3. Public opinion—East Asia. 4. East Asia—Politics
and government—21st century. I. Zhu, Yunhan. II. Title.

JQ1499.A91H69 2008
321.8095—dc22
                         2008007235

∞

Columbia University Press books are printed on permanent and
durable acid-free paper.
This book is printed on paper with recycled content.

Printed in the United States of America
c 10 9 8 7 6 5 4 3 2 1

References to Internet Web sites (URLs) were accurate at the time
of writing. Neither the author nor Columbia University Press is
responsible for URLs that may have expired or changed since the
manuscript was prepared.

Note to Readers
For more published and unpublished research based on the surveys,
please see www.asianbarometer.org.

To Professor Fu Hu,
Pioneer, Inspiration, Example:
His research and teaching over the decades
set the agenda for our work.

CONTENTS

FIGURES AND TABLES

ACKNOWLEDGMENTS

This is the first book to emerge from the Asian Barometer Survey, a comparative survey of democratization and value change across the region. The project was launched in 2000 under the name East Asia Barometer, with a three-year grant from the Ministry of Education of the Republic of China (Taiwan). Headquartered in the Department of Political Science of National Taiwan University (NTU) under the codirectorship of Yun-han Chu and Fu Hu, the East Asia Barometer survey involved more than twenty leading scholars from across the region and the United States.

This path-breaking project was built upon a substantial base of completed scholarly work in a number of East Asian localities. In Taiwan, Fu Hu launched the island's first scientific survey on citizens' political attitudes and political participation in 1975. Since then the NTU research team has conducted over seventeen island-wide face-to-face surveys under his leadership. In Hong Kong, Hsin-chi Kuan and Siu-kai Lau of the Chinese University of Hong Kong launched their first Hong Kong–wide survey research on popular values in the social, economic, political, and cultural realms in 1985. Since then they have implemented a series of extensive surveys on voting, political participation, and social indicators. In the Philippines, the country's first nonpartisan social research institute, the Social Weather Stations, established in 1985 and led by Mahar Mangahas and Linda Luz Guerrero, evolved into the country's leading nonprofit survey organization. In South Korea, Doh Chull Shin launched the Korean Democratization Survey (which later became known as the Korean Democracy Barometer

Survey) in 1988. Since then the project has been continually monitoring a triple transition—political democratization, cultural democratization, and economic liberalization—and its consequences for the quality of life. With the support of the Chiang Ching-Kuo Foundation, National Science Foundation, and Henry Luce Foundation, between 1991 and 1994 the Taiwan and Hong Kong teams collaborated with Tianjian Shi, Andrew J. Nathan, and James Tong in a collaborative project for the comparative study of political culture and political participation in the three culturally Chinese societies—Taiwan, Hong Kong, and mainland China. This collaboration laid the foundation for the region-wide initiative that came into being in late 1999.

All the research teams and advisors who participated in the East Asia Barometer survey contributed to the development of the research agenda, conceptual framework, and survey instrument, in addition to implementing rigorous methodological criteria in their fieldwork. Hearty thanks are due to the following people and their survey teams: Ken'ichi Ikeda, Masaru Kohno, and Yasuo Yamada (Japan); Chong-Min Park, Hyeon-Woo Lee, and Ah-Ran Hwang (South Korea); Damba Ganbat and the team of the Academy of Political Education (Mongolia); Huoyan Shyu, Yu-tzung Chang, Yangchih Fu, Yung-tai Hong, and Alfred Hu (Taiwan); Hsin-Chi Kuan, Wai-man Lam, Timothy Ka-ying Wong, and Ma Ngok (Hong Kong); Tianjian Shi, Chih-yu Shih, Yung-tai Hong, and Yu-tzung Chang (mainland China); Mahar Mangahas and Linda Luz Guerrero (the Philippines); Robert Albritton and Thawilwadee Bureekul (Thailand).

For intellectual advice and guidance we thank Michael Bratton, Russell Dalton, Ronald Inglehart, Marta Lagos, Robert Mattes, William Mishler, and Richard Rose. For indispensable research assistance at various stages of the project we thank Nathan Batto, Tse-hsin Chen, Takashi Ooyama, David Da-hua Yang, and Fu-yi Yang. The talented and dedicated administrator of the project has been Kai-Ping Huang.

Taiwan's Ministry of Education, National Science Council, Academia Sinica, and National Taiwan University provided major funding support. Additional funding for individual surveys came from the Hong Kong Research Grants Council, the Chiang Ching-Kuo Foundation, and the Ministry of Education of the Republic of Korea. The Henry Luce Foundation and the Taiwan Foundation for Democracy financed many of our conferences and field trips. Since 2005, the headquarters of the East Asia Barometer has been cohosted by the Institute of Political Science of the Academia Sinica (IPSAS) and the Institute for the Advanced Studies of Humanities and Social Sciences (ASHSS) of National Taiwan University; the project benefited greatly from the generous support of these two institutions. We express particular thanks to Yu-shan Wu, director of IPSAS, and Tzong-ho Bao, dean of ASHSS. We are also grateful to the following institutions for their support: the Department of Political Science of National Taiwan University; the Hoover Institution and the Center for Democracy, Development, and the Rule of Law at Stanford University; the Department of Political Science and the Weatherhead East Asian Institute at Columbia University; and the Department of Political Science at the University of Missouri.

HOW EAST ASIANS VIEW DEMOCRACY

1

INTRODUCTION

Comparative Perspectives on Democratic Legitimacy in East Asia

Yun-han Chu, Larry Diamond,.
Andrew J. Nathan, and Doh Chull Shin

EAST ASIAN THIRD-WAVE DEMOCRACIES are in distress. From Bangkok to Manila, Taipei, Ulaanbaatar, and Seoul, democratically elected governments have been embroiled in political turmoil. Most East Asian third-wave democracies have suffered inconclusive or disputed electoral outcomes, incessant political strife and partisan gridlock, and recurring political scandals. Frustrated citizens in Manila and Taipei more than once lost confidence in the efficacy of democratic procedures to the point where they tried to bring down incumbent leaders through the extraconstitutional means of "people's power." In Thailand in 2006, a crippling political crisis triggered a military coup.

Democracies in Asia are in trouble because they suffer from fragile foundations of legitimation. Nostalgia for the authoritarian past shadows these new democracies, many of which succeeded seemingly effective progrowth soft-authoritarian regimes. In Thailand, the Philippines, and Taiwan, a significant number of citizens harbor professed reservations about democracy and lingering attachments to authoritarianism. In the eyes of many citizens, the young democracies have yet to prove themselves. Even in Japan, the region's oldest democracy, citizens show low enthusiasm for the political system. If Japanese democracy is secure, it owes more to a lack of support for less democratic alternatives—what we call authoritarian detachment—than to positive feelings about the performance of democracy itself. Such luke-warm support for its own system prevents Japan from promoting the soft power of democracy effectively in the region. Instead, paradoxically, it is the confident regime of authoritarian China whose public seems satisfied.

Many forces affect the emergence and stability of democracy. Among them are elite interactions, economic development, and the international environment. But popular attitudes are a crucial factor. Beliefs and percep-tions about regime legitimacy have long been recognized as critical influ-ences on regime change, with particular bearing on the maintenance or breakdown of democracy (Dahl 1971; Linz 1978). As early as the late 1950s, Lipset presented evidence demonstrating a strong positive relationship be-tween economic development and democracy. He also showed that politi-cal beliefs, attitudes, and values were important intervening variables in this relationship (Lipset 1981). The path-breaking work of Almond and Verba and Inkeles and Smith showed that countries differ significantly in their pat-terns of politically relevant beliefs, values, and attitudes and that within na-tions these elements of political culture are shaped by life experiences, edu-cation, and social class (Almond and Verba 1963; Inkeles 1969; Inkeles and Smith 1974). In 1980, Inkeles and Diamond presented more direct evidence of the relationship between a country's level of economic development and the prevalence among its people of such democratic cultural attributes as tolerance, trust, and efficacy (Inkeles and Diamond 1980). Subsequently, Inglehart showed that life satisfaction, interpersonal trust, and rejection of revolutionary change are highly correlated not only with economic devel-opment but also with stable democracy. He thus argued that "political cul-ture may be a crucial link between economic development and democracy" (Inglehart 1988, 1990; Inglehart and Welzel 2005).

Theorists of the 1960s and early 1970s took political culture seriously as an autonomous factor shaping democracy's evolution, while emphasizing the formative role of elite patterns and decisions in the early phases of sys-tem evolution or transition. Dankwart Rustow was the pioneer of his gen-eration in advancing our understanding of the genesis of democratization and its stages. In his now classic model of democratic transition, Rustow identified four phases. His model begins with one prerequisite condition—national unity—founded on a widely shared allegiance to a given political community. Second, the democratization process is set off by a prolonged, inconclusive struggle over important socio-economic-political cleavages. What follows is a decision phase, which results in the institutionalization of some crucial aspect of democratic procedure. The last phase is habituation, during which elites and citizens both submit to the democratic rules of contestation (Rustow 1970). Progress in the habituation phase—subsumed under the concept of consolidation in most present-day democratization literature—is gauged by the strengthening of the normative commitment of elites and citizens to democratic procedures. Rustow's seminal work, although not immediately influential among his contemporaries, paved the way for the second generation of theory on democratic transition that emerged a quarter century later.

Political and intellectual trends in the social sciences during the 1970s and 1980s challenged or dismissed political culture theory. Most political scientists writing at that time placed emphasis on social structure, elite transactions, and political institutions. For example, in his work on the authoritarian turn of Latin America, Guillermo O'Donnell (1973) pointed to the structural connection between the deepening of late industrialization and what he called bureaucratic authoritarianism, arguing that the experiences of many Latin American countries directly challenged earlier predictions that modernization would entail parallel processes of economic development and democratization. Other analysts of regime transition, such as Juan Linz and Alfred Stepan (1978), challenged the determinacy of these structural models and applied elite-actor models to analyze the uncertainty surrounding democratic breakdowns. Other scholars followed the lead of Samuel Huntington's *Political Order in Changing Societies* (1968) to explore the role of political institutionalization in shaping dynamics in developing countries. This second generation of democratic-transition theory, led by the multivolume work of O'Donnell, Schmitter, and Whitehead and the writings of Adam Przeworski, stressed the analysis of choices and strategic interactions among contending elites within both the authoritarian regime and its democratic opposition (O'Donnell, Schmitter, and Whitehead 1986; Przeworski 1991).

Only in the 1990s with the surge of theoretical and empirical attention to the process of democratic consolidation—and the growth of mass belief in democratic legitimacy as the core element of this process—has political culture recovered a central place in the comparative study of democracy. Among recent scholars writing on democratic transition and consolidation, Linz and Stepan stand out for their appreciation of the importance of mass-level changes in political culture and their efforts to link the elite and mass levels of behavior and belief (Linz and Stepan 1996a; also see Gunther et al. 1995).

To be sure, public attitudes are not the sole determinant of the fragility or robustness of democratic regimes, but work in combination with other factors. One of us has suggested viewing the complex process of democratic consolidation in terms of six domains (Diamond 1999:68–69; also see Linz and Stepan 1996a:5–7). The argument is summarized in table 1.1.[1] Consolidation takes place in two dimensions—normative and behavioral—and at three levels—political elites, organizations (such as parties, movements, and civic organizations), and the mass public. Although it is but one of six domains, the domain of mass norms and beliefs is crucial to consolidation. No democratic system can be secured that does not command long-term deep support at the mass level. Without such support, the regime is vulnerable to decay in the other five domains and then to collapse. It is in this sense that "the core process of consolidation is legitimation" (Diamond 1999:21).

Democracies therefore become consolidated only when both significant elites and an overwhelming proportion of ordinary citizens see democracy, in Linz and Stepan's incisive phrase, as "the only game in town" (1996a:15). The consolidation of democracy requires "broad and deep legitimation, such that all significant political actors, at both the elite and mass levels, believe that the democratic regime is the most right and appropriate for their society, better than any other realistic alternative they can imagine" (Diamond 1999:65).

Thus the state of normative commitment to democracy among the public at large is crucial for evaluating how far the political system has traveled toward democratic consolidation (Chu, Diamond, and Shin 2001). Regardless of how international donors or academic think tanks rate the extent of democracy in a given country, this form of regime will consolidate only if the bulk of the public believe that democracy is the best form of government for their society, and that democracy of an acceptable quality is being supplied. The citizens are the final arbiters of democracy's legitimacy.

In response to the third-wave transitions and associated developments in theorizing about democracy, a new generation of public opinion studies has arisen. Three large-scale regional survey projects came into being during the 1990s: the Latinobarómetro, launched by Marta Lagos; the Afrobarometer, co-led by Michael Bratton and Robert Mattes; and the New Europe Barometer (formerly the New Democracy Barometer), launched by Richard Rose.[2] In the late 1990s, a global network of comparative surveys of attitudes and values toward politics, governance, democracy, and political reform began to take shape. Increasingly, the regional barometers have cooperated with one another to standardize questions and response formats in order to achieve global comparability.[3]

TABLE 1.1 **INDICATORS OF DEMOCRATIC CONSOLIDATION**

	NORMS AND BELIEFS	BEHAVIOR
Elite	Most significant leaders of opinion, culture, business, and social organizations, and all major leaders of government and politically significant parties, believe that democracy is the best form of government, and that the constitutional system merits support.	Leaders of government, state institutions, and significant political parties and interest groups respect each other's right to compete peacefully for power, eschew violence, and obey the laws, the constitution, and mutually accepted norms of political conduct.
Organizations	All politically significant parties, interest groups, and social movements endorse (or at least do not reject) in their charters and statements the legitimacy of democracy, and of the country's specific constitutional rules.	No politically significant party, interest group, movement, or institution seeks to overthrow democracy or employs violence or antidemocratic methods to pursue power or other political goals.
Mass Public	More than 70% of the mass public consistently believes that democracy is preferable to any other form of government, and that the democracy in place in the country is the most suitable form of government for the country. No more than 15% of the public actively prefers an authoritarian form of government.	No antidemocratic movement, party, or organization enjoys a significant mass following, and ordinary citizens do not routinely use violence, fraud, or other illegal or unconstitutional methods to express their political preferences or pursue their political interests.

Source: Adapted from Larry Diamond, *Developing Democracy: Toward Consolidation* (Baltimore: Johns Hopkins University Press, 1999), table 3.1, p. 69.

Parallel to this emerging global network is the World Values Surveys (WVS), developed by Ronald Inglehart of the University of Michigan and other social scientists around the world, which assesses the sociocultural, moral, religious, and political values prevalent in many cultures. The WVS focuses on changing patterns of mass belief systems and examines their economic, political, and social consequences from the perspective of modernization theory (Inglehart and Welzel 2005). During the past decade, the WVS has extended its coverage to a number of emerging democracies in Eastern Europe, Latin America, and Asia.

The East Asia Barometer (EAB), launched in 2000, was this region's first collaborative initiative toward a network of democracy studies based on surveying ordinary citizens.[4] The regional initiative was built on a substantial base of completed scholarly work in a number of East Asian localities (for examples, Chu and Hu 1996; Kuan and Lau 1988; Shin 1999; Shi 1997). Between June 2001 and February 2003, the EAB implemented its first-round comparative survey in eight political systems that have experienced different trajectories of regime evolution or transition: Japan, South Korea, Mongolia, Taiwan, the Philippines, Thailand, Hong Kong, and China.[5] The EAB was the region's first systematic and most careful comparative survey of attitudes and values toward politics, governance, democracy, reform, and citizens' political actions. Table 1.2 and appendices 1 through 4 provide more details about the individual surveys.

In 2005 the East Asia Barometer began a second cycle of surveys. During the second wave, the project expanded to include Indonesia, Vietnam, Cambodia, Malaysia, and Singapore. In addition, the EAB formed a collaboration with a similar project coordinated by the New Delhi–based Centre for the Study of Developing Societies, which aims to assess the state of democracy in five South Asian countries: India, Pakistan, Bangladesh, Sri Lanka, and Nepal. The Asia-wide network of thirteen East Asian and five South Asian countries took the name Asian Barometer Survey of Democracy, Governance, and Development (ABS). The Asian Barometer Survey stands as the largest link in the global survey network for the study of democracy, covering eighteen political systems, more than 48% of the world's population, and the bulk of the population living in the developing world.

TABLE 1.2 **SURVEY SCHEDULES AND SAMPLE SIZES OF FIRST-WAVE EAB**

LOCATION	SURVEY SCHEDULE	VALID CASES
Taiwan	Jun–Jul 2001	1415
Hong Kong	Aug–Oct 2001	811
Thailand	Oct–Nov 2001	1546
Philippines	Mar 2002	1200
China	Mar–Jun 2002	3183
Mongolia	Oct–Nov 2002	1144
Japan	Jan–Feb 2003	1418
South Korea	Feb 2003	1500

Note: Ns (sample size) in some tables and figures vary because of the effects of weighting.

The first-wave eight-regime study reported in this volume permits a series of nested comparisons. The data from South Korea, Mongolia, Taiwan, the Philippines, and Thailand allow us to compare the popular legitimation of democracy across the region's five new democracies. Data collected from Japan, Hong Kong, and China throw light on popular beliefs and attitudes in societies living under different kinds of regimes: the only long-established democracy in the region; a former British colony that has enjoyed the world's highest degree of economic freedom but witnessed its momentum of democratic transition slow after retrocession to Chinese control in 1997; and a one-party authoritarian system wrestling with the political implications of rapid socioeconomic transformation while resisting a fundamental change of political regime. Thanks to the existence of comparable data from other regional barometer surveys, we are also able to compare patterns of mass attitudes toward democracy in our region with those in other regions, as examined in the conclusion to this volume.

As we conduct these multilevel comparisons, we focus on the following questions. What do citizens of East Asia think of the state of their political regimes today? How is the current regime in each society perceived in comparison to the system of the past? To what extent do citizens in each society support or demand democracy as a system of government? Is the embrace of democratic legitimacy backed up by beliefs in fundamental liberal-democratic values? How many people in these societies still consider authoritarian arrangements as desirable alternatives? Do attachment to democracy and detachment from authoritarianism reinforce each other, yielding a coherent attitudinal foundation for sustainable democracy? What are the constituencies for and against democracy? Do they come predominantly from rural or urban areas, higher-income or lower-income strata, more- or less-educated sectors of the population, or younger or older generations?

The EAB survey looks more closely at attitudes toward democracy than other surveys that have been conducted in the region. As a consequence, it is able to treat popular support for democracy as a dynamic phenomenon with multiple dimensions and levels. Support for democracy is dynamic because citizens of new democracies compare the current regime with the previous one and often shift their views of democratic politics as they gain knowledge and experience. It is multidimensional because it involves beliefs about democracy's preferability, efficacy, and suitability and also rejection of nondemocratic alternatives. It is multilevel because most citizens simultaneously evaluate democracy as both an ideal political system and a system in practice. With questionnaire batteries designed to test each of these attitudes toward democracy, the EAB surveys offer the most comprehensive analysis of the depth and dynamics of popular support for democracy among East Asian citizens.

The methodological challenge of establishing comparability in any cross-national survey is formidable. We are comparing national responses to questions that are identically worded but must be translated into a number of different languages and administered in different cultural and institutional contexts. Throughout this project, we struggled with the challenge of achieving a sufficiently high degree of standardization in questionnaire design and administration so that the answers would be comparable across our eight countries. As Gary King and his colleagues have pointed out (2004), standardization by itself does not solve the problem of cross-cultural validity.[6] Our analyses take this issue into consideration by striking a balance between generalizing cross-national comparisons and contextualizing the meaning and significance of our data in their specific cultural and political settings.

This introductory chapter presents some highlights in comparative perspective across the region as well as some comparisons with other regions of the world. The following eight chapters interpret the findings for each political system in historical and institutional context, in order to assess how much progress has made toward consolidating democracy and what challenges it faces to reach that goal. The conclusion reviews the state of democratic consolidation in the region in comparison with regions where the other third-wave democracies are clustered, and probes more deeply into the theoretical relationship of mass public attitudes to regime consolidation.

EAST ASIAN DEMOCRACIES IN THE GLOBAL PERSPECTIVE

East Asia presents five major puzzles to students of democratization. First, the region has partially defied the global movement toward democracy. Since the current wave of democratization began in 1974, more than eighty countries have made significant progress toward democracy by expanding political freedoms and holding competitive elections (Diamond and Morlino 2004). During the same period in East Asia, however, the movement toward democracy has remained limited (Chu 2006). According to Freedom House's standards of political rights and civil liberties, in 2005 only six of the eighteen sovereign states and autonomous territories in the region were ranked "free" (Freedom House 2005). Among the six, only five—the Philippines, South Korea, Taiwan, Thailand, and Mongolia—became democratic in the time span typically referred to as the third wave. (All are included in the East Asia Barometer survey.) The region's remaining authoritarian and semidemocratic regimes seem well positioned for an extended lease of life.

Second, the region presents a perplexing juxtaposition for modernization theory. On the one hand, it delivers two of the most compelling cases, Taiwan and South Korea, in support of the claim that modernization is a coherent process that produces a certain uniformity of economic and political institutions across different regions and cultures (Fukuyama 1998:224–225). On the other hand, the region contains some of the most prominent cases—in particular, Malaysia and Singapore—that challenge such predictions (e.g., Boix and Stokes 2003). Indeed, Singapore is the most economically developed authoritarian state ever. And China appears poised to join the list of developed countries with large middle classes and nondemocratic regimes.

Third, authoritarianism remains a fierce competitor to democracy in East Asia. In the ideological arena, East Asia and the Islamic world remain the two notable exceptions to the general observation that "the democratic ideal has become the 'spirit of the times'" (Linz and Stepan 1996a:74–76). The sustained interest in the "Asian values" debate among elites suggests that liberal democracy has not yet established itself as "the only game in town." While the region's new democratic regimes struggle with governance challenges of disputed elections, partisan gridlock, corruption scandals, slow growth, and weak economic outlooks, the region's resilient authoritarian and semiauthoritarian regimes, such as Singapore, Malaysia, and China, seem capable of coping with complex economies, diverse interests, and globalization.

Fourth, few of the region's former authoritarian regimes were thoroughly discredited before they fell. Many of our respondents remember the old regimes as having delivered social stability and economic growth and as being less susceptible to money politics than the new regimes. During the authoritarian years, most of the countries that later became East Asia's new democracies experienced limited pluralism, including some forms of electoral contestation as well as the existence of some form of opposition. As a result, citizens in many new East Asian democracies did not experience as dramatic an increase in the area of political rights and freedom as did citizens in many other third-wave democracies.

Last but not least, with the shift of the center of regional economic gravity from Japan to China, East Asia is becoming one of the few regions in the world where the characteristics of political systems pose no barrier to trade and investment, and perhaps the only region in the world where newly democratized countries become economically integrated with and even to some extent dependent on nondemocratic countries. The region's emerging multilateral institutions are increasingly orbiting around China. For its socialist neighbors, China is seen as having demonstrated a viable path for growing out of a planned economy and as showing how sequencing political and economic change makes possible a transition from communism to postcommunist authoritarianism. The adaptability and resiliency of China's communist regime has made the region's overall environment much more hospitable for nondemocratic regimes.

The above analyses lend some support to the idea of "Asian exceptionalism" (Fukuyama 1998). The region's unique history of political development carries important implications for the growth of democratic legitimacy in emerging democracies. Citizens in democratic parts of East Asia tend to compare their current regimes with two readily available benchmarks: either with progrowth soft-authoritarian regimes that they experienced in their lifetimes or with prosperous nondemocratic neighbors. Either way, these region-specific benchmarks tend to generate dauntingly high expectations for the performance of democratic systems. Thus, while East Asian democracies are endowed with many favorable socioeconomic conditions (such as sizable middle classes, well-educated populations, and highly internationalized economies) that should promote the growth of democratic legitimacy, the region's culture, political history, and the overall geopolitical configuration put a drag on the development of a robust democratic culture.

POPULAR UNDERSTANDING OF DEMOCRACY

The starting point of our analysis concerns the people's conception of "democracy," a cognitive issue that has been taken for granted by most students of democratization. We do not assume that ordinary citizens share one common understanding of democracy or conceive of democracy in the same way as political scientists do. Before we can make sense out of our data about people's attitudes and orientations toward "democracy," we need to explore how people understand the concept.

Previous survey studies showed that democracy is a contested concept that means different things to different people (Miller, Hesli, and Reisinger 1997; Shin 1999; Bratton, Mattes, and Gyimah-Boadi 2005). In distinguishing democracy from nondemocracy, ordinary citizens often disagree over the specific characteristics of political and social life that they take into account. The particular characteristics or terms they emphasize most are likely to serve as the main standards for their appraisal of how well the current democratic political system performs and their decision to support or not to support it on a continuing basis (Shin et al. 2003).

To explore respondents' understanding of democracy, the EAB survey employed an open-ended question: "What does democracy mean to you?" This question encouraged respondents to think about their own notions of democracy and allowed them to name up to three elements of democracy in their own words. For the sake of presentation, we condense the various verbal answers down to eight substantive categories, a residual category, and a Don't Know/No Answer (DK/NA). The frequency distributions are displayed in table 1.3.

A large majority in every survey was able to offer some sort of meaningful answer. This is probably due to the fact that the rhetoric of democracy has been pervasive in the political life of every East Asian society, including China, for a century. In most countries, the percentage of DK/NA responses ranged from 10% to 25%, which is not high for this cognitively demanding question. There were three notable exceptions. In Japan, China, and Mongolia, the figures were all above 30%. The reasons for this are quite different among the three. In China and Mongolia, the high percentage of DK/NA responses is related to the higher illiteracy rate and the limited exposure to national media in the countryside. In Japan, it reflects the self-effacing character of Japanese people when they are asked to express opinions.[7]

Across East Asia citizens conceive democracy in positive rather than negative terms. Few anywhere associate democracy with chaos, corruption, violence, or inefficiency. Respondents also regard democracy in both procedural and substantive terms. A procedural perspective emphasizes attributes like civil rights, freedom, political institutions, and process. A substantive view emphasizes social justice, good governance, general welfare, and government "by and for the people."

In the majority of societies, citizens most frequently associate democracy with "freedom and liberty." This is comparable to what the Afrobarometer has found among Africans (Bratton, Mattes, and Gyimah-Boodi 2005:68). In the age of globalization there is a floor of shared understanding across cultures. However, the divergence both within each country and across nations remains great. In Thailand, Mongolia, Taiwan, and even China, many people are capable of defining democracy in Schumpe-

TABLE 1.3 MEANING OF DEMOCRACY

(Percent of total sample mentioning this meaning)

CATEGORIES	CHINA	HONG KONG	TAIWAN	KOREA	MONGOLIA	THAILAND	PHILIPPINES	JAPAN
Freedom and liberty	25.4	34.1	29.9	59.5	58.9	35.0	48.2	29.9
Political rights, institutions, and processes	24.3	16.9	18.6	11.0	25.2	27.1	4.9	8.7
Market economy	0.1	0.0	1.4	9.9	7.0	0.0	0.0	2.1
Social equality and justice	4.4	10.7	6.3	34.0	33.4	10.4	4.0	17.5
Good government	2.7	0.5	3.2	4.7	11.6	1.3	1.2	1.8
By and for the people	28.8	5.4	17.1	5.1	7.5	6.6	1.8	5.9
In general positive terms	8.0	6.0	24.1	25.5	20.3	26.4	16.3	18.1
In negative terms	0.0	5.3	5.2	0.5	4.8	0.1	2.1	3.4
Other	7.1	9.3	8.2	7.0	1.7	2.1	3.9	5.9
Don't know/No answer	34.7	21.3	17.0	1.5	31.4	20.2	26.7	35.5
N =	3183	811	1415	1500	1144	1546	1200	1418

Note: Totals exceed 100% because respondents could give up to three meanings.

terian terms (i.e., associating democracy with "political rights, institutions, and processes"), but this type of answer is relatively scarce among Filipino and Japanese respondents.[8] On the other hand, many respondents in Mongolia and South Korea associate democracy with "social equality and justice." A large percentage of the answers offered by our respondents in China do not fit into any of our categories and are placed in the residual category of "Others." As we will explore in chapter 9, because Chinese live under a political regime that promotes its own conception of "socialist democracy," they adhere to distinctive ideas that are not part of the conventional understanding.[9]

It is also interesting to notice what kind of answers are missing. In all eight political systems, few respondents associate democracy with the market economy or private property. This is in contrast with Eastern Europe where many citizens view democratization and market-oriented economic reform as synonymous. Overall, the East Asians we have interviewed seem to conceive democracy as a system based on a mixture of liberal, participatory, and populist elements. Except for the Chinese, their conceptions of democracy are compatible with the views held by citizens on other continents, rather than being Asia-specific.

POLITICAL EFFICACY

Effective democratic governance depends not only on the presence of formal rules and structures but also on effective citizenship. In a democracy, an effective citizen is expected to take an interest in public affairs and to possess a sense of "internal political efficacy"—i.e., "beliefs about one's own competence to understand and to participate effectively in politics" (Niemi, Craig, and Mattei 1991:407). Many studies show that a subjective sense of confidence propels people to join voluntary organizations, contribute to communal projects, and vote in local and national elections (Seligson 1980).

Do East Asian citizens believe that they have the capacity to understand and participate in politics? Some answers can be gleaned from a pair of items that the EAB survey employed to probe respondents' internal efficacy.[10] The first asked if the respondent agreed with the statement, "Sometimes politics and government seem so complicated that a person like me can't really understand what is going on"; the second asked for agreement or disagreement with the statement, "I think I have the ability to participate in politics."

Table 1.4 presents the percentage of respondents with different levels of subjective sense of self-confidence in each regime. The level of internal efficacy among East Asians is relatively low as compared with comparable figures from the established democracies (Pharr and Putnam 2000). In all the regimes we surveyed except Mongolia, fewer than 18% of the respondents felt that they were capable of both understanding and participating in politics. In Hong Kong, China, Taiwan, and Japan more than half of the respondents believed that they had neither the ability to understand nor to participate in politics. Hong Kong registered the lowest level of internal efficacy, with less than 2% believing that they were both cognitively and behaviorally capable and more than 82% believing that they lacked both the ability to understand politics and the capacity to take part.

There are some exceptions to this pattern. Thais were distinguished by an extraordinary level of confidence in their active participatory capacities. Mongolians were also more optimistic about their political efficacy than other East Asians. In both cases, we ran into many more citizens with a sense of political self-confidence than we found in the socioeconomically more advanced societies of Japan, Taiwan, and Hong Kong. This suggests that the perceived characteristics of political institutions are more important in setting the tone of citizens' orientations toward the state than the level of social modernization.

EVALUATION OF REGIME TRANSITION

The eight regimes in the EAB project had followed different trajectories of development at the time of our surveys. We wanted to know how much progress citizens thought each political system had made in the direction of democratic change. The survey asked respondents to compare the level of democracy of the old regime and that of the current regime on a scale of 1 to 10, where 10 represents complete democracy and 1 represents complete dictatorship. The old regime was defined as the last authoritarian regime. For the Japanese it was the prewar military regime, for Koreans the military regime under Chun Doo Hwan before 1987, for residents of Taiwan the one-party hegemony before the lifting of martial law in 1988, for Filipinos the Marcos regime, for Thais the military regime before 1992, and for the Mongolians the communist regime before 1991. For Hong Kong, the old regime was defined as the British colonial administration before the 1997 handover.

TABLE 1.4 CITIZEN EMPOWERMENT

(Percent of respondents)

	CHINA	HONG KONG	TAIWAN	KOREA	MONGOLIA	THAILAND	PHILIPPINES	JAPAN
Neither	63.3	82.5	60.8	38.5	21.0	37.5	12.9	59.2
Can understand politics	9.9	13.9	11.4	36.3	16.9	31.6	2.8	16.9
Can participate in politics	19.1	2.1	17.7	7.3	32.7	17.7	71.7	13.8
Both	7.4	1.5	10.0	17.8	29.4	13.2	12.5	10.2
N =	3184	811	1415	1500	1144	1203	1544	1419

For China, it was defined as the system before the start of Deng Xiaoping's economic reforms in 1979. For the sake of presentation, we grouped the scores that respondents gave the two regimes into four categories: 1–2 stands for very dictatorial, 3–5 somewhat dictatorial, 6–8 somewhat democratic, and 9–10 very democratic. The rating for the old regime is presented in table 1.5 and that for the current regime in table 1.6.

In all societies, more than two-thirds of respondents were capable of rating their past and current regimes with this numerical yardstick. The fact that some of the respondents did not personally experience the old regime did not dissuade them from offering their opinion. The DK/NA responses increase only slightly when the question is shifted from rating the current to the old regime. The highest proportion of DK/NA (32%) is found in China. This is consistent with our earlier finding that a large number of Chinese respondents do not possess a basic awareness of democracy.

Table 1.5 shows that across East Asia a majority of the citizens considered their respective old regimes either somewhat dictatorial or very dictatorial with the exception of Hong Kong, where most citizens believed that the former system was somewhat democratic. In Taiwan, South Korea, Mongolia, and China, majorities viewed the old regime as somewhat dictatorial, while in Japan, Thailand, and the Philippines there were almost as many people who considered the old regime as very dictatorial as those who believed it was only somewhat dictatorial.

In a similar vein, citizens in most East Asian countries considered the current system to be somewhat democratic as opposed to very democratic (see table 1.6). In Japan, only 12.4% of the respondents believed that their current regime was very democratic, significantly lower than what we observed in some new democracies, such as Taiwan, Thailand, and the Philippines. It is clear that when evaluating democratic changes, most East Asian citizens subscribe to a subjective benchmark based on country-specific historical experiences as well as their own expectations. In a maturing democracy like Japan, a demanding electorate has probably raised the bar for evaluating the system as "very democratic." In the emerging democracies, the euphoria surrounding the dawning of a new political era may have prompted some citizens to give the new system high marks.

The same logic helps explain why, in China, the popular tendency to associate democracy with freedom and the dramatic improvement in living conditions brought about by economic reform, induced close to 60% of the citizens to view their system as "somewhat democratic," and almost a quarter to believe that they live under a "very democratic" system. In contrast,

TABLE 1.5 PERCEPTIONS OF THE PAST REGIME

(Percent of valid sample)

RATING	CHINA[a]	HONG KONG	TAIWAN	KOREA	MONGOLIA	THAILAND	PHILIPPINES	JAPAN
Very dictatorial (1–2)	14.0	3.1	15.3	16.5	32.3	48.4	34.0	41.9
Somewhat dictatorial (3–5)	54.2	23.4	60.0	55.0	51.4	42.6	39.2	48.3
Somewhat democratic (6–8)	25.4	63.8	22.1	27.6	14.5	6.2	18.8	9.1
Very democratic (9–10)	6.3	9.7	2.6	0.9	1.8	2.9	8.1	0.7
Total	100.0	100.0	100.0	100.0	100.0	100.0	100.0	100.0
DK/NA	31.6	12.5	17.7	0.2	4.4	14.7	0.6	16.4
N=	3184	811	1415	1500	1144	1544	1203	1419

Notes: Scale runs from 1, "complete dictatorship," to 10, "complete democracy."
DK/NA = Don't know/no answer, percent of total sample.
[a] Past regime defined as before 1979.

TABLE 1.6   PERCEPTIONS OF THE CURRENT REGIME

(Percent of valid sample)

RATING	CHINA	HONG KONG	TAIWAN	KOREA	MONGOLIA	THAILAND	PHILIPPINES	JAPAN
Very dictatorial (1–2)	1.6	6.1	1.5	0.5	0.5	0.7	4.6	0.5
Somewhat dictatorial (3–5)	14.6	53.6	14.9	17.8	17.8	6.4	25.7	14.9
Somewhat democratic (6–8)	59.3	37.4	60.9	79.5	79.5	47.3	47.3	72.2
Very democratic (9–10)	24.5	2.9	22.7	2.3	2.3	45.7	22.5	12.4
Total	100.0	100.0	100.0	100.0	100.0	100.0	100.0	100.0
DK/NA	25.1	12.1	12.9	0.0	2.6	4.9	0.2	9.1
N =	3184	811	1415	1500	1144	1544	1203	1419

Notes: Scale runs from 1, "complete dictatorship," to 10, "complete democracy."
DK/NA = Don't know/no answer, percent of total sample.

Hong Kong people today enjoy substantially more civil liberty and political rights than citizens in the Chinese mainland. But the popular perceptions in the two Chinese societies are reversed. In this sense, the legitimacy crisis the Hong Kong government faces today is more serious than that of the communist regime.

In table 1.7, we have identified six patterns of perceived change based on the difference between the respondent's rankings of the current and past regimes. Across East Asia most citizens recognize that their country has undergone a "moderate change to democracy." A majority do not see the transition as a quantum leap. Most believe that the old regime was somewhat dictatorial rather than highly repressive, and that the new system is only somewhat democratic rather than very democratic. Only in Thailand are almost as many people recognizing "dramatic change to democracy" as those perceiving moderate change.

This means that most East Asian citizens believe there is still ample room for their current system to improve. Hong Kong is again the outlier against this regional upward trend. Forty percent of our Hong Kong respondents felt that there had been backsliding in the level of democracy after the 1997 handover. In contrast, in China 44.5% of our respondents believed that their country had made a moderate change to democracy while 14.1% perceived "dramatic change." This again reflects the fact that Chinese citizens evaluate the trajectory of their political system in light of their country's history of totalitarian rule.

In every country there are significant minorities who hold very different views about the nature of past and current regimes. In Taiwan and South Korea, 19.2% and 25% of our respondents respectively fell into the category of "continuing democracy," meaning that they believed their old regimes were already democratic and perceived no significant difference between the past and the current regime. This attitude is a symptom of authoritarian nostalgia, reflecting the fact that both countries enjoyed miraculous records of economic growth during the authoritarian years.

POPULAR SUPPORT FOR DEMOCRACY

One of the central tasks of the EAB survey was to measure the extent to which East Asian democracies have achieved broad and deep legitimation, such that all significant political actors, at both the elite and mass levels, believe that the democratic regime is the most desirable and suitable for their society and

TABLE 1.7   PERCEIVED CHANGE FROM PAST TO CURRENT REGIME

(Percent of valid sample)

REGIME CHANGE	CHINA	HONG KONG	TAIWAN	KOREA	MONGOLIA	THAILAND	PHILIPPINES	JAPAN
More dictatorial	5.7	40.3	5.2	3.5	4.2	0.8	10.4	0.9
Equally dictatorial	4.4	16.8	7.4	6.2	7.9	1.1	9.1	3.5
Less dictatorial	5.3	2.6	3.7	8.6	15.3	4.4	10.7	11.0
Moderate change to democracy	44.5	6.0	48.4	55.6	51.6	44.0	36.4	64.3
Dramatic change to democracy	14.1	0.9	16.0	1.1	8.9	41.5	16.9	11.7
Continuing democracy	25.9	33.5	19.2	25.0	12.1	8.1	16.5	8.5
Total	100.0	100.0	100.0	100.0	100.0	100.0	100.0	100.0
DK/NA	32.1	15.3	19.7	0.2	5.9	15.4	0.8	18.6
N=	3184	811	1415	1500	1144	1544	1203	1419

Notes: Entries are the percent of respondents perceiving the given kind of change from the past to the current regime. Regime categories are based on the respondent's ranking of the current and the past regime on a scale from 1, "complete dictatorship," to 10, "complete democracy." Scores of 5 and below are degrees of dictatorship and scores of 6 and above are degrees of democracy. Where C = score of current regime and P = score of past regime, "more dictatorial" means C≤5 and P≥6; "equally dictatorial" means C and P are both ≤5 and C-P<2; "less dictatorial" means C and P are both ≤5 but C-P>2; "moderate change to democracy" means P<6 and 6≤C≤8; "dramatic change to democracy" means P≤5 and C≥9; "continuing democracy" means both C and P≥6.

DK/NA = Don't know/no answer, percent of total sample.

better than any other realistic alternative. We employed a set of five questions to estimate the level of support for democracy. These questions address democracy's desirability, suitability, efficacy, preferability, and priority.

We measure the "desirability" dimension by asking respondents to indicate on a 10-point scale how democratic they want their society to be, with 1 being "complete dictatorship" and 10 being "complete democracy." The first row of percentages in table 1.8 shows that in most societies, except China and Taiwan, overwhelming majorities (87% or higher) expressed a desire for democracy by choosing a score of 6 or above. In Taiwan, 72.2% of the electorate expressed their desire for democracy, which is not a very impressive ratio in comparison with South Koreans' near unanimity (95.4%). On this score, Taiwan trails behind not only all East Asian democracies, but also Hong Kong.[11]

Next, respondents were asked to rate the suitability of democracy for their society on a 10-point scale, 10 being perfectly suitable and 1 being completely unsuitable. The second row of table 1.8 indicates that in most East Asian societies at least 75% of respondents considered democracy suitable. The gap between the desirability and suitability measures suggests that there are many East Asians who in principle desire to live in a democracy, but who do not believe that their political system is ready for it. Taiwan again fares unimpressively on this measure, with only 59% of the respondents looking favorably on the suitability issue, trailing behind Hong Kong's 66.8% and China's 67%. It may not be coincidence that a sizable minority is skeptical about the suitability of democracy in all three culturally Chinese societies. This reflects the lingering influence of their common cultural values, which privilege order and harmony.

The EAB survey asked respondents whether they believed that "democracy is capable of solving the problems of our society." East Asians hold divergent views on this efficacy question. When sampled in late 2001, Thais overwhelmingly (89.6%) believed that democracy is capable of addressing their problems, while only 39% of Hong Kong respondents answered the question in the affirmative. In most regimes, a majority expressed their belief in democracy's efficacy for solving their societies' problems. Nevertheless, across all eight of these cases, the proportion of people who registered their doubt about democracy's problem-solving potential was substantially higher than those questioning democracy's desirability or suitability. This suggests many East Asians attached themselves to democracy as an ideal, but not as a viable political system.

The EAB survey also included a widely used item for measuring popular support for democracy as a preferred political system.[12] Respondents were

TABLE 1.8 SUPPORT FOR DEMOCRACY

(Percent of respondents)

DEMOCRACY IS...	CHINA	HONG KONG	TAIWAN	KOREA	MONGOLIA	THAILAND	PHILIPPINES	JAPAN
Desirable for our country now[a]	72.3	87.6	72.2	95.4	91.6	93.0	88.1	87.1
Suitable for our country now[a]	67.0	66.8	59.0	84.2	86.3	88.1	80.2	76.3
Effective in solving the problems of society[b]	60.5	39.0	46.8	71.7	78.4	89.6	60.7	61.4
Preferable to all other kinds of government[c]	53.8	40.3	40.4	49.4	57.1	82.6	63.6	67.2
Equally or more important than economic development[d]	40.3	19.6	23.5	30.1	48.6	51.3	21.8	44.0
None of the above	13.6	7.2	13.0	0.7	1.4	0.5	1.5	5.7
All of the above	17.8	7.0	7.4	15.7	25.9	35.6	6.7	23.4
Mean number of items supported	2.9	2.5	2.4	3.3	3.6	4.0	3.1	3.4

[a] Six or above on a 10-point dictatorship-democracy scale of where the country should or could be now.

[b] Dichotomous variable.

[c] Trichotomous variable recoded into a dichotomous variable.

[d] Five-way variable recoded into dichotomous variable.

asked to choose among three statements: "Democracy is always preferable to any other kind of government," "Under some circumstances, an authoritarian government can be preferable to a democratic one," and "For people like me, it does not matter whether we have a democratic or a nondemocratic regime." It turns out that popular belief in the preferability of democracy is lower in East Asia than in other third-wave democracies. In Spain, Portugal, and Greece, more than three-quarters of the mass public say democracy is always preferable in survey after survey (Dalton 1999:69). In East Asia, only Thailand (82.6%) had reached that threshold. In Japan, only 67.2% of respondents said they always prefer democracy to other forms of government, lower than the average (above 70%) of the twelve sub-Saharan countries surveyed by Afrobarometer around 2000 (Bratton, Mattes, and Gyiman-Boadi 2005:73). In Taiwan and South Korea, more than half of those surveyed either supported a possible authoritarian option or showed indifference to the form of government, pushing the support level down to 40.4% and 49.4% respectively. Outside East Asia, such low levels of support are found only in some struggling Latin American democracies such as Ecuador (Latinobarómetro 2005). This low level of popular support in the two East Asian tigers in spite (or because) of their higher level of socioeconomic development underscores the point we have already made: in societies where people have experienced a variant of soft authoritarianism that was efficacious in delivering social stability and economic development, democracy will have a difficult time winning people's hearts.

To measure the priority of democracy as a societal goal, the EAB survey asked, "If you had to choose between democracy and economic development, which would you say is more important?" Across the region, democracy lost to economic development by a wide margin. Only about one-third of Japanese respondents and slightly over a quarter of Mongolian respondents favored democracy over economic development, while fewer than one-fifth of respondents felt that way in Hong Kong, Taiwan, South Korea, and the Philippines. On this score, East Asians and Latin Americans look very much alike, despite the fact that most East Asian countries have enjoyed an extended period of rapid economic expansion. According to the 2001 Latinobarómetro, 51% of Latin Americans believed that economic development was more important than democracy; 25% thought democracy was more important; and 18% stated that both are equally important.[13] One possible reason for an overwhelming emphasis on the priority of economic development in East Asia is the psychological impact of the region's financial crisis of 1997 and 1998. In the aftermath of this economic shock, most

East Asian citizens no longer took sustained growth for granted. In China and Mongolia, the two countries that were relatively insulated from the financial meltdown, more people were willing to put democracy before economic development than elsewhere.

To summarize the overall level of attachment to democracy, we constructed a 6-point index ranging from 0 to 5 by counting the number of prodemocratic responses on the five items discussed above. On this 6-point index, Japan registered the highest level of overall support with an average of 3.4, while Taiwan and Hong Kong registered the lowest, with 2.4 and 2.5 respectively. Across East Asia, few people gave unqualified support for democracy. Even in Japan, only around 19% of respondents reached the maximum score of 5. This suggests that East Asia's democracies have yet to prove themselves in the eyes of many citizens.

Our findings make clear that normative commitment to democracy consists of many attitudinal dimensions and the strength of citizens' attachment to democracy is context-dependent. The more abstract the context, the stronger the normative commitment; the more concrete the context, the weaker the commitment. The conclusion will develop this point further on the basis of the country chapters: citizens' commitment to democracy responds sensitively to the democratic regime's perceived performance—its ability to deliver political goods. Democracy as an abstract idea was widely embraced. But not so many people endorsed it as the preferred form of government under all circumstances, and few preferred it to economic development.

DETACHMENT FROM AUTHORITARIANISM

While we did not find a full-blown democratic culture in most of our surveys, this does not mean that democracy is in imminent danger. Richard Rose and his colleagues have put forward an argument about the competitive justification of democratic regimes. Referring to Winston Churchill's famous line "Democracy is the worst form of government except all those others that have been tried from time to time," they argued a democracy may survive not because a majority believes in its intrinsic legitimacy, but because there are no viable alternatives (Rose, Mishler, and Haerpfer 1998:31). This suggests that authoritarian detachment is as important as democratic commitment in sustaining the legitimacy of a democratic regime.

TABLE 1.9 AUTHORITARIAN DETACHMENT

(Percent of respondents)

ITEM	CHINA	HONG KONG	TAIWAN	KOREA	MONGOLIA	THAILAND	PHILIPPINES	JAPAN
Reject "strong leader"[a]	—	71.5	68.3	84.4	59.2	76.6	69.4	79.1
Reject "military rule"	61.4	85.7	81.6	89.8	85.8	81.2	62.7	94.4
Reject "no opposition party"[a]	—	62.4	70.3	86.7	72.4	61.3	69.6	66.7
Reject "experts decide everything"	74.5	73.5	71.3	82.3	66.1	77.7	76.8	85.4
Reject all authoritarian options	57.9[b]	49.4	50.0	65.1	37.0	43.1	35.6	54.3
Reject no authoritarian options	22.0[b]	9.0	10.1	0.9	4.0	5.5	4.1	3.6
All of the above	17.8	7.0	7.4	15.7	25.9	35.6	6.7	23.4
Mean number of items rejected (0 to 4)	2.7[c]	2.9	2.9	3.4	2.8	3.0	2.8	3.3

Notes: [a] Not asked in China.
[b] Based on two questions.
[c] Mean score multiplied by two for comparison with other countries.

To assess East Asian citizens' antipathy for authoritarian alternatives, the EAB survey asked respondents whether they would favor the return to any of the four likely authoritarian alternatives: strongman rule, military rule, single-party rule, and technocratic rule.[14] As shown in table 1.9, a greater than two-thirds majority in each political system except Mongolia rejected the idea of replacing democracy with strongman rule. Military rule was rejected even more vigorously, at levels over 80%, everywhere except the Philippines and China. Rejection of single-party rule was less emphatic but still exceeded two-thirds in five regimes. Finally, at least two-thirds in every political system rejected the option of technocratic rule.

The survey identified pockets of authoritarian inclination among the populace in most countries. In Mongolia, the yearning for a return to strongman rule remains, with only 59.2% of respondents opposing it. In the Philippines, fewer than two-thirds of the people rejected military rule. Also, there was substantial support for single-party rule in Hong Kong and Thailand.

When all four measures are considered jointly, the aggregate picture raises some cause for concern. In only three political systems—Korea, Japan, and Taiwan—did more than half the people reject all four alternatives. In Mongolia and the Philippines, fewer than 40% of respondents

TABLE 1.10 CORRELATION BETWEEN AUTHORITARIAN DETACHMENT AND SUPPORT FOR DEMOCRACY

	PEARSON CORRELATION	N
Hong Kong	0.424**	811
Japan	0.414**	1419
Korea	0.205**	1500
Mongolia	0.305**	1144
Philippines	0.044	1203
Taiwan	0.400**	1415
Thailand	0.152**	1546
China	N/A	N/A
East Asia	0.321**	12219

*<.05; ** <.01

Note: The support for democracy scale was the sum of agreement to: democracy is desirable for our country now, suitable for our country now, effective in solving the problems of society, preferable to all other kinds of government, equally as or more important than economic development. Authoritarian detachment was measured by the number of authoritarian options rejected of a possible four.

rejected all four authoritarian options. This makes the average (48%) of our seven survey sites (excluding China) identical to that reported by the New Europe Barometer covering nine Central and Eastern European new democracies (Rose, Mishler, and Haerpfer 1998:116). This is not reassuring, considering that most postcommunist countries suffered much more severe and protracted economic turmoil during the transition to democracy than East Asian countries did, even taking into account the Asian financial crisis of 1997 and 1998.

To estimate overall levels of detachment from authoritarianism, we combined the responses into a 5-point scale, with 4 meaning complete detachment and 0 meaning full attachment to authoritarian rule. The last row of table 1.9 reports the mean score in each regime. The cross-country variation is not as great as that in support for democracy. However, the two summary measures do tend to move in tandem. A correlation analysis at the level of the individual respondent (reported in table 1.10) shows that growth in citizens' positive orientations toward democracy goes along in most countries with a decline in their attachment to authoritarianism. Only in the Philippines were these two indexes not correlated at a statistically significant level. However, the correlation is below .50 everywhere. As Doh Chull Shin and Chong-Min Park explicate the issue in the Korean context, for citizens with little experience in democratic politics, both democracy and dictatorship may fail to provide satisfying solutions to their problems. Confronting such uncertainty, some citizens embrace democratic and authoritarian political propensities concurrently (Shin and Park 2003).

LOCATING THE PRINCIPLED BELIEVERS IN DEMOCRACY

A principled believer in democracy not only expresses favorable orientations toward democracy but also rejects authoritarian alternatives. The greater the number of principled believers living under a new democracy, the more robust its foundation of legitimation. In table 1.11, we define a "very strong supporter of democracy" as someone who rejects all four authoritarian alternatives and embraces at least four of the five items measuring support for democracy. At the other end of the spectrum, we identify a "strong opponent to democracy" as someone who agrees with two or more of the authoritarian alternatives and embraces two or fewer of the five prodemocracy items. In between, as shown in the notes to the table, we define several intermediate levels of belief in democracy.

TABLE 1.11 PATTERNS OF COMMITMENT TO DEMOCRACY

(Percent of valid sample)

TYPE	CHINA[a]	TAIWAN	KOREA	MONGOLIA	THAILAND	PHILIPPINES	JAPAN	HONG KONG
Very strong supporters	15.89	16.65	33.87	27.07	16.48	35.72	36.52	N/A
Strong supporters	21.05	20.58	24.73	24.81	22.60	28.65	23.27	N/A
Less dictatorial	5.3	2.6	3.7	8.6	15.3	4.4	10.7	11.0
Moderate supporters	20.41	16.46	21.20	16.65	22.57	15.98	15.74	34.46
Skeptical supporters	17.14	18.96	11.40	11.94	16.21	5.18	11.60	13.24
Weak opponents	10.07	8.80	4.33	4.98	7.81	2.30	4.93	11.43
Strong opponents	11.45	14.67	1.00	3.31	2.65	1.38	4.98	22.45
Mixed	3.99	3.88	3.47	11.24	11.68	10.78	2.95	18.42
Total	100.00	100.00	100.00	100.00	100.00	100.00	100.00	100.00

Notes: Types of supporters and opponents are defined as follows: a very strong supporter has an authoritarian detachment (AD) score of 4 and a democratic support (DS) score of 4 or 5 out of a possible 5; for a strong supporter AD = 4 and DS = 3, or AD = 3 and DS = 4 or 5; for a moderate supporter AD = 3 and DS = 3, or AD = 2 and DS = 4 or 5; for a skeptical supporter AD = 4 and DS = 0 or 1, or AD = 3 and DS = 1 or 2; for a weak opponent AD = 3 and DS = 0, or AD = 2 and DS = 1 or 2, or AD = 1 and DS = 2; for a strong opponent AD = 2 and DS = 0, or AD = 1 and DS = 0 or 1, or AD = 0 and DS = 0, 1, or 2; for mixed, AD = 0 or 1 and DS = 3, 4, or 5.

[a] Only two authoritarian detachment questions were asked in China.

As table 1.11 shows, across East Asia only Japan, South Korea, and Thailand enjoy a robust foundation of legitimation in which principled believers in democracy (i.e., the sum of "very strong supporters," "strong supporters," and "moderate supporters") constitute majorities, respectively 75.5%, 79.8%, and 80.4%. In Taiwan, the three categories of clear supporters constitute barely above 55% of the sample, suggesting a weak cultural foundation for democracy. The comparable figures for Mongolia and the Philippines (68.5% and 61.7%) are in the middle. While Japan has the largest percentage of very strong supporters (36.5%) Taiwan has the largest share of "strong opponents" (14.7%).

In Thailand, Mongolia, and the Philippines, there also exist a large number of disoriented and confused citizens, as defined by the "mixed" category, whose inconsistent political orientations burden their democracies with a fragile foundation of legitimation. Subsequent to our surveys, all three countries experienced various forms of political instability, as described in this volume's country chapters. In Hong Kong the prodemocracy parties faced dwindling support for their agenda of sweeping reform.

Our analysis suggests that except for South Korea and Japan, most East Asian democracies do not enjoy deep legitimation. The young democracies have yet to prove themselves in the eyes of many citizens.

PERCEPTIONS OF THE FUTURE

Even when citizens harbor reservations about democracy, a new democracy may generate such a sense of momentum that it makes other forms of government increasingly unthinkable. To assess whether this bandwagon effect might be occurring in East Asia, we asked respondents where they expected their political system to be in five years on the 10-point scale from complete dictatorship to complete democracy. Based on the difference between respondents' ratings of the future and current regimes, we identified seven patterns of predicted change. These are reported in table 1.12. Across the region citizens are both optimistic and realistic about their countries' futures. On average people anticipate incremental change in the direction of further democratization. Citizens in China, Mongolia, and South Korea are bit more optimistic about the future, with a change in mean score greater than 1.2, while citizens in other societies are more modest. Even in Hong Kong, where many people perceived a political setback after the handover to Chinese rule, citizens are hopeful. The smallest difference in mean scores is found in Japan, where

TABLE 1.12 EXPECTED CHANGE FROM CURRENT TO FUTURE REGIME

(Percent of valid sample)

REGIME CHANGE	CHINA	HONG KONG	TAIWAN	KOREA	MONGOLIA	THAILAND	PHILIPPINES	JAPAN
Authoritarian persistence	2.8	39.3	7.5	2.9	4.4	1.5	9.8	10.6
Authoritarian reversal	0.5	2.4	5.0	2.1	3.5	2.3	7.9	4.4
Limited democratic transition	7.6	19.3	5.3	13.8	16.2	2.6	11.4	4.4
Advanced democratic transition	5.4	2.2	1.9	1.6	6.3	2.4	9.1	0.2
Struggling democracy	17.1	29.7	38.6	54.3	32.2	20.9	29.9	57.7
Developing democracy	43.2	5.4	23.3	23.3	28.2	28.4	17.7	12.3
Consolidating democracy	23.3	1.7	18.5	1.9	9.3	41.9	14.1	10.4
Total	100.0	100.0	100.0	100.0	100.0	100.0	100.0	100.0
DK/NA[a]	29.8	30.0	32.6	0.3	9.0	8.9	2.0	20.3

Notes: Entries are the percent of respondents expecting the given kind of change from the current to the future regime, defined as the regime five years from now. Categories are based on the respondent's ranking of the current and the future regime or a scale from 1, "complete dictatorship," to 10, "complete democracy." Scores of 5 and below are degrees of dictatorship and scores of 6 and above are degrees of democracy. Where C = score of current regime and F = score of future regime, "authoritarian persistence" means C ≤ 5 and F ≤ 5; "authoritarian reversal" means C ≥ 6 and P ≤ 5; "limited democratic transition" means that C ≤ 5 and 6 ≤ F ≤ 8; "advanced democratic transition" means C ≤ 5 and F ≥ 9; "struggling democracy" means C ≥ 6 and 6 ≤ F ≤ 8 and 6 ≤ C ≤ 8 and F ≥ 9; "developing democracy" means 6 ≤ C ≤ 8 and F ≥ 9; "consolidating democracy" means C ≥ 9 and F ≥ 9.

[a] Percent of total sample who answered don't know or no answer to one or both of the regime type questions.

democracy has been established for more than half a century and the momentum for democratic deepening is exhausted. In the three culturally Chinese societies (China, Hong Kong, and Taiwan), significant proportions of respondents did not make any prediction. Since the fate of the three systems is intimately entangled, uncertainty about the future has become contagious.

Citizens in Taiwan, South Korea, and Japan, who gave on average a modest rating of their current regimes, tend to predict a pattern of "struggling democracy," i.e., being stuck in a state of "somewhat democratic," with a rating of between 6 and 8, for the foreseeable future.[15] However, in all five emerging democracies, there are significant numbers of citizens who are more optimistic, predicting a pattern of "developing democracy", i.e., moving up from the state of "somewhat democratic" to "very democratic," reaching a score of 9 or 10. Thailand stood out among the five emerging democracies in having the largest number of citizens who gave a rating of 9 or 10 for their current system and believed (erroneously, as it turned out) that the country would stay at this highly democratic level in five years. In stark contrast, in South Korea only 1.9% of our respondents were equally positive about their country's democracy in either the present or the future. In China, respondents were positive and optimistic, with more than two-fifths predicting a pattern of "developing democracy" for their country.

COMMITMENT TO RULE OF LAW

To probe further popular commitment to democratic legitimacy, it is helpful to employ questionnaire items that avoid the "d" word. In our time the concept of "democracy" has been embraced by virtually all politicians everywhere, including leaders of regimes that are actually nondemocratic. Items carrying the "d" word run the danger of eliciting what survey researchers call socially desirable answers from respondents. The EAB survey therefore included a series of questions that probed respondents' value orientations toward some of the fundamental organizing principles of liberal democracy, including political equality, rule of law, and government accountability. Responses to this battery reveal both the substance and depth of respondents' commitment to democratic values.

To save space, we present only selected items that measure popular commitment to rule of law. We focus on this dimension because according to many works on Asian political culture (Pye 1995; Tu 1998; Ling and Shih 1998; Fukuyama 1995), among all the principles of liberal democracy, Asian people have the greatest difficulty embracing rule of law. This concept contradicts traditional Asian notions of good governance as rule by benevolent and virtuous leaders. To probe how strongly our Asian respondents believe in rule of law, we used four items that tap different dimensions of the concept. All four statements were worded in the negative direction to avoid acquiescence and impose a higher psychological threshold.

Table 1.13 provides the summary statistics of answers to this four-item battery. Across East Asia, a majority of citizens embraced the idea that government should not disregard the law even if the country is facing a difficult situation. More than two-thirds of the citizens of Hong Kong, Japan, South Korea, and the Philippines and close to three-fifths of the electorate in Taiwan and Mongolia expressed opposition to the arbitrary use of power by the government. However, only half of the citizens in Thailand supported this idea. Next, more than three-quarters of the citizens in Hong Kong, Taiwan, and South Korea, and a majority in the Philippines and Japan believed that a leader should follow procedures. However, only 41% of respondents in Mongolia and 43% in Thailand endorsed this idea. Overall, a robust popular commitment to the liberal constitutionalism of a *Rechtstaat*, a law-bound state (O'Donnell 1996, 1998), is found in only a few East Asian societies, notably South Korea and Hong Kong. It is not widespread or firm elsewhere in the region. The new democracies remain vulnerable to the encroachment of populist leaders.

The remaining two items in our battery are designed to address the notion of separation of power, an important pillar of rule of law. On the issue of judicial independence, we found majority support for the idea that "judges should decide cases independently" in only four of our eight societies: Mongolia, South Korea, Japan, and Taiwan. In the Philippines and Thailand, the level of support for the principle of judicial independence is quite low, and it is still lower in China, where the guiding authority of the Communist Party is enshrined in the constitution.

The notion of legislative supervision over the executive has even fewer subscribers across the region. Only in two countries, South Korea and Japan, did popular endorsement of the idea that "the legislature should check the executive" exceed 50%, though by a thin margin. In Taiwan, the level of popular acceptance was quite low at 24.7%. There are two possible reasons why the notion of horizontal accountability has not gained widespread acceptance in East Asia. First, most East Asian societies inherited a tradition of a strong state, which finds its embodiment in the executive. Next, in most East Asian countries citizens had bad experiences with political gridlock

TABLE 1.13 COMMITMENT TO RULE OF LAW

(Percent of respondents)

ITEM	CHINA	HONG KONG	TAIWAN	KOREA	MONGOLIA	THAILAND	PHILIPPINES	JAPAN
Government should not disregard law[a]	–	69.8	58.3	76.7	59.6	49.2	70.2	72.0
Leader should follow procedure	47.3	76.3	75.5	77.1	41.0	43.4	61.5	54.4
Judges should decide cases independently	30.9	46.7	53.7	69.0	71.0	40.1	38.7	62.2
Legislature should check executive	34.2	46.8	24.7	53.8	38.8	47.4	49.9	50.2
None of the above	36.1[b]	9.4	11.1	2.7	7.2	15.2	7.6	9.9
All of the above	13.0[b]	23.4	15.0	30.1	11.8	8.2	15.0	24.9
Mean level of commitment to rule of law (0–4 scale)[c]	1.5[d]	2.4	2.1	2.8	2.1	1.8	2.2	2.4

[a] Not asked in China.

[b] Based on three questions.

[c] Each item is scored as follows: strongly support or somewhat support the rule of law principle = 1; strongly oppose, somewhat oppose, don't know, or no answer = 0.

[d] Mean score multiplied by 4/3 for comparison with other countries.

between the executive and the legislature. In Taiwan, partisan gridlock virtually paralyzed the DPP government after the 2000 power rotation, as described in chapter 4.

In the last row of table 1.13, we report the mean scores of commitment to rule of law. We combine the responses to the four questions into a 5-point scale from 0 to 4. South Korea registers the highest average score, followed by Japan and Hong Kong. Among the five emerging democracies, Thailand registers the lowest at 1.8. Overall across East Asia, popular commitment to rule of law is weak. The specter of what Fareed Zakaria calls "illiberal democracy" (1997) hangs over most East Asian societies.

This analysis reinforces our earlier finding that liberal democracy enjoys a more robust cultural foundation in South Korea and Japan than elsewhere in the region. Where we found a low level of popular commitment to the rule of law, such as in Thailand and Mongolia, we also found the largest number of opponents to democracy and people holding mixed and incoherent views. In Thailand, strong support for the "d" word (table 1.8) coexists with a weak commitment to liberal democratic values. Thus, a seemingly strong popular base of democratic legitimacy is actually quite shallow because it is not backed by a belief system revolving around democratic values. This helps explain why Thai citizens tend to give their democracy a very generous rating while South Koreans are so critical. In countries where there are many stalwart believers in core democratic values the political system is expected to meet a higher benchmark, while in countries where democracy is a favored label but democratic values are not widely held, even a pseudodemocracy might get wide popular acceptance. On this score South Korea and Thailand represents two polar examples. Japan and Hong Kong come closer to the case of South Korea while Mongolia, Taiwan, and the Philippines are somewhere in between.

In a similar vein, when we evaluate the observed level of support for democracy in China, we have to take into account the fact that respondents in China exhibit the lowest overall level of commitment to rule of law. This suggests that when Chinese citizens express positive orientations toward democracy as an idea, or give generous ratings of the level of democracy of their political system, most are using frames of reference that deviate substantially from what political scientists define as "liberal democracy." To understand what our respondents are saying, we must interpret their responses in context. This is what the country chapters of this volume are meant to accomplish.

ORGANIZATION OF THE BOOK

The chapters that follow are unified by their common research questions, scope, and structure. This uniformity makes possible systematic cross-national comparison. But our interpretations of the findings are contextualized, with each chapter applying expert knowledge of a given society's trajectory of regime transition, evolving institutional setting, changing social and economic conditions, and national political dynamics.

Each chapter is organized into seven sections. The first discusses the historical and institutional characteristics of a given political system's democratization (or regime evolution) to provide background for the interpretation of the EAB survey findings. The second section examines how the citizens in the society understand the meaning of democracy. The third section deals with their perceptions of how far their society has traveled on the road of democratization, based on their ratings of past and current regimes. It also examines how citizens evaluate the characteristics and performance of the current regime in comparison with the old one with respect to major indicators of good governance. The fourth section assesses quality of democracy by exploring respondents' perceptions of their roles as citizens, the responsiveness of government, the extent of corruption, and the trustworthiness of political and government institutions. The fifth section deals with the depth of popular attachment to democracy and the degree of popular detachment from authoritarianism. The sixth section discusses the popular perception of the regime's political future. The seventh and final section of each chapter highlights the key findings of the EAB survey and explores their implications from the perspective of democratic development.

The first five chapters introduce the cluster of new democracies that form the core focus of the EAB survey. We find support for democracy in Korea to be firm but not unconditional. In the Philippines, democracy is deeply challenged by deficiencies in the performance of the new regime. In Taiwan, support for democracy is heavily qualified and has been falling as political turmoil has increased, yet attraction to authoritarian alternatives is not widespread. In Thailand, our survey revealed that the mass public, especially in rural areas, strongly supported democracy, but elite and urban support was weaker, helping to explain the political system's vulnerability to the coup that took place in September 2006. Mongolia is unique among our cases in having made its democratic transition from a communist base, undergoing at once a political transition to democracy and an economic transition to the market economy. With their political system struggling to meet public expectations, Mongolians showed comparatively low levels of both democratic support and authoritarian detachment. In all, none of the new democracies in East Asia appear firmly consolidated at the level of mass public opinion, and all are vulnerable to public disaffection.

The next three chapters place the new democracies in comparative perspective by focusing on regimes of other types in the same region. Japan is a democracy that has to be considered consolidated in view of the long survival of its democratic institutions, where we nonetheless find that citizens' attitudes are no less critical and sometimes more so than those in their newly democratized neighbors. Hong Kong is a partial democracy where citizens are thoroughly committed to democratic values and chafe under restrictions imposed by Beijing. China is by our definition an authoritarian system, whose citizens nonetheless see much of what goes on as consistent with their own understanding of democracy. These comparative perspectives help reinforce the point that citizens understand democracy differently in different countries (and in various ways within any given country) and that they see both democracy and their own regimes multidimensionally in terms of policy performance and compatibility with various kinds of values.

The conclusion tries to make sense of the patterns we observe within East Asia and to compare these to patterns in other regions of the world where global barometer surveys provide comparable data. Even though mass attitudes toward democracy are only one of a number of domains in which democratic consolidation occurs or fails to occur, we argue that it is a crucial domain with implications for all the rest. Consolidation is a long-term and zigzag process, responding both to public evaluations of regime performance and to the evolution of political values. We find that for now East Asian citizens are favorably disposed to democracy but not irreversibly committed to it. Democracy is a valued idea, but as an actual regime it has to earn support through performance. So far the new democracies in the region have not attained this standard. It would be wrong to view their futures with complacency.

NOTES

1. This argument applies to the consolidation of democratic regimes only. The dynamics of authoritarian regime consolidation are different, involving, among other things, more mobilization from the top down and more intense, deliberate, and openly ideological indoctrination.
2. These regional barometers may be accessed, respectively, at www.latinobarometro .org, www.afrobarometer.org, and (for the New Europe Barometer) www.abdn

.ac.uk/cspp/nebo.shtml. In addition to these three regional barometers and our own East Asia Barometer, a new South Asia Barometer conducted its first wave of surveys in 2004, and an Arab Barometer is now under construction. For information on the South Asia Barometer, see www.asianbarometer.org/ newenglish/introduction/. The new Arab Barometer is being coordinated from the University of Michigan and Princeton University with participation from a number of research centers in the Arab world.

3. The survey instrument that has generated the data analyzed in this book drew a number of items from the other barometers. These survey projects have, in turn, borrowed from one another, from the longer-established Eurobarometer, and from some unique questions developed in longitudinal studies of public opinion in Taiwan and Korea. For information about the interaction among the regional barometers in the emerging global barometer of democracy, see www.globalbarometer.net.

4. Besides the Asian Barometer Survey, the region is home to another cross-national public opinion research project which monitors and compares how urban residents live their lives, and what they value and worry about most for themselves their countries. This project is called the AsiaBarometer, and has been conducted since 2002 under the coordination of Professor Takashi Inoguchi and his colleagues at the University of Tokyo (Inoguchi et al. 2005).

5. To avoid overusing terms like "political system," we sometimes refer to the eight survey locales collectively as "countries." In matter of fact, Hong Kong is a Special Autonomous Region of China, and China claims sovereignty over Taiwan. Throughout the volume, China refers to mainland China exclusive of Hong Kong. As noted in appendix 1, the China sample also excludes Tibet owing to its sparse population and difficult terrain.

6. We did not adopt the approach proposed by King and his colleagues known as "anchoring vignettes" for two reasons: it is too costly in terms of questionnaire space and it is difficult to design anchoring vignettes that are themselves free of cultural and institutional embeddedness.

7. Please refer to chapters on Japan and China for elaboration of these points.

8. Typical answers that fall into this category include election, check-and-balance, majority rule, and party competition. Please refer to appendix 3 for details.

9. Please refer to the chapter on China for further analysis.

10. The items the EAB applied to measure internal efficacy are two of the original seven items proposed by Richard Niemi, Stephen Craig, and Franco Mattei (1991).

11. The ratio of "don't know" and "no answer" varies considerably across the seven cases. A higher ratio of DK/NA, which is counted as a non-positive response, brings down the percentage of positive responses shown in our tables. However, this technical reason only partially explains why Taiwan and Hong Kong trail behind other Asian countries on virtually every prodemocracy indicator.

12. This item has been employed by Latinobarómetro, Afrobarometer, and World Values Survey. See Klingemann (1999).

13. See http://www.Latinobarometro.org/uploads/media/2001_01.pdf. Since then more and more Latin Americans (51% in 2003) have agreed with the statement, "I would not mind a nondemocratic government in power if it could solve the economic problems."

14. Because the questions on "strongman" and "single-party rule" were not suitable in the context of China, they were dropped from the China survey.

15. Please refer to the note at the bottom of table 1.11 for the operational definition of each category.

2

THE MASS PUBLIC AND DEMOCRATIC POLITICS IN SOUTH KOREA

Exploring the Subjective World of Democratization in Flux

Doh Chull Shin and Chong-Min Park

SOUTH KOREA (KOREA HEREAFTER) has achieved a reputation in the contemporary world as one of the four "tiger economies" of East Asia. Like Hong Kong, Singapore, and Taiwan, Korea transformed one of the world's poorest societies into an economic powerhouse within a single generation (Kim and Hong 1997). With a current population of forty-six million, Korea produces a gross domestic product (GDP) larger than that of many Western European states. It is also one of the six new democracies (together with the Czech Republic, Hungary, Mexico, Poland, and the Slovak Republic) admitted in the past decade to the Organization for Economic Cooperation and Development (OECD) and is only the second Asian country to join the exclusive organization.

In the late 1980s, Korea began its political transformation from military rule to representative democracy. It was the only new democracy that not only transferred power peacefully to an opposition party but also fully transformed an entrenched system of crony capitalism into a competitive and transparent market economy. In the scholarly community, Korea is acknowledged as one of the most vigorous and analytically interesting third-wave democracies (Chu, Diamond, and Shin 2001; Diamond and Kim 2000; Diamond and Shin, 2000; S. Kim 2003). In policy circles, it is increasingly regarded as a model of market liberalization and political democratization (Bremner and Moon 2002; Haggard 2000; Lemco 2002).

Yet many researchers wonder how much progress Korea has really made in democratizing its authoritarian institutions and transforming the cultural values that for nearly three decades supported military dictatorships. What challenges does the country face in furthering democratization? What are its prospects for consolidating democratic rule? In the literature on the current wave of global democratization, there is a general agreement that nascent democratic rule becomes consolidated when ordinary citizens not only embrace its principles, but also endorse its practices. Therefore, this chapter examines the reactions of ordinary Koreans to democracy both in principle and in action, using data from the East Asia Barometer (EAB) survey. This survey was conducted during February 2003, when Koreans were commemorating the fifteenth anniversary of the democratic Sixth Republic and reflecting on the election of the republic's fourth president, Roh Moo Hyun. (For information about the fieldwork undertaken for the EAB survey, see appendix 1 and Garam Research Institute 2003.)

1. HISTORICAL AND INSTITUTIONAL BACKGROUND

Between 1987 and 1988, Korea accomplished a peaceful transition from a military dictatorship, led by former general Chun Doo Hwan, to a democratic state that allowed the people to choose their president and other political leaders through free and competitive elections. For nearly three decades prior to the advent of democracy (1961–1987), the military ruled the country as a developmental dictatorship with a rationale of promoting economic development and strengthening national security against the communist North (Moon 1994). Institutionally, the developmental state provided the president with unlimited powers, both executive and legislative in character, to the extent that he was authorized to dissolve the National Assembly and take emergency measures whenever he deemed such actions necessary (Lim 1998, 2002).

By invoking the National Security and Anti-Communist laws, the military dictatorship, led successively by former generals Park Chung Hee and Chun Doo Hwan, suppressed political opposition and curtailed freedoms of expression and association (Moon and Kim 1996). Through security agencies such as the Korean Central Intelligence Agency and the National Security Command, the military regime placed the news media under strict censorship and kept labor unions and educational institutions under constant surveillance. The regime controlled opposition parties and other nonpolitical civic and business organizations through a variety of tactics including co-optation and intimidation. By suppressing political opposition and deterring individual citizens and civic groups from taking part in the political process, the military dictatorships insulated policymaking from the pressures of social and political groups (Jang 2000). In predemocratic Korea, technocrats and bureaucrats, rather than elected representatives, played the key roles in policymaking.

The constitution of the democratic Sixth Republic, ratified in a national referendum held in October 1987, laid out a new institutional foundation for representative democracy. It provided for direct election of the president with a single, nonrenewable five-year term. The president's powers to rule by emergency decree and dissolve parliament were abolished, while the National Assembly's power to oversee the executive branch was strengthened. The constitution also established the Constitutional Court and created measures to guarantee the independence of the judiciary, broaden civil liberties, protect political parties from being disbanded by arbitrary government action, and mandate the political neutrality of the military.

The second and third presidents of the Sixth Republic—both opposition figures in the era of military rule—implemented reforms to consolidate the spirit of the new constitution. Kim Young Sam (1993–1998) established civilian supremacy over the military and enacted legislation to mandate the use of real names in financial transactions in order to dismantle the structure of political corruption (Kil 2001:58–63). Kim Dae Jung (1998–2003) expanded the social security system to include health insurance, unemployment insurance, pension insurance, and workers' accident compensation insurance (Shin and Lee 2003). With these reforms, the Korean political system moved beyond electoral democracy toward democratic consolidation.

The institutionalization of free and fair elections for both local and central governments expanded the involvement of the mass public. Farmers, factory workers, women, the elderly, the urban poor, businesspeople, and journalists formed new public interest groups as competing forces against the existing government-controlled representational institutions. By the turn of the century, more than six thousand nongovernmental organizations were known to be operating in Korea (Lim 2000; see also S. Kim 2000). As a result, civic associations and interest groups became formidable players in the policy process, which had previously been dominated by bureaucrats and technocrats.

At the time of our survey in 2003, Korean democracy met the criteria for procedural democracy or polyarchy as specified by Dahl (1971) and many other scholars (Przeworski et al. 2000; Rose, Mishler, and Haerpfer 1998; Schmitter and Karl 1991). It was a regime characterized by free and fair elections, universal adult suffrage, multiparty competition, civil liberties, and a free press. In the words of Kim Byung-Kook (2000:52), "Electoral politics has become the only possible game in town for resolving political conflicts." Between 1993 and 2003, Korea received an average score of 2.0 in Freedom House's ratings of political rights and civil liberties, placing it within the ranks of the world's liberal democracies.

Nonetheless, serious problems remain. Institutionally, Korea is a presidential system with multiple minority parties and staggered presidential and parliamentary elections (Kim and Lijphart 1997). But while the president may serve for only a single term of five years, lawmakers can serve multiple terms of four years each. Due to a complex system combining single member legislative districts and proportional representation, in all four parliamentary elections held after the democratic regime change in 1988 up to the time of our survey, more than three parties participated (Jaung 2000). Because these parties have regionally concentrated bases of support in the country, no president's party ever obtained a majority in the legislature. The system often produced immobilizing institutional deadlocks, especially during periods of divided government (Mo 1998, 2001; Park 2002).

To overcome this problem, even democratically elected presidents sometimes resorted to extralegal tactics. They merged political parties and intimidated opposition lawmakers. Their use of prosecutorial power for political purposes undermined the political neutrality of the judicial system. Their frequent use of tax audits for political purposes threatened freedom of expression, as evidenced in the Kim Dae Jung's government investigations of newspapers critical of its policy toward North Korea. Frequent refusal by the executive branch to be accountable to the National Assembly opened the door to what O'Donnell (1994) termed "delegative democracy" and undermined the institutional foundations of representative democracy (Park 1998).

What did the Korean people think of the state of Korean democracy? How was the democratic regime perceived in comparison to the authoritarian system of the past? In the following sections, we examine the Korean people's evaluations of democratic rule as they experienced it on a daily basis for the first fifteen years.

2. CONCEPTIONS OF DEMOCRACY

To explore the Korean people's divergent interpretations of democracy, the EAB survey asked an open-ended question, "What does democracy mean to you?" The responses are displayed in chapter 1, table 1.3.

Virtually all Koreans surveyed (98%) were able to identify at least one constituent or element of democracy. More than one-half (57%) could identify a second element of democracy, and nearly one-fifth (19%) were able to supply a third one.

Nearly 60% associated democracy with freedom and liberty, while 11% defined it in terms of political rights, institutions, and processes. These choices reflect the strength of constitutional values among the Korean public in reaction to decades of political repression under military rule. Another one-third (34%) associated democracy with social justice and equality, and 10% mentioned market economy. The percentages for these two categories were the highest of any country in the survey, perhaps reflecting the history of crony capitalism and labor repressive policies that characterized the generals' regime. Other positive views were mentioned by 26% of respondents. Only half a percent of Korean respondents characterized democracy in negative terms, one of the lowest levels of dissatisfaction in any of the eight countries surveyed. Of the eight East Asian societies surveyed, moreover, Korea registers the highest level of attachment to the rule of law (see chapter 1, table 1.13). Because it associates democracy primarily with freedom and the rule of law, Korea appears to have established a more solid foundation for liberal democracy than other nations in the region.

3. EVALUATING THE TRANSITION

Given their favorable conceptions of democracy, it is interesting to ask to what extent Koreans perceived their current regime as democratic, and how wide a gap they saw between it and the former system of military rule.

3.1. PERCEPTIONS OF REGIME CHANGE

The EAB survey asked respondents to rate their current and past regimes on a 10-point scale, with 1 indicating "complete dictatorship" and 10 indicating "complete democracy." Table 2.1 reports the scores and mean ratings for the two regimes.

Koreans clearly view the current regime as a democracy and the past regime as a dictatorship. More than four out of five Koreans (82%) rated the current regime as democratic by placing it at 6 or above on the scale. The mean rating of 6.5, however, was only the fifth highest among the eight countries surveyed, suggesting that even after a decade of democratic rule by two long-time leaders of the democracy movement, the country remained a partial or limited democracy in the eyes of its people.

The past regime scored 4.4 on the 10-point scale, with nearly three-quarters of the Korean public (71%) rating the past regime as undemocratic by placing it at 5 or below. However, four of the eight EAB surveys rated the old regime as more dictatorial than the Korean survey did, suggesting a nuanced view of the old regime by Koreans today. Indeed, among Koreans who rated the old regime as undemocratic, the less critical were more numerous than the more critical. While 55% rated the military regime as "somewhat dictatorial," fewer than 17% perceived it as "very dictatorial."[1]

In an analysis not shown here, we found that both those who perceived the past regime to be democratic and those who perceived the current regime to be democratic were significantly more numerous among older people (sixty and older), the less educated (elementary education and less), and residents of rural communities. That is, these three segments of the

TABLE 2.1 **PERCEPTIONS OF PAST AND CURRENT REGIMES: KOREA**

(Percent of total sample)

REGIME TYPES	PAST REGIME	CURRENT REGIME
Very dictatorial (1–2)	16.5	0.5
Somewhat dictatorial (3–5)	54.9	17.8
Somewhat democratic (6–8)	27.5	79.5
Very democratic (9–10)	0.9	2.3
DK/NA	0.2	0.0
Total	100.0	100.0
Mean on a 10-point scale	4.4	6.5

Notes: Regime types are based on the respondent's ranking of the regime on a scale from 1, "complete dictatorship," to 10, "complete democracy." Scores of 5 and below are degrees of dictatorship and scores of 6 and above are degrees of democracy.

N = 1500.

DK/NA = Don't know/no answer.

Korean population were the least likely to perceive any fundamental difference between the old and the new regimes. As the members of Korean society most limited in their cognitive capacity to differentiate democratic and nondemocratic regimes, these groups appear the least likely to demand or support further democratic reform. On the other hand, respondents who understood democracy in liberal terms (the first two categories in table 1.3, chapter 1) tended to set more demanding standards for both the old and the new regimes than those with nonliberal views of democracy; they were most likely to see both the past and the current regimes as nondemocratic.

Figure 2.1 displays the distribution of regime change scores. While the majority of Koreans perceived some movement toward greater democracy, the extent of the changes was seen to be limited. About 7% of our respondents perceived no democratic progress, and another 7% reported retrogression toward authoritarianism. Even among those who perceived progress, the majority found it to be limited. A substantial majority of three-fifths (60%) perceived an advance of 3 points or less on the scale, while only 24% perceived substantial improvements of 4 to 9 points.

Based on the ratings of the past and current regimes, we identified six patterns of perceived regime change (see chapter 1, table 1.7). Of these six views, moderate change to democracy was the most popular with 56%. This was followed by continuing democracy (25%), with the other categories all below 10%. Overall, 57% of the Korean people perceived a transition to

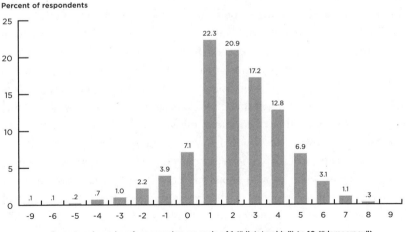

Percent of respondents

Current regime minus former regime on scale of 1 ("dictatorship") to 10 ("democracy")

FIGURE 2.1   **Perceived Regime Change: Korea**

democracy in the aftermath of military rule. Yet even after more than a decade, more than two-fifths (43%) had yet to perceive a regime change. This figure is comparable to what was observed in three of the four other East Asian new democracies, including Mongolia (40%), the Philippines (47%), and Taiwan (36%). Yet it is clearly indicative of a low level of sophistication concerning democratic politics among the Korean people.

3.2. COMPARING PAST AND PRESENT REGIMES

To evaluate the perceived consequences of democratic transition, the EAB survey asked respondents to rate each of nine major government performance domains on a 5-point scale, ranging from "much better than before" (+2) to "much worse than before" (-2).

The mean and PDI scores reported in table 2.2 show that democratic transition has brought about positive consequences in all five areas of democratic performance. Sixty-three percent more respondents saw positive than negative change in the area of freedom of speech, despite government efforts to curb the news media during the last two years of the Kim Dae Jung government (Kirk 2001; Larkin 2001). And nearly half saw improvement in freedom of association. Such public perceptions are consistent with changes in Korea's ratings in the Freedom House index of political rights and civil liberties. On the 7-point index of political freedom (1 being the highest), Korea scored an average of 4.6 during the authoritarian period between 1980 and 1987, but between 1988 and 2002 averaged 2.0, close to the scores for the consolidated democracies in the West. On the index of civil liberties, Korea experienced a similar improvement, moving from 5.4 to 2.4 between the two periods (Freedom House 2003). According to these ratings, democratic rule has indeed transformed Korea into a free country. In the area of judicial independence, however, Koreans were reluctant to rate the current regime as significantly better than the old regime, suggesting that at the time of our survey the public was fed up with the government's frequent use of prosecutorial power against opposition parties.

In the second category of government performance, more Koreans perceived negative change, with economic equality being the most adversely affected. Popular perceptions of changes in the economy appear consistent with objective indicators. According to the Korea National Statistical Office (2003), Korea's annual GDP growth rate averaged 8.7% during the authoritarian Chun Doo Hwan period (1980–1988), but began to decline after the inauguration of the Sixth Republic. By the time of the Kim Dae Jung government

TABLE 2.2 PERCEIVED PERFORMANCE OF CURRENT AND PAST REGIMES: KOREA

	MEAN[a]	SD[a]	NEGATIVE CHANGE[b]	POSITIVE CHANGE[b]	NO CHANGE[b]	PDI[c]	VALID %[d]
Democratic performance							
Freedom of speech	0.74	0.76	6.4	69.7	23.9	63.3	100.0
Freedom of association	0.52	0.76	7.9	53.1	39.0	45.2	99.9
Equal treatment	0.24	0.78	14.8	37.7	47.5	22.9	100.0
Popular influence	0.22	0.82	17.1	37.6	45.3	20.5	100.0
Independent judiciary	0.04	0.78	20.9	26.3	52.8	5.4	99.9
Average	0.35	0.78	13.4	44.9	41.7	31.5	100.0
Policy performance							
Anticorruption	-0.15	0.88	33.4	23.2	43.4	-10.2	100.0
Law and order	-0.17	0.89	36.5	24.7	38.8	-11.7	99.9
Economic development	-0.25	0.97	42.5	24.9	32.6	-17.7	100.0
Economic equality	-0.70	0.86	60.9	8.1	30.9	-52.8	100.0
Average	-0.32	0.90	43.3	20.2	36.4	-23.1	100.0

Notes: N = 1500.

Past regime is defined as pre-1987.

[a] Scale ranges from -2 (much worse) to +2 (much better).
[b] Percent of valid sample.
[c] PDI (percentage difference index) = percent seeing positive change minus percent seeing negative change.
[d] Percent of sample giving a valid answer to this question.

(1998–2003) it averaged only 4.6%, a slowdown of nearly 50% from the Chun period. On economic inequality, the Korea National Statistical Office (2001) reported that the country's Gini coefficient, which averaged 0.309 during the Chun period, fell below 0.3 under the first two democratic governments, but rose sharply to an average of 0.317 during the Kim Dae Jung presidency, when the country suffered its worst economic crisis since the Korean War.

More respondents saw negative change in corruption in the aftermath of the regime change. This reflects the exposure of a number of spectacular political corruption cases in the period before we conducted our survey, including one that resulted in the imprisonment of President Kim Dae Jung's two sons and other close associates.

In short, democratization has been a mixed blessing in the eyes of the Korean people, delivering gains in democratic performance but mostly losses in policy performance.

A demographic analysis (not shown here) showed that respondents with lower levels of education and income were in general more supportive of both the democratic performance of the new regime and its policy performance. These segments of the population are apparently less demanding of the new democratic order than are more sophisticated respondents who understand that democracy differs from its alternatives in providing political freedom and pluralistic competition. Thus, Koreans with lower levels of education and income are more likely to express satisfaction with whatever benefits government supplies.

We also found that the perceived impact of regime change on performance was correlated with views of the transition. Those who perceived a democratic regime change were the most positive about its consequences, while those who said they perceived an authoritarian reversal were also the most critical of the new regime's policy performance. On average, the former rated 3.4 domains of public life positively and 2.3 negatively. The latter, however, rated only 2.0 domains positively and 3.5 negatively. Evidently, many Koreans do not judge democratic regime change solely in terms of what happened to their constitution and political institutions. Instead, they judge it in terms of the substantive policy outcomes from which they have personally benefited.

4. APPRAISING DEMOCRATIC INSTITUTIONS

The effective functioning of democratic institutions depends on the capacity of ordinary people to participate in the political process and on popular confidence in the country's political leaders and various institutions of state and society. In this section, we examine public evaluations of three aspects of the democratic system—political efficacy, political corruption, and trust in institutions. We will ask how satisfied Korean citizens are with the performance of the system as a whole and the extent to which they would endorse it as the best system for the nation.

4.1. POLITICAL EFFICACY

To estimate Korean citizens' perceived participatory capacity, we selected a pair of items from the EAB survey that tapped into these issues. Respondents were asked about their self-perceived ability to understand the complexities of politics and government and their perceived capacity to participate in politics (see chapter 1, table 1.4).

Roughly two-fifths (39%) of respondents believed they could neither understand nor participate in politics, while only 18% felt capable of both. These numbers confirm earlier findings suggesting a low level of cognitive and behavioral participatory capacity on the part of the Korean public (Shin, Park, and Jang 2002). Yet by comparative Asian standards, Koreans' level of citizen empowerment was relatively high. Korea had one of the lowest percentages of those self-rated as fully incapable and the second-highest percentage after Mongolia of those rating themselves as fully capable.

To assess further the perceived efficacy of popular participation, we asked respondents how strongly they agreed or disagreed with the following statements: "The nation is run by a powerful few and ordinary citizens cannot do much about it," and "People like me don't have any influence over what the government does." On both statements, 41% of our respondents disagreed. Taken together, about one-quarter (24%) disagreed with both statements, while 43% agreed with both. This pattern of prevalent skepticism about the impact of one's own participation on the political system is widespread among the countries included in the EAB project.

4.2. PERCEPTIONS OF CORRUPTION

The EAB survey asked a pair of questions concerning perceived corruption among local and national government officials (see table 2.3). In a region where corruption is a widespread concern, Korea was no exception, with

TABLE 2.3 PERCEPTION OF POLITICAL CORRUPTION AT NATIONAL AND LOCAL LEVELS: KOREA

(Percent of respondents)

	NATIONAL GOVERNMENT					
LOCAL GOVERNMENT	Hardly anyone is involved	Not a lot of officials are involved	Most officials are corrupt	Almost everyone is corrupt	DK/NA	Total
Hardly anyone is involved	0.1	0.6	0.3	-	-	1.1
Not a lot of officials are involved	0.3	**42.8**	**10.4**	1.1	0.1	**54.7**
Most officials are corrupt	-	8.0	**24.4**	3.3	-	**35.7**
Almost everyone is corrupt	0.1	0.8	2.5	5.0	-	8.4
Don't know / No answer	-	0.1	0.1	-	-	0.1
Total	0.5	**52.3**	**37.7**	9.5	0.1	**100.0**

Notes: N = 1500.

Blank cell means no cases.

Percentages above 10 are in boldface.

47% of respondents believing that most or almost all national level officials are corrupt and 44% believing that most or all local level officials are corrupt. Yet the Korean sample was markedly bimodal: while more than half (56%) the respondents expressed concern over corruption, a large minority of 44% stated that "hardly any" or "not a lot" of officials at either the national or local level were involved in corruption. This was, after Thailand and Hong Kong, the highest percentage in the upper left quadrant of the table among all the countries we surveyed.

4.3. INSTITUTIONAL TRUST

The EAB survey asked respondents how much trust they had in eleven state and societal institutions. The results are presented in figure 2.2. Only about 15% of Koreans expressed trust in political parties and the parliament, which constitute two key institutions of democratic politics. Although just under half (44%) of our respondents considered local governments trustworthy, only a quarter (27%) expressed trust in the national government. These results imply that the key political institutions of Korean democracy are not performing properly in the eyes of the public.

By comparison, the Korean public expressed more faith in the administrative organs of the state, especially those that were once the coercive apparatus

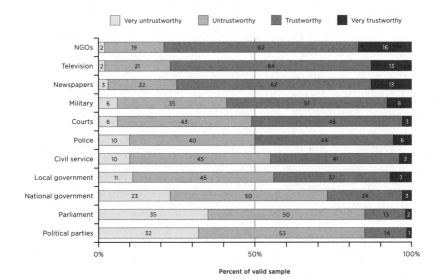

FIGURE 2.2   **Trust in Institutions: Korea**

of authoritarian rule. More than half (51%) of respondents expressed trust in the judiciary, nearly three-fifths (59%) trusted the military, and 50% trusted the police. Relatively speaking, the technocratic elite fared less well. Only 44% expressed trust in the civil service, despite the fact that it was arguably the most successful pillar of the old developmental authoritarian state.

These findings suggest that significant progress has been made in depoliticizing the security forces and the administrative agencies in the aftermath of the democratic transition. It is notable that the major institutions of the former bureaucratic-authoritarian regime have managed to attain greater levels of public trust, while those of the democratic regime have failed to do so. More notable is the fact that the Korean people were significantly less trusting of state institutions than societal institutions, including the news media and nongovernmental organizations (NGOs). All of these societal institutions enjoyed the trust of over three-quarters of the public.

Compared to other third-wave democracies in the survey, however, the overall level of trust is low, suggesting that these institutions have failed to deliver what Korean citizens expected from their new democracy.

4.4. OVERALL ASSESSMENT OF REGIME QUALITY

For a comprehensive assessment of the regime's overall quality, we selected another pair of items from the EAB survey. The first item asked, "On the whole, how satisfied or dissatisfied are you with the way democracy works in our country?" Contrary to what one may expect given the low levels of institutional trust and perceived political efficacy, more than three-fifths (62%) of the Korean people expressed at least some degree of satisfaction with the current regime at the time of the survey, which was conducted just before the inauguration of a new president in February 2003. However, when asked to evaluate the statement "Whatever its faults may be, our form of government is still the best for us," only 36% agreed. Even among those who expressed satisfaction with the performance of Korean democracy, only a minority (43%) endorsed it as the best for their nation.

Finally, in our assessment of the regime's overall perceived quality, we considered responses to the items above along with the perceived character of the current regime and identified four different views of the current system. Respondents viewed the regime as: (1) an undemocratic system; (2) an ill-performing democracy; (3) a well-performing democracy; and (4) a best-performing democracy.[2] We found that fewer than one-quarter (23%) of respondents placed the current system in the most positive category. Thirty-one percent considered the current system a well-performing democracy, 27% an ill-performing democracy, and 19% did not consider the current regime democratic at all. Overall, those who held a positive view of the current system outnumbered those who held a negative view by eight percentage points (54% versus 46%).

Older and less-educated Koreans were significantly more positive in their assessments of the current regime than their younger and college-educated counterparts. Residents of rural communities were also far more positive than those in large metropolitan areas. In all groups, however, at least half of the respondents recognized the current regime as a democracy and expressed at least some degree of satisfaction with the way it performs. This finding suggests that democracy as a system of government has succeeded in appealing to all segments of the Korean population.

5. COMMITMENT TO DEMOCRACY

To citizens with little experience and limited knowledge of democratic politics, both democracy and dictatorship may fail to provide satisfying solutions to the many problems facing society. Confronting this reality, citizens with little democratic experience, more often than not, embrace both democratic and authoritarian propensities concurrently (Rose, Mishler, and Haerpfer 1998; Shin 1999; Shin and Shyu 1997). Growth in their prodemocratic orientations does not necessarily bring about a corresponding decline in their authoritarian attachment. Popular support for democracy in emerging democracies, therefore, depends on a majority that not only accepts democracy, but also rejects its alternatives.

5.1. ATTACHMENT TO DEMOCRATIC POLITICS

A set of five questions allowed us to estimate the level of support for democracy in principle as well as in practice. These questions address democracy's desirability, suitability, preference, efficacy, and priority (see chapter 1, table 1.8). An overwhelming majority (95%) of Korean respondents expressed a desire for democracy by choosing a score of 6 or above on the 10-point scale of how democratic they wanted the current political regime to be, with nearly one-third (31%) selecting either 9 or 10 on the scale.

Levels of attachment to democracy-in-practice were somewhat lower than its desirability. A large majority (84%) considered democracy suitable for Korea by selecting a score of 6 or above on a 10-point scale. However, only a quarter (25%) of respondents selected 9 or 10. Obviously there are many Koreans who, in principle, desire to live in a democracy, but do not believe that it is highly suitable for their country given its current situation.

The EAB survey asked respondents whether or not they believed that "democracy is capable of solving the problems of our society." A substantial majority (72%) replied affirmatively, but the number is lower than for suitability. In other words, even among those Koreans who see democracy as a suitable political system, many question its viability. When responses affirming democratic suitability and efficacy are considered together, less than two-thirds (62%) answered both questions in the affirmative. When we compare this figure with that of democratic desirability (95%), we see that one-third of the Korean electorate remains attached merely to the idea of democracy as an ideal without embracing it as a viable political system.

Close to one-half (49%) of the Korean public agreed with the statement, "Democracy is always preferable to any other kind of government." One-third (33%) was willing to entertain an authoritarian alternative while just under one-fifth (17%) expressed no particular regime preference. Fewer than one out of five (19%) said that democracy is somewhat more (15%) or far more (4%) important than economic development. Roughly one-tenth (11%) considered economic and democratic development to be of equal importance. On the other hand, a large majority (70%) replied that economic development is far more (30%) or somewhat more (40%) important. Even among those who said that democracy is preferable to all other kinds of government, a majority (62%) considered it to be less important than economic development.

These findings make clear that in Korea as elsewhere in East Asia, attachment to democracy depends on context. When viewed as a political ideal, almost everyone embraces it. Most of them also consider it a suitable and effective political system. Yet when asked to consider alternatives, only about half endorse democracy as the preferred model of governance, and relatively few prefer it to economic development. The higher the level of abstraction, the greater the level of attachment; the broader the basis of comparison, the lower the level of attachment.

An overall measure of support for democracy can be obtained by constructing a 6-point composite index ranging from 0 to 5, counting the number of positive responses regarding desirability, suitability, efficacy, preference, and priority. On this index, Koreans averaged 3.6, indicating a

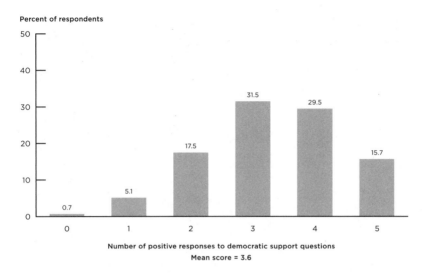

FIGURE 2.3   **Democratic Support: Korea**

relatively robust level of democratic support in the Asian comparative context. However, figure 2.3 shows that only 16% of Koreans were completely attached to democracy by responding affirmatively to all five questions. Fewer than one-third (30%) received a score of 4. This pattern of less-than-majority support for democracy appears common across the Asian democracies.

5.2. AUTHORITARIAN DETACHMENT

To what extent have Korean citizens detached themselves from the temptations of authoritarian rule? To address this question, the EAB survey asked respondents whether or not they would favor the return to one of four types of authoritarian regime (see chapter 1, table 1.9).

A compelling majority (84%) in Korea—the highest percentage in the regimes surveyed—opposed a return to strongman rule, and an even larger majority (90%), the second highest in the region, rejected the return of military dictatorship. Similar majorities rejected the option of single-party dictatorship (87%), and nearly as many (82%) rejected the option of rule by technocrats. At 65%, rejection of all authoritarian options was the most emphatic of all the regimes surveyed (see figure 2.4). An additional one-fifth (19%) rejected three out of four authoritarian options. After more than a decade of democratic rule, the vast majority of Koreans appeared to have

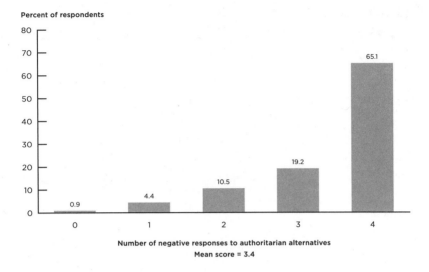

FIGURE 2.4   **Authoritarian Detachment: Korea**

dissociated themselves substantially from authoritarianism. Yet as shown earlier, support for democracy is not very deep. Full rejection of authoritarianism is apparently to some extent independent of the full embrace of its alternative, democracy. This suggests that at the level of culture, democratization is a process with different dimensions or stages that do not necessarily change in full synchronization.

5.3. OVERALL COMMITMENT TO DEMOCRACY

As argued in chapter 1, the consolidation of democratic rule requires commitment to democracy among a majority of the citizenry, combining attachment to democracy with detachment from authoritarianism (Alexander 2002; Diamond 1999; Inglehart 2000; Linz and Stepan 1996a). Otherwise, the cultural norms of the previous authoritarian regime may cohabit with the institutions and procedures of democratic rule (O'Donnell 1996; Shin and Shyu 1997). If this happens, citizens embrace democratic and authoritarian propensities concurrently, "not as hypothetical alternatives but as lived experiences" (McDonough, Barnes, and Lopez Pina 1994:350; see also Rose and Mishler 1994).

Figure 2.5 identifies seven patterns of regime orientation, taking into account both levels of democratic attachment and authoritarian detachment as

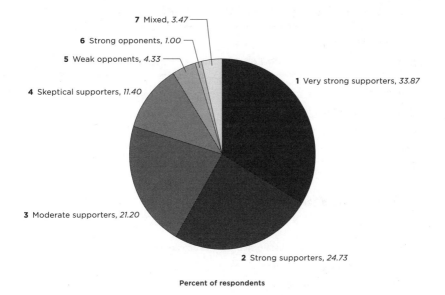

Percent of respondents

FIGURE 2.5 **Patterns of Commitment to Democracy: Korea**

defined in the notes to table 1.11, chapter 1. Among the political systems in the EAB survey, Korea has the highest proportion of supporters and the lowest proportions of opponents and persons with mixed regime orientations. Nearly two-thirds of the Korean people were supporters of democracy, outnumbering opponents by over eighteen to one (91% to 5%). Although 5% of the public had yet to accept democracy as the "only game in town," compared to their neighbors, Korean citizens were the most democratically committed in East Asia.

6. EXPECTATIONS OF KOREAN DEMOCRACY

What changes do the Korean people anticipate in their political order? Are they optimistic about its future? In the EAB survey, respondents were asked to indicate their evaluations of the current and future standings of the political system on a 10-point scale, with 10 representing "complete democracy." The results for Korea are presented in table 2.4. According to the mean ratings reported in the table, Korean citizens anticipated significant democratic improvements in their political system. On the 10-point scale, they expected the system to progress toward an advanced democracy by 1.2 points from 6.5 to 7.7 in the next five years. More than one-

TABLE 2.4 **CURRENT AND EXPECTED FUTURE REGIME TYPE: KOREA**

(Percent of respondents)

RATING	CURRENT REGIME	FUTURE REGIME	CHANGE[a]
Very dictatorial (1–2)	0.5	0.1	-0.4
Somewhat dictatorial (3–5)	17.8	4.9	-12.9
Somewhat democratic (6–8)	79.5	68.0	-11.5
Very democratic (9–10)	2.3	26.7	24.5
DK/NA	0.0	0.3	0.3
Total	100.0	100.0	
Mean on a 10-point scale[b]	6.5	7.7	1.2

Notes: N = 1500.

Scale runs from 1, "complete dictatorship," to 10, "complete democracy."

Future regime is five years from time of survey.

DK/NA = Don't know/no answer.

[a] Change in percent of respondents rating the regime at the given level when the object of evaluation shifts from the current to the future regime.

[b] DK/NA excluded

quarter (27%) believed that in five years they would live in an advanced democracy, a more than thirteen-fold increase from the 2% who placed the present regime in the same category. Even among those respondents who considered the current regime to be undemocratic, most expected progress toward greater democracy. While 18% considered the present regime to be very or somewhat dictatorial, only 5% expected the system to remain so in five years. Nearly every Korean (95%) expected to live in a democracy soon (as compared to 82% who believe they live in a democracy now) and a substantial minority (27%) expected to live in an advanced democracy. That 27% would represent a nearly 12-fold increase from the number of Koreans who appraised their democracy so highly at the time of the survey. Such optimism about increasing democracy may fuel demands for continued democratization and promote Korea's consolidation as a new democracy.

We classified our respondents' current and future regime ratings into seven patterns of expected regime change (see chapter 1, table 1.12). The majority of Koreans (54%) expected the persistence of a struggling democracy. This is followed by those who expected continuing democratic development from a limited to an advanced democracy (23%). Among those who considered the current regime to be undemocratic, the majority anticipated at least some degree of democratic progress. About 14% anticipated the transition to a limited democracy, while only 3% expected the persistence of authoritarian rule. A tiny minority of 2% anticipated authoritarian retrogression.

7. SUMMARY AND CONCLUSIONS

Koreans' rejection of authoritarianism is unambiguous, and they are optimistic that the process of democratization will continue in the future. Popular sovereignty is practiced at all levels of government through regularly scheduled free and fair elections. Normative support for democracy as an ideal political system has become nearly universal, while support for democracy-in-action, which involves the endorsement of democracy as a suitable and effective system, is pervasive through every segment of the population.

Korea is thus one of the most firmly consolidated of the new democracies in our survey. Yet Korea remains at some distance from full democratic consolidation both institutionally and culturally. Institutionally, the operations of government are often stymied by a system that blends semipresidentialism with multipartyism, using staggered presidential and parliamentary elections. This system often produces divided governments and immobilizing institutional deadlocks, which help to sustain low levels of public trust in political institutions. Meanwhile, long-standing problems of corruption and economic inequality, among others, remain to be tackled. Culturally, only a small minority of Koreans unconditionally embrace democracy as the best form of government. Support for democracy is not unconditional, and large majorities in Korea as elsewhere in Asia consider it less important than economic development (see also Shin 2003b; Shin et al. 2003). Considering Korea's vulnerable economic and geostrategic position in the world, its leaders will need both wisdom and luck to sustain the kind of policy performance that can fortify the public's commitment to the new democratic system.

NOTES

An earlier version of this chapter was presented at an international conference, "How People View Democracy: Public Opinion in New Democracies," organized by Stanford University's Center for Democracy, Development, and the Rule of Law,

July 21–22, 2003. The authors wish to thank Anita Harrison for helpful comments and suggestions on earlier drafts and Byong-Kuen Jhee for research assistance.

1. The 28% who rated the old regime as a democracy rather than a non-democracy in our 2003 survey was higher than in previous Korean Democracy Barometer surveys—19% in 1996, 19% in 1997, 18% in 1998, 13% in 1999, and 14% in 2001 (Shin 2003a). Our data do not enable us to explain why this proportion has increased.

2. These four types of regime quality are identified in three successive steps. In the first step, respondents were divided into two groups according to their perception of the current regime. Those who perceived it as a non-democracy were grouped into category 1. In the second step, we divided those who perceived it as a democracy into two subgroups depending on whether or not they were satisfied with its performance. Those who were not satisfied became category 2. In the third step, we subdivided into two types those who were satisfied with the performance of the current regime as a democracy on the basis of their relative assessment of its quality. Those who expressed agreement with the statement that "Whatever its faults may be, our form of government is still the best for us" formed category 4. Those who did not agree with this statement were placed into category 3.

3

MASS PUBLIC PERCEPTIONS OF DEMOCRATIZATION IN THE PHILIPPINES

Consolidation in Progress?

Linda Luz Guerrero and Rollin F. Tusalem

THE PEOPLE POWER UPRISING of 1986 that reinstalled democracy in the Philippines after fourteen years of martial law marked the start of the third wave of democratization in East Asia (Carothers 2002; Lapitan 1989). Among third-wave democracies globally, the Philippines was the first make the transition through mass protest. The Philippine transition was cited as an inspiration for the protest movement in Czechoslovakia that toppled the communist regime and for the 1989 prodemocracy movement in China's Tiananmen Square (Hedman and Sidel 2000).

The Philippines' revolutionary transition to democracy differed from the smooth and stable pacted transitions in Spain and other Southern European and Latin American countries, as well as in some of the new democracies of East Asia. The latter type of transition is thought to facilitate the consolidation of nascent democratic rule (Diamond 1999; Huntington 1991; Linz and Stepan 1996a; O'Donnell and Schmitter 1986b; Pereira 1993; Zhang 1994). The revolutionary or "unpacted" path to democratic regime change, however, rejects the gradual liberalization of the previous dictatorship, but risks burdening the new regime with political turmoil, institutional instability, class conflict, and economic underdevelopment. Whether pacted or unpacted, polities in transition are more likely to experience turmoil and instability than more established ones (Hegre et al. 2001).

In the Filipino case, such predictions are reinforced by the long, turbulent history of democratization, for the post-1986 democratic regime is not a new experiment as in most other third-wave countries, but a second try. The country had already tried to establish democracy during the post–World War II period that transition theorists call the second wave. In 1946, when the Philippines gained independence from the United States, it kept in place a presidential democratic system patterned after the American one, which had been initiated over a decade earlier under the colonial tutelage arrangement called the Philippine Commonwealth. Starting in 1946, the Philippine system was a functioning and apparently stable democracy, with freedom of the press, regular elections, and robust popular legitimacy.

By the late 1960s, however, it became apparent that procedural democracy had not generated social justice and equity. Half of the population remained poor. The regime was challenged on several fronts: by a rural insurgency, a Maoist-oriented political movement, and eventually a massive urban protest movement. In response, President Ferdinand Marcos declared martial law in 1972 and "constitutional authoritarianism," with the declared intent of increasing the institutionalization of the state.

The 1986 People Power movement that overthrew Marcos marked a new attempt to make democracy work. The 1987 Constitution restored the presidential democratic and unitary system Filipinos had been familiar with before Marcos. At the same time, however, the new system brought back, and even strengthened, key patterns of dynastic elite control of the masses behind the screen of procedural democracy. The deep roots of these patterns of political and social inequality, and popular resignation to their inevitability, may explain the survival of the highly imperfect post-Marcos democratic system through four presidents. The president in office at the time of our survey in 2002, Gloria Macapagal-Arroyo, had come to power a year earlier after her predecessor, Joseph Estrada, was ousted by People Power. She struggled to maintain normal government operations in the face of constitutional and extraconstitutional challenges to her administration. After nearly two decades of restored democracy, Filipino democracy continued to encounter enormous obstacles to consolidation (Rose and Shin 2001). In the classic Huntingtonian sense, it still suffered from the underinstitutionalization of the state, resulting in persistent challenges to the rule of law and constitutional governance.

How much progress has the Philippines made toward democratic consolidation? This chapter seeks to address this question from the perspective of ordinary Filipinos who experienced the transition process as part of their daily lives. Almost two decades after the rebirth of Filipino democracy, were the citizens who fought to usher in the new regime still willing to rally to its defense? In the following pages we offer some answers to this question, using data from the East Asia Barometer (EAB) survey conducted in March and April 2002, with a random sample of twelve hundred voting age citizens drawn from across the country.

We found that Filipinos perceived the least degree of progress toward democracy among all the recent democracies in this study. The perceived level of corruption was the highest among the countries surveyed, and most institutions of the state were distrusted by the public. Although the country is endowed with one of the most vibrant civic cultures in the region, commitment to democratic governance was weak. However, the vast majority of Filipinos remained hopeful that the shortcomings of the current system could be overcome, and by a ratio of five to one envisioned a more democratic future for their country. Although it is a work in progress, democracy is not a project that the Filipino people are ready to abandon.

1. DEMOCRATIC AND AUTHORITARIAN EXPERIMENTS IN PHILIPPINE HISTORY

The Philippines is the only Asian nation that experienced both Spanish and American colonization (Karnow 1989; McCoy and de Jesus 1982). Spanish colonial rule was exercised with a high level of political and social repression principally by way of religious institutions and the monarchy. Dissenters were repressed as both religious heretics and political rebels. American colonial rule over the islands began in 1898 with the signing of the Treaty of Paris, which marked the conclusion of the Spanish American War. The Americans established what may be regarded as a form of colonial administration grounded on constitutionalism and the rule of law. Nevertheless, throughout the period of American possession of the Philippines, traditional political elites remained in power. These elites benefited from the democratic institutions established by the Americans in the 1935 Constitution.

After gaining independence in 1946, the Philippines continued to adhere to the principles of the 1935 Constitution, which made a wide range of civil liberties, personal freedoms, and political rights an integral part of the country's embryonic democracy. Until the late 1950s, the country faced the problem of land tenure among the peasants. The peasant struggle was carried out by the Communist Party of the Philippines and its armed wing, the Hukbong Bayan or People's Army.

In 1965 Ferdinand Marcos was elected president amid accusations of electoral fraud and corruption on both sides. In the succeeding years, the government was confronted with several challenges, notably an insurgency led by the reestablished Communist Party of the Philippines and its armed wing, the New People's Army (NPA). The situation in the southern Philippines worsened with the founding of the Moro National Liberation Front (MNLF). As Marcos approached the end of his second term, after which he could not run again under the 1935 Constitution, he declared martial law in 1972 ostensibly to address these threats (Grossholtz 1973; Overholt 1986; Thompson 1995).

Under martial law the Philippines was transformed from an elitist democracy into a "constitutional authoritarian" system (Landé 1965; Hernandez 1985). Marcos's rule (1965–1986) was of the personalist type. His friends and associates monopolized major industries, and cronyism and patron-client relations became a regular part of the governing process (Hawes 1987; Hutchcroft 1991; Manapat 1991; Kerkvliet and Mojares 1992).

The year 1986 marked a turning point for Filipino democracy. After the assassination of his political opponent, Benigno "Ninoy" Aquino, which led to mounting questions about the legitimacy of his regime, Marcos called a snap election marked by fraud, and then declared victory. In response, approximately one million citizens packed the streets of Manila to demand that Marcos step down. This huge gathering was apparently triggered by an attempted power grab on the part of Marcos's defense minister, Juan Ponce Enrile, and a former chief of staff, General Fidel Ramos (later to become president himself). Marcos was forced to flee the country. Corazon Aquino, widow of Ninoy and considered to be the real winner in the snap election, replaced him as president. The new regime promulgated a constitution restoring most of the civil liberties and political rights abrogated by Marcos in 1972.

Aquino's tenure was marked by a string of attempted coups by disgruntled military factions, the growth of the communist insurgency, and chronic economic underdevelopment (Danguilan-Vitug 1990; Thompson 1992). Political stability was gradually restored under the leadership of Fidel Ramos, who succeeded Aquino as president in 1992. Relying on his long experience in the military, Ramos was able to bring the military factions to heel and reach settlements with the Moro secessionists in the south and the communists in the rural areas. He did not, however, make much headway in redressing the nation's economic disparities, even though his term was characterized by unprecedented economic growth, the regional financial crisis of 1997 and 1998 notwithstanding.

Ramos finished his term in 1998. The presidency passed to Joseph Estrada, a former actor who was elected on a populist platform promising to deliver the country's masses from economic hardship. Although Estrada won a convincing victory, his campaign polarized the nation between the so-called haves and have-nots. When Estrada was implicated in a series of corruption scandals early in his tenure, pressure began mounting for his removal. Opponents of the embattled president were usually identified with the middle classes and other elite segments of society, while many lower class Filipinos continued to support him and launched a counteroffensive complete with its own People Power uprising, which failed. Before long, the military and members of the cabinet withdrew their support from Estrada, and the Supreme Court appointed Vice President Gloria Macapagal Arroyo as the new president. Arroyo was the daughter of a former president, Diosdado Macapagal, who ran against Marcos in 1965 (Leroy 2003). Estrada supporters bitterly denounced the turn of events as a "judicial coup d'état" and an "untamed mobocracy of the rich and connected."

The conflict-ridden power handover inflicted considerable damage to the political fabric of the nation. Critics charged that Estrada's ouster was mostly a middle- and upper-class revolt, and that the lower classes, which make up over two-thirds of the population, did not support the overthrow. In their view, Estrada's ouster signified a major setback to the process of democratic consolidation in that a legitimately elected president was cast out by a vocal minority through rebellion in the streets. After taking office in January 2001, Arroyo had to contend with two abortive coups against her administration, a renewal of the Islamist and communist insurgencies, and a crushing devaluation of the peso, which lost half its value against the dollar in three years. Corruption and poverty continued to fester. Arroyo was nonetheless reelected to the presidency in May 2004 after opposition charges of massive vote fraud and a dramatic all-night session of the Filipino Congress.

At the time of our survey in the spring of 2002, Filipino democracy had achieved much in the nearly two decades since the fall of the Marcos dictatorship, yet a great deal more remained to be done. On the positive side, the country scored highly on the Freedom House indices of political rights and civil liberties.[1] The vibrancy of Filipino civil society was the envy of Southeast Asia (Silliman and Noble 1998). National and local elections were regularly held and were generally considered free even though they were often marred by vote-buying and violence (Putzel 1995). Although power alternated among parties, the party system was characterized by a lack of programmatic coherence and a predominance of personalities. New parties and alliances took shape with dizzying regularity (Magno 1992).

In the midst of this complex evolution, we examine the views of ordinary citizens whose lives have been directly touched by the country's political system.

2. CONCEPTIONS OF DEMOCRACY

About three-quarters of our respondents were able to offer at least one answer to the open-ended question, "What does democracy mean to you?" (see chapter 1, table 1.3). Nearly half associated democracy with freedom and liberty. This was the most popular answer not only in the Philippines but in all but one of the other countries in the EAB survey. Only a few respondents, totaling no more than 5%, were able to associate democracy with specific institutions and procedures, the lowest percentage in the study. The emphasis on freedom over institutions may have provided a permissive context for the practice of People Power in the Philippine system, as in the case of the fall of Estrada.

Also noteworthy was that only 4% of respondents associated democracy with substantive notions of social justice, again the lowest level among the countries surveyed. As we will suggest in the next section, the lack of association of democracy with social justice may help explain the democratic regime's weak performance in this area.

3. EVALUATING THE TRANSITION

At the time of our survey, almost two decades had passed since People Power overthrew the Marcos dictatorship. Our data suggest that while most Filipinos recognized some degree of democratic progress, a significant minority—the largest of any third-wave democracy in the survey—perceived no progress, or even perceived regression toward authoritarianism since the Marcos era. In evaluating regime performance, Filipinos also registered the lowest level of perceived improvements in the political domain among the countries in our survey that underwent recent democratization. However, the new democratic regime was perceived as having avoided deterioration in the policy domain.

3.1. RECOGNITION OF DEMOCRATIC REGIME CHANGE

The EAB survey included an item asking respondents to rate the current and past regimes on a 10-point scale (from 1, "most dictatorial," to 10, "most democratic"). The results for the Philippines are summarized in table 3.1. Seven out of ten Filipinos rated the current regime as democratic. An even larger percentage (73%) rated the Marcos regime as dictatorial. While the average rating for the current regime was 6.7, the average for the past regime was 4.1. Clearly, despite whatever misgivings they may have had, the majority of Filipinos regarded their political system as a democracy while perceiving the past regime as a dictatorship.

Yet, close to one-third (30%) of Filipinos perceived their political system under the Arroyo presidency (in power at the time of our survey) as authoritarian, a high percentage in the region. Figure 3.1 shows a wide range of views on the nature of change from Marcos to Arroyo. Although most of our respondents recognized some democratic progress, 11% perceived no progress at all (a zero score) and 16.8% perceived authoritarian retrogression (negative scores). These scores are by far the most negative for any

TABLE 3.1 **PERCEPTIONS OF PAST AND CURRENT REGIMES: THE PHILIPPINES**

(Percent of total respondents)

REGIME TYPES	PAST REGIME	CURRENT REGIME
Very dictatorial (1–2)	33.8	4.6
Somewhat dictatorial (3–5)	38.9	25.6
Somewhat democratic (6–8)	18.7	47.2
Very democratic (9–10)	8.0	22.4
DK/NA	0.6	0.2
Total	100.0	100.0
Mean on a 10-point scale	4.1	6.7

Notes: Regime types are based on the respondent's ranking of the regime on a scale from 1, "complete dictatorship," to 10, "complete democracy." Scores of 5 and below are degrees of dictatorship and scores of 6 and above are degrees of democracy.

N = 1200.

DK/NA = Don't know/no answer.

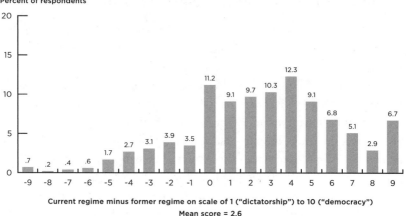

Percent of respondents

Current regime minus former regime on scale of 1 ("dictatorship") to 10 ("democracy")
Mean score = 2.6

FIGURE 3.1   **Perceived Regime Change: The Philippines**

recent democracy in our survey and are second in negative magnitude only to Hong Kong's. Even with the invigoration of civil society and the restoration of political rights and civil liberties, many Filipinos evidently remained deeply disaffected with the new regime.

The polarizing conflict that surrounded Arroyo's ascension to the presidency was most likely a major contributing factor to this pattern. In addition, after Arroyo took office, she cracked down on pro-Estrada demonstrations using the military and the police, leading to a number of deaths and injuries. In fact, Arroyo initially held Estrada inside a military detention facility before later transferring him to his house in the outskirts of Manila. Critics accused the government of relying on autocratic methods to compensate for its wobbly popular support, a charge Arroyo supporters denied.[2] Many respondents seem to have believed that Arroyo was repressing dissenters, especially those close to the former president, who was seen as a populist leader.

3.2. COMPARING THE PAST AND PRESENT REGIMES

Especially in transitional democracies, citizens are conscious of the effects of regime change on the quality of their lives and their country's situation (Colton 2000). Table 3.2 shows that Filipinos perceived appreciable improvements in all five items of democratic performance that our survey asked

TABLE 3.2 PERCEIVED PERFORMANCE OF CURRENT AND PAST REGIMES: THE PHILIPPINES

	MEAN[a]	SD[a]	NEGATIVE CHANGE[b]	POSITIVE CHANGE[b]	NO CHANGE[b]	PDI[c]	VALID %[d]
Democratic performance							
Freedom of speech	0.62	1.11	16.9	58.7	24.4	41.8	99.8
Freedom of association	0.47	1.02	13.7	49.5	36.8	35.8	99.6
Equal treatment	0.28	0.99	18.1	40.0	41.9	21.9	99.8
Popular influence	0.27	0.96	17.6	39.0	43.4	21.4	99.6
Independent judiciary	0.13	1.03	23.2	36.1	40.7	12.9	99.6
Average	0.35	1.02	17.9	44.7	37.4	26.8	99.7
Policy performance							
Anticorruption	-0.02	1.05	28.1	29.5	42.4	1.4	99.7
Law and order	0.08	1.10	27.1	35.9	37.0	8.9	99.7
Economic development	0.00	1.12	30.6	34.2	35.2	3.6	99.7
Economic equality	-0.05	0.99	25.8	26.5	47.7	21.9	99.8
Average	0.00	1.07	27.9	31.5	40.6	8.9	99.7

Notes: N = 1200.

Past regime is defined as pre-1986.

[a] Scale ranges from -2 (much worse) to +2 (much better).

[b] Percent of valid sample.

[c] PDI (percentage difference index) = percent seeing positive change minus percent seeing negative change.

[d] Percent of sample giving a valid answer to this question.

about—especially in the area of civil liberties—but little improvement in the domain of socioeconomic policy performance. This is consistent with the earlier discussion of the conception of democracy as being associated with freedom and liberties in the minds of Filipinos. The democratic domain averages a numerical score of 0.35 and a PDI score of 26.8, modest compared to the country's third-wave neighbors, but a clear improvement nevertheless. The policy domain, however, registers no improvement on the numerical scale and a PDI of only 8.9. Considering the disastrous policy performance of the Marcos regime, the barely positive PDI score is hardly a surprise.

These results reveal that while democratization was perceived as having delivered greater freedom and more popular participation in government, it did little to improve the quality of life in the eyes of the Filipino public. It is ironic that economic equality received the lowest rating given that surging economic inequality was one of the social ills that led to Marcos's downfall. Twenty-two years of Marcos's rule had left the Philippines with a two-tier class system, composed of a large lower class mired in poverty and a small upper class that controlled most of the nation's wealth (Doronila 1992). Yet almost two decades after the transition to democracy, the new regime had done little to reduce poverty or to create a healthy middle class. The government's perceived ineffectuality in closing the income gap may prove an obstacle to democratic consolidation.

4. ASSESSMENTS OF DEMOCRATIC INSTITUTIONS

In this section, we examine self-perceived political efficacy, perceptions of corruption in government, and popular trust in political and social institutions. Compared to many of their neighbors, Filipinos were more confident of their participatory capacities and were especially conscious of the power of popular collective action. Nongovernmental institutions of Filipino society enjoyed robust levels of public confidence. But respondents believed the country was saddled with one of the most corrupt political elites in East Asia, especially at the highest levels of government. Most institutions of the state were distrusted by the public.

4.1. POLITICAL EFFICACY

The EAB survey used two questions to assess whether Filipinos believe that they have the capacity to understand and influence the political process (see chapter 1, table 1.3). While 13% of the Filipino public felt capable of both, nearly three times as many (38%) felt incapable of either. In addition, 32% believed that they could understand the complexities of politics but lacked confidence in their ability to participate, whereas another 18% chose not to let their perceived lack of understanding get in the way of active participation. Overall, the Filipino numbers compare favorably with most of the country's neighbors in terms of citizens' perceived political efficacy.

The tradition of People Power appears to have made an impact on how the efficacy of popular participation is understood. When asked to evaluate the statement, "The nation is run by a powerful few and ordinary citizens cannot do much about it," 46% of Filipinos disagreed. When asked to evaluate the proposition "People like me don't have any influence over what the government does," 52% disagreed. These disagreement ratios are the highest of any country in our survey. The triumphs of People Power may have convinced the Filipino public of their collective strength, even if many citizens remain diffident about their abilities as individuals. These figures suggest the existence of an untapped participatory potential in Filipino society, a potential currently restrained by barriers to participation for many individuals.

4.2. PERCEPTIONS OF CORRUPTION

According to a report by the World Bank, corruption in the Philippines costs the government some $47 million a year, contributing to a growing fiscal deficit. Moreover, corruption has led to continual abuse of the rule of law, erosion of the moral fabric of Philippine society, and chronic economic underdevelopment. The report concludes with the grim appraisal that "corruption in the public and private sectors in the Philippines is pervasive and deep-rooted, touching even the judiciary and the media" (World Bank 2003b). The low rankings the Philippines received on the Global Corruption Perceptions Index corroborate the bank's conclusions.[3] On a scale of 1 to 10, 10 being the least corrupt, the Philippines averaged an annual ranking of 2.6 from 1995 to 2005, a score that compares poorly to those of its East Asian neighbors.

The EAB survey examined corruption from the perspective of the public, with a pair of questions concerning the extent to which local and national governmental officials were perceived to be corrupt. The results are presented in table 3.3. At the national level of government, close to

TABLE 3.3 **PERCEPTION OF POLITICAL CORRUPTION AT NATIONAL AND LOCAL LEVELS: THE PHILIPPINES**

(Percent of respondents)

LOCAL GOVERNMENT	NATIONAL GOVERNMENT					
	Hardly anyone is involved	Not a lot of officials are involved	Most officials are corrupt	Almost everyone is corrupt	DK/NA	Total
Hardly anyone is involved	4.2	3.0	2.4	1.5	—	**11.1**
Not a lot of officials are involved	1.1	**16.5**	**13.7**	5.5	—	**36.8**
Most officials are corrupt	0.7	6.7	**22.9**	6.2	—	**36.4**
Almost everyone is corrupt	0.4	1.7	2.0	**11.1**	—	**15.2**
Don't know/ no answer	—	0.1	0.1	—	0.3	0.5
Total	6.3	**27.9**	**41.1**	**24.4**	0.3	**100.0**

Notes: N = 1200.
Blank cell means no cases.
Percentages above 10 are in boldface.

two-thirds of our respondents perceived corruption in almost all (24.4%) or most (41.1%) officials. Corruption among local officials was felt to be somewhat less widespread, amounting to 15.2% for "almost everyone" and 36.4% for "most." More than 42% of the public perceived widespread corruption in both national and local governments, whereas only about a quarter did not believe corruption to be common at either level. If, as some Filipino scholars have argued (e.g., Magno 1992), political corruption in the Philippines is driven primarily by the country's electoral financing system, then the perceived difference between the two levels may be attributed to the greater financial demands and higher stakes involved in national politics.

4.3. INSTITUTIONAL TRUST

Public trust in democratic institutions constitutes an essential foundation for democratic consolidation. In the EAB survey, respondents were asked to indicate their level of trust in twelve key institutions of state and society. The results are presented in figure 3.2. The average trust level for societal institutions (newspaper, television, and NGOs), was highest at 57%, followed by governmental institutions (the civil service, military, courts, and election commission) at 51%, and political institutions (national and local government, political parties, and parliament), at 46%. In other words, the institutions of representative democracy were the least trusted among the Filipino people.

However, within each category there was considerable variation. Local governments were tied with the civil service as the second most trusted of all institutions (58%). This high level of trust may be due to the responsive performance of the Local Governmental Units (LGUs), which have gained prominence since the end of the Marcos dictatorship. These subsidiary organizations of municipal governments have been instrumental in assisting infrastructure development in urban and rural areas, channeling state resources for the support of urban and rural renewal projects, supporting local cottage industries, promoting environmental protection efforts, and providing emergency financial assistance to the poor.[4]

Nevertheless, political parties were the least-trusted institutions in the survey. As mentioned previously, Filipino political parties generally do not have consistent programmatic identities but are instead vehicles for the fluctuating mass appeals of individual politicians (Magno 1992; Rocamora 1999). Parties are as numerous as they are ephemeral, and partisan defections occur regularly. Their representative and aggregating potential have been offset by their elitist leaderships.

Among governmental institutions, the civil service and the military received favorable ratings from more than half of the Filipinos surveyed. The confidence Filipinos placed in the civil service may be an indication that the post-Marcos administrative reforms were bearing fruit and that meritocracy was perceived to be taking the place of nepotism (Thompson 1996). The high level of trust enjoyed by the military, however, may be a result of its perceived successes in counterinsurgency campaigns as well as public sympathy for soldiers' grievances, such as inadequate pension benefits. Although the military was the source of much political instability under the Aquino presidency (Danguilan-Vitug 1990), it largely maintained political neutrality during the Ramos and Estrada eras. Even renewed rumblings of

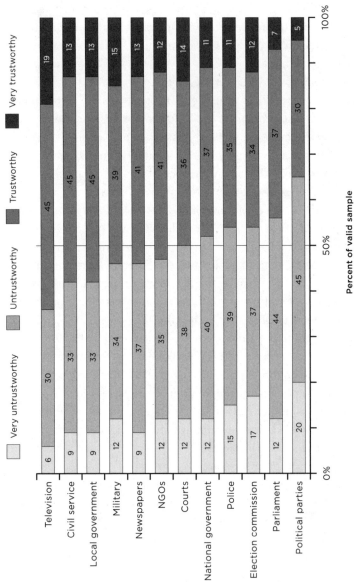

	Very untrustworthy	Untrustworthy	Trustworthy	Very trustworthy

Television	6	30	45	19
Civil service	9	33	45	13
Local government	9	33	45	13
Military	12	34	39	15
Newspapers	9	37	41	13
NGOs	12	35	41	12
Courts	12	38	36	14
National government	12	40	37	11
Police	15	39	35	11
Election commission	17	37	34	12
Parliament	12	44	37	7
Political parties	20	45	30	5

Percent of valid sample

FIGURE 3.2 **Trust in Institutions: The Philippines**

coup conspiracies under the Arroyo administration probably did not impair the military's prestige, as these merely mirrored the restive mood of the public.

Finally, institutions in the societal category were the most highly trusted. As in Mongolia and Thailand, television was trusted by more Filipinos (64%) than any other institution. Newspapers (54%) and NGOs (53%) were both trusted by more than half of the respondents. Free from censorship and government regulations, the media's prestige has been enhanced by respected independent news agencies such as the Philippine Center for Investigative Journalism,[5] which produced documentaries shown on national television exposing corruption among top politicians in all branches of government. On the other hand, the high regard for NGOs may emanate from their prominence in advocacy on behalf of the rural and urban poor. Proliferating after the end of the Marcos dictatorship, NGOs provided industrial training, financial support, and legal assistance to include farmers, factory workers, indigenous groups, women, teachers, rural nurses, doctors, and local entrepreneurs (Silliman and Noble 1998).

In recent years NGOs have become significant players in electoral politics, assuming a role as channels of interest aggregation when the mainstream political parties were slow to respond to the policy demands of the electorate. The participation of NGOs in elections is made possible by a party list system that allows up to one-fifth of the seats in the House of Representatives (up to fifty seats depending on the number of votes received by the party lists above the minimum threshold) to be filled from party lists elected nationally. The other members of the House run as individuals in electoral districts. The House of Representatives is one of two houses of Congress, the other being the Senate, whose members are elected individually and at large. NGOs have formed coalitions in areas such as environmental preservation, human rights protection, and promotion of local cottage industries to offer party lists to the voters. In doing so, they have played an important role not only in redressing social inequalities, but also in facilitating democratic citizenship.

5. SUPPORT FOR DEMOCRACY

In this section, we explore the extent to which Filipinos have embraced democracy and dissociated themselves from the authoritarian practices of the past.

5.1. ATTACHMENT TO DEMOCRATIC POLITICS

Filipinos were asked to assess the desirability, suitability, efficacy, preferability, and priority of democracy (see chapter 1, table 1.8). Eighty-eight percent articulated a clear desire for democracy by choosing a score 6 or above on a 10-point scale, with some 40% selecting the maximum score of 10. As with desirability, a large majority of Filipinos (80%) believed that democracy is suitable for their nation, choosing a score of 6 or higher on a 10-point scale. Such results are consistent with one another. Only a relatively small minority of 20% rated democracy to be unsuitable.

In addition to desirability and suitability, the level of efficacy citizens assign to democratic governance is often a test of the depth of their democratic attachment. Despite widespread corruption and the absence of a healthy party system, we found that a majority of Filipinos (61%) agreed with the statement, "Democracy is capable of solving the problems of our society."

Finally, the EAB asked two questions that measured citizen support for democracy in practice. Nearly two-thirds (64%) expressed unconditional support for democracy, agreeing with the statement, "Democracy is always preferable to any other kind of government." The question on the priority of democracy as a policy goal vis-à-vis economic development produced the lowest level of prodemocratic response in all eight societies surveyed, and the Philippines were no exception. In the Philippines, only about one-fifth (21.8%) replied that democracy is of greater or equal importance.

On our 6-point index of overall attachment to democracy, Filipinos averaged 3.3, which is on the low end of the third-wave democracies surveyed (see figure 3.3). Only about 7% responded affirmatively to all five questions, with an additional 37% responding affirmatively to four out of five questions. But these numbers are again lower than those of most of the new democracies in the survey. In short, Filipino citizens, like their neighbors in the rest of East Asia, are enthusiastic supporters of democracy in principle, but their enthusiasm tends to recede when faced with the realities of democracy in practice.

5.2. DETACHMENT FROM AUTHORITARIANISM

Between 1986 and 1992, the Aquino-led Philippine government faced a series of coup attempts launched by elements of the armed forces. All of these

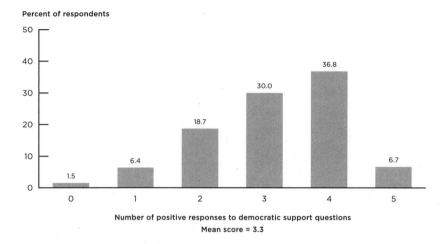

FIGURE 3.3   **Democratic Support: The Philippines**

attempts failed due to lack of popular support. Given the problems of the democratic regime in subsequent years, we asked how Filipinos would feel about antidemocratic alternatives at the time of our survey.

We asked respondents if they would support the return to a strongman dictatorship or oligarchic rule in some other form. The results were clearly negative. A compelling majority (69%) of Filipinos were against the dictatorial rule of a strong leader, while 63% were against military rule. A one-party dictatorship was likewise rejected (70%), and more than three-quarters (78%) were opposed to rule by technocratic experts (see chapter 1, table 1.9). The distaste for the last alternative may be explained by the current prominence of "business politicians"—skilled political entrepreneurs with connections in the public and private spheres. Many citizens consider them to be influential peddlers mediating between corporations and the agencies of the state (Kang 2002).

To measure the overall level of detachment from authoritarianism, we counted the number of antiauthoritarian responses, using them to construct a 5-point index ranging from 0 to 4. The mean score was 2.8, indicating that the average Filipino was still willing to contemplate one or another form of authoritarian alternative despite the overall rejection of dictatorial rule. Figure 3.4 shows that fewer than 36% of our respondents were fully detached from authoritarianism, whereas a slightly larger number remained open to at least two types of nondemocratic rule.

Percent of respondents

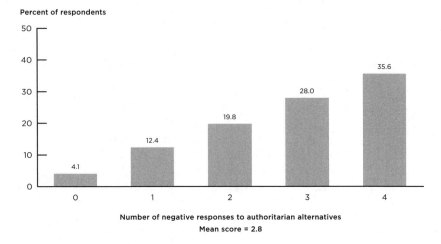

Number of negative responses to authoritarian alternatives
Mean score = 2.8

FIGURE 3.4 **Authoritarian Detachment: The Philippines**

5.3. OVERALL COMMITMENT TO DEMOCRACY

Taking into account both the depth of democratic support as well as the completeness of authoritarian detachment, we identified seven patterns of regime orientation. The results for the Philippines are presented in figure 3.5. The analysis shows the nuances in perceptions and attitudes toward democratic institutions and processes. The single largest segment, at 28%, consists of those with mixed regime orientations and skeptical supporters. Together, moderate to strong supporters of democracy amount to only about two-thirds (62%) of the electorate, one of the lowest proportions in the countries surveyed. If the benchmark of democratic consolidation is majority acceptance of democracy as the only game in town, then it may be said that the Philippines is still in the midst of a long, complicated, and thorny process of democratic consolidation.

6. EXPECTATIONS OF PHILIPPINE DEMOCRACY

In 1986, the Philippine nation brimmed with optimism that democracy would promote economic prosperity and restore the political rights and freedoms that the Marcos dictatorship took away. Sixteen tumultuous years and four presidencies later, how much of that optimism remained? To gauge

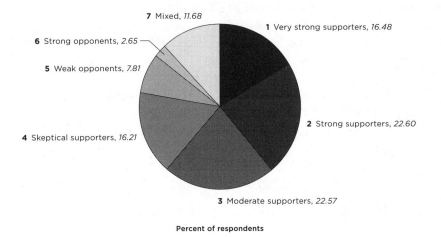

7 Mixed, *11.68*

1 Very strong supporters, *16.48*

6 Strong opponents, *2.65*

5 Weak opponents, *7.81*

4 Skeptical supporters, *16.21*

2 Strong supporters, *22.60*

3 Moderate supporters, *22.57*

Percent of respondents

FIGURE 3.5 **Patterns of Commitment to Democracy: The Philippines**

popular expectations for the future of democracy, we asked respondents to indicate where they expected the country's political system to stand on a 10-point scale five years into the future.

According to the mean ratings reported in table 3.4, the Filipino people as a whole anticipated improvement in the democratic level of their political system. On the 10-point scale, they expected their system to progress toward greater democracy by 1 point from 6.7 to 7.7 in the next five years. Forty percent believed that five years from now they would live in a complete democracy, nearly double the 22% who considered the current regime to be in the same category. Conversely, although nearly one-third (30%) of respondents considered the current regime to be at least somewhat dictatorial, only 17% expected their government to remain so five years from now. Given these anticipated shifts across regime categories, more than eight out of ten Filipinos believed that in five years they would live in a democracy of at least a limited sort by their own standards. This level may not represent a strong sense of optimism, but it is still characterized by a sense of hopefulness that the future will be better than the past or the present.

What specific patterns of regime transformations did the Filipino people expect in the near future? We identified seven patterns based on the respondents' current regime ratings and expected future ratings (see chapter 1, table 1.12). A large majority (62%) of Filipino citizens expected democratic persistence over the next five years, although just under half

TABLE 3.4   **CURRENT AND EXPECTED FUTURE REGIME TYPE: THE PHILIPPINES**

(Percent of respondents)

RATING	CURRENT REGIME	FUTURE REGIME	CHANGE[a]
Very dictatorial (1–2)	4.6	3.2	-1.4
Somewhat dictatorial (3–5)	25.6	14.1	-11.4
Somewhat democratic (6–8)	47.2	40.4	-6.7
Very democratic (9–10)	22.4	40.3	17.9
DK/NA	0.2	1.9	1.7
Total	100.0	100.0	
Mean on a 10-point scale	6.7	7.7	1.0

Notes: N = 1200.

Scale runs from 1, "complete dictatorship," to 10, "complete democracy."

Future regime is five years from time of survey.

[a] Change in percent of respondents rating the regime at the given level when the object of evaluation shifts from the current to the future regime.

of this group expected their government to remain only a limited democracy. Even among those Filipinos who considered the current regime to be authoritarian, the majority expected significant progress toward greater democracy in the near future. Eleven percent expected the transition to a limited democracy and 9% expected the transition to an advanced democracy. Only about 10% of the respondents expected their political system to remain authoritarian in the next five years, in addition to a small number (8%) who foresaw authoritarian retrogression. In short, those who anticipated significant democratic progress outnumbered those who anticipated authoritarian reversal by a ratio of nearly five to one (38% versus 8%). On the basis of this finding, the Filipino people's confidence in the ensuing democratic consolidation process appears unshaken.

7. CONCLUSIONS

The 2002 survey provides only a snapshot of the post-Marcos democratic regime. And this at perhaps one of its most legitimacy-challenged moments, when the Arroyo administration had recently emerged out of the intense factionalism that attended the ouster of President Estrada. A survey during the Ramos administration, for example, might have shown significantly different results, and the interadministration comparisons would have been interesting.

With that caveat, our data nonetheless suggest that the reestablished democratic institutions were unable to overcome traditions of corruption and elitist politics, nor were they able to harness effectively the dramatic increase in civil society participation to buttress their legitimacy. The EAB results show a high degree of civic activism through NGOs and LGUs, and these institutions received the highest trust ratings among those we looked at. Civil society institutions are a dynamic force for channeling the people's participation in politics and governance. As it is, the institutions of the new regime pale by comparison; they are neither responsive nor effective enough for ordinary citizens to consider them trustworthy.

The current regime in the Philippines is characterized by persistent challenges to the constitutional order emanating, ironically, from the same institutions that led to the demise of the old order under Marcos—People Power. Until Filipinos forge an acceptable and peaceful process for the settlement of political conflicts, politics will remain open to challenges by nonconstitutional means.

The Philippines has the highest incidence of poverty in the region, with a middle class still in the formative stages (World Bank 2003a, 2003b). The failure of the democratic regime to deliver economic prosperity may be one reason why the Philippines is characterized by one of the lowest levels of popular commitment to democracy in our survey. Such support as democracy commands is apparently due to its effectiveness in bringing about some political freedom, but not to any achievements it can claim in promoting prosperity or equity. In a society where economic deprivation is widely and urgently felt, this condition does not augur well for democratic consolidation.

The present situation as can be discerned from the survey may not be completely promising, but it does indicate the pitfalls and obstacles facing a polity in transition. This is a reality that has striking similarities, as well as dissimilarities, to other polities within the region and beyond. Philippine democracy, now on its second phase, continues to be a work in progress.

NOTES

1. Since achieving democratic transition in 1986, the Philippines has consistently scored an average of 2.43 for political rights and a 3.06 for civil liberties. Its

democratic status has alternated between partly free and free. Data for the Philippines accessed from www.freedomhouse.org.

2. For a full journalistic account of the mass rebellion that occurred shortly after Arroyo became president, refer to *Focus on the Global South: A Program of Development Policy Research, Analysis, and Action.* Accessed at: http://www.focusweb.org/publications/Bulletins/Fop/2001/FOP20.htm.

3. Every year, Transparency International conducts a global survey of corruption perceptions based on a "Corruption Perceptions Index" or CPI score. This CPI score pertains to perceptions of the degree of political corruption assessed by industrialists, risk analysts, and academics. For more specifics refer to Transparency International's database accessed at: http://www.transparency.org/policy_research/surveys_indices/cpi.

4. Philippine Institute for Development Studies, 2001. "Indicators of Good Governance: Developing an Index of Governance Quality at the LGU level." Accessed at http://serpp.pids.gov.ph/details.php3?tid=635.

5. For a more detailed description of the PCIJ's policy goals and objectives, refer to its website: http://www.pcij.org.

4

HOW CITIZENS VIEW TAIWAN'S NEW DEMOCRACY

Yu-tzung Chang and Yun-han Chu

TAIWAN'S YOUNG DEMOCRACY is endowed with a sizable middle class, a well-educated population, and a vibrant and highly internationalized economy with a relatively flat wealth distribution. It also enjoys the advantage of having emerged from an unusually smooth and peaceful transition process, during which the incumbent elite carried out a series of incremental changes that transformed the political system from an authoritarian party-state system to a democratic one-party dominant regime and subsequently to a competitive multiparty system.[1] However, the peaceful transition process left the new democracy burdened with two unresolved authoritarian legacies: First, there is widespread nostalgia for the seeming efficacy of the authoritarian era. Second, China's claims on Taiwan produces a unique set of challenges for the young democracy: an unsettled status in the international system, a looming military threat from mainland China, and a polarized internal conflict over national identity.

Under the circumstances, one might wonder how much progress Taiwan could really make in transforming the political culture that sustained the one-party authoritarian regime for four decades. To what extent have authoritarian legacies limited the options and shaped the nature of the new regime? To what extent has the new regime been able to promote congruent shifts in popular orientations toward democracy? What challenges does Taiwan face in furthering democratization? And what are the prospects for democratic consolidation?

To address these questions, this chapter uses first-wave East Asia Barometer survey data collected through face-to-face interviews of randomly selected eligible voters during July 2001.

1. HISTORICAL OVERVIEW

Our survey was conducted about a year after the first victory of an opposition-party presidential candidate in Taiwan's history. The March 18, 2000, election of Democratic Progressive Party (DPP) candidate Chen Shui-bian marked the culmination of a transition process that began in 1987 with the opposition party's formal establishment under the regime of authoritarian ruler Chiang Ching-kuo (president 1978–1988). Chiang's death meant that his successor, Lee Teng-hui (president 1988–2000), completed the abolition of martial law that Chiang had begun. When the DPP assumed power, the Kuomintang (KMT, or Nationalist Party) had ruled Taiwan for fifty-five years after emigrating from mainland China near the end of the protracted Chinese Civil War (1927–1949).

The peaceful transition of power presented a classic opportunity to consolidate the new democracy. To do so, both the newly installed ruling party and the former ruling party had to tackle the young democracy's deficiencies and weaknesses left to them by Taiwan's distinctive political history. For the first time in history, they had to work toward their goals in the unfamiliar roles of oppositional parties.

The democratization process faced at least four obstacles. First, in Taiwan, regime transition did not involve *redemocratization* but *democratization*. Unlike many third-wave democratizers elsewhere, Taiwan was a society with no prior democratic experiences. It had been governed as a colony of Japan (1895–1945) and then as a provincial-level unit of the authoritarian Republic of China (ROC) under the KMT from 1945 onward.[2] In 1949 the KMT imposed martial law, under which it banned many elements of the institutional infrastructure for liberal democracy, including a free press, independent judiciary, autonomous civic associations, and opposition political parties. The party-state instituted various forms of corporatist control over social groups and economic sectors. The small political opposition, known as the *dangwai* ("outside the KMT"), because it was forbidden to organize itself as a political party, faced grave difficulties in building broad-based social support for its political reform agenda (Chu 2001).

Second, unlike some of the authoritarian regimes that fell in the third wave, Taiwan's regime was a deeply rooted Leninist-style party system that had been in existence for four decades and was well known for its resiliency and stability (Winckler 1984). In Latin America, the military was able to return to the barracks when its authoritarian rule was no longer sustainable. There was no such natural fallback for Taiwan's ruling party, which was blended into the state in both organizational and personnel terms. Partisan control of the mass media, military, judiciary, and bureaucracy was institutionalized. This structural fact imposed dual impediments to Taiwan's democratization—the need to separate the ruling party from the state apparatus and the need to depoliticize the military-security apparatus. The first challenge is similar to the major constraint on transitions from authoritarianism in Eastern Europe. The second is similar to the major constraint on the transitions from authoritarianism in Latin America.

Third, unlike most Latin American and Eastern European cases, the political opening in Taiwan was not triggered by any major socioeconomic crisis or external market shock. To be sure, it drew some of its momentum from the exogenous shock of American diplomatic derecognition of Taiwan in 1979, when Washington normalized diplomatic relations with Beijing. But since the KMT's management of the economy had continued to pay off in growth rates averaging 8.73% in the period leading up to the transition, there was no popular demand for major socioeconomic reform.[3] Mass defection from the ruling party looked unlikely. The prodemocracy opposition lacked the leverage to impose political reforms on the incumbent elite with means utilized elsewhere, such as large-scale strikes or mass rallies of the economically disadvantaged.

Finally, the transition to democracy in Taiwan involved more than just a legitimacy crisis of the regime. It also called into question the legitimacy of the state—its claims over sovereignty status, boundary of jurisdiction, and what its citizenship encompasses. At the start of the transition, the KMT considered Taiwan a province of China, not an independent state (a position that it would modify later, during the course of the transition under Lee Teng-hui). The opposition leaders had long linked the goal of democratization to the issue of Taiwanese identity, claiming that democracy entailed self-determination and the right to independence from China. The opposition used identity in lieu of socioeconomic dissatisfaction to mobilize public support for democratization, so the demand for democratization became for many citizens an expression of identity. This merging of issues made the transition more intensely conflictual than elsewhere because the identity issue, much like the issue of ethnic conflict in some other transitions, involved a symbol of worth on which there was no compromise. In Taiwan's case, however, the issue of identity did not bear the threat of state disintegration, as it did, for example, in the Soviet Union and Yugoslavia, because Taiwan was already de facto autonomous. What was involved was the question of whether to claim de jure independence at the risk of eliciting a military reaction from China. Even though there was no risk of tearing the state in Taiwan apart, the dangers of internal political polarization and of external intervention were real.

Despite these obstacles, three historical conditions made a peaceful extrication from authoritarian rule politically manageable. First, the KMT's official ideology and the constitutional arrangements it brought over from the mainland contained democratic elements. The party propounded the Three People's Principles of its founder, Sun Yat-sen, and claimed to be exercising authoritarianism as a period of "tutelage" until the society was mature enough to implement democratic self-rule. The constitutionally mandated state structure included a hierarchy of local elections and a national-level legislature (the Legislative Yuan) that was in principle elected, although its full reelection had been stalled because of separation from the mainland. As Taiwan society became increasingly wealthy and educated, tutelage seemed less defensible and martial law—justified as a response to the national emergency caused by "communist rebellion"—also grew less credible as China entered the period of "reform and opening" and became a quasi-ally of the United States.

Second, the KMT had started recruiting native Taiwanese members (as opposed to those who had immigrated from the mainland) and establishing local electoral machines throughout the island as early as the 1950s, allowing it to face the prospect of democratic transition with strong roots in local political society. In the late 1970s the KMT began to promote native Taiwanese to leading party and state positions, giving it a high expectation of surviving democratic competition at the leadership level as well.

There was also a contingent factor that facilitated the transition. Chiang Ching-kuo, the last authoritarian strongman, lacked a credible successor within either his family or the broader mainlander party elite. He had already appointed a Taiwanese, Lee Teng-hui, as his vice president, and as illness encroached Chiang did nothing to disturb Lee's claim to the succession. In keeping with the constitution, Lee succeeded Chiang as president, and ended up serving two and a half four-year terms (1988–2000). To the surprise of many, Lee emerged as a potent democratic reformer, completing the transition that Chiang had barely begun. He carried out the series of democratizing reforms that would culminate in Chen Shui-bian's presidential victory in 2000, while holding in check the tendency of the entrenched incumbent elite within the party-state to restrict the scope of democratic reform. Meanwhile, in mainland China affairs, he redirected the regime toward fostering the growth of Taiwanese identity and away from commitment to broad Chinese nationalism, changing Taiwan's stance on cross-strait issues in ways that established greater separation from the mainland.

Thanks to these facilitating conditions, democratic transition proceeded more smoothly and quickly than observers expected (Cheng 1992; Winckler 1992). First social mobilization, in the form of various movements of the 1980s and early 1990s, loosened the grip of the authoritarian state on civil society at the grassroots level. Then in 1986 a genuine competitive party system came into being when Chiang Ching-kuo allowed the formation of the DPP, which competed in elections for so-called supplementary seats in the Legislative Yuan. Third, Chiang Ching-kuo declared the end of martial law in 1987. With the end of martial law, the provisions of Taiwan's constitution returned to effect. The constitution had been written in China in 1946, setting up institutions to rule over the entire country. But Lee sponsored amendments which refitted the constitution for rule over the actual territory of the Republic of China, consisting of Taiwan and several smaller islands. On that basis, Taiwan's new democracy finally held a series of founding democratic elections starting with the first reelection of the National Assembly (the constitution-amending body) in 1991, the first reelection of the Legislative Yuan in 1992, and then the first-ever popular election for president in 1996. Lee himself won this election, but the next presidential contest in 2000 saw the elite turnover that is the defining culmination of a democratic transition.

But the smoothness and swiftness of the transition was not an unalloyed blessing. Many residual authoritarian elements were preserved and rolled over into the new regime, leaving a series of challenges for the new democracy to face as it slogged along the road toward consolidation. The first issue was the politicization of the military and security apparatus. This privileged branch of the state had long been a political instrument of the KMT and was prominently featured in its formal power structure. Until the end of Lee's presidency, the KMT leadership continued the practice of placing political surveillance on its political rivals both within its own party and the opposition in the name of national security.

Second, the new competitive party system was endowed with the established patterns of ubiquitous presence of partisan politics in all organized sectors of the society (including the civil service, mass media, academia, religious groups, secondary associations, and unions), all-encompassing social mobilization in electoral contests, and a monopoly by political parties in elite recruitment and organizing the political process. The omnipresent political parties almost eliminated free public discourse and stifled the development of autonomous civil society. While the opposition parties (there were several besides the DPP) aimed to curtail the reach of the dominant party, they themselves were forced to try to become mirror images of the KMT in order to compete with it.

A third problematic legacy was the lack of a level playing field for competitors in the party system. During the period of authoritarian repression, the opposition had not been able to establish itself as a viable alternative to the KMT. It lacked both the grassroots electoral machinery and the national level policy experience that made the KMT such a formidable organization. During and after the transition, the KMT resisted pressure to relinquish its grip on electronic mass media, especially the three national television networks, and its ownership of large, privileged, profitable, quasi-public business enterprises. The KMT's undisrupted hegemonic presence in many local electoral constituencies aggravated the prevalent problem of so-called money politics and mafia politics with troubling implications for the legitimacy of Taiwan's new democracy. With the opening of an electoral avenue to national power, structured corruption was quickly transmitted into the national representative bodies. This tendency toward corruption was exacerbated by the speedy indigenization of the KMT's power structure in the early years of the new democracy. In short, democratic competition weakened the institutional insulation that had formerly protected the party's central leadership from the infiltration of social forces via interpersonal connections and lineage networks.

Fourth, as already noted, the issue of national identity shaped the new democratic system around the clash of apparently irreconcilable emotional claims about Taiwan's statehood and the identity of its people. Mirroring Taiwan's internal conflict, a cross-strait standoff continued between the two competing nation-building processes, as China attempted to impose its one-country–two-system model on Taiwan and vowed to use military force if necessary to stop any move toward independence. Lee Teng-hui tried to moderate the internal conflict over national identity by calling for the formation of "a sense of shared destiny among the twenty-one million people [residents of Taiwan]" and backing away from the KMT's historical commitment to the principle of a unified China (Lee 1997). But KMT-DPP electoral competition tended to focus on this issue, unintentionally inviting further external intervention. This, in turn, has created an additional burden on the new democracy. The perceived need to deter a potential military threat and contain the political infiltration of China has visibly clashed with the respect for political pluralism, minority rights, and due process.

Last but not least, an important challenge that Taiwan's new democracy faced at the end of Lee Teng-hui's tenure was the underdevelopment of constitutionalism. Among the third-wave democracies, Taiwan's democratic transition was often cited as a unique case where a quasi-Leninist party not only survived an authoritarian breakdown but also capitalized on the crisis to its advantage.[4] From the late 1980s through the late 1990s, with the principles of popular accountability and open political contestation steadily becoming more legitimized and institutionalized, the KMT managed to keep its political dominance largely intact through an impressive streak of electoral successes (Tien and Chu 1998). Under these circumstances, Lee Teng-hui, in his dual capacities as national president and KMT party leader, managed four phases of constitutional revision between 1990 and 1997. The passage of these constitutional amendments carried a strong flavor of unilateral imposition. For the expected era of continued one-party dominance, Lee designed a semipresidential system, somewhat akin to that of the French Fifth Republic, that gave great authority to both the legislature and the cabinet, but allowed the president to control these branches of government behind the scenes in his role as leader of the ruling party. Although the Temporary Articles, which had authorized martial law, were abolished, some of their key elements were transplanted into the new constitutional amendments, including the emergency power of the president and the creation of the National Security Agency under the presidential office. In the name of presidential prerogative, the military and security apparatuses continued to evade direct supervision by the Legislative Yuan.

Because of these elements of strongman government, the ensemble of Lee's constitutional revisions failed to achieve broad and deep legitimation.[5] Even more seriously, the constitutional arrangements proved to have been poorly designed for the unanticipated scenario of a divided government. This came up after the DPP unexpectedly won the presidency in 2000 with only 39.3% of the vote (thanks to a split in the KMT camp), while the KMT retained control over the Legislative Yuan.

Despite such challenges, a majority of Taiwan's electorate held an optimistic outlook for the dawning of a new political epoch and wished Chen

Shui-bian well. In a postelection survey, 78% of the electorate said that their view of Taiwan's future had stayed the same or become more optimistic after the election.[6] During the first month of his presidency, Chen Shui-bian's approval rate surged to 77%.[7] In particular, he was applauded for his conciliatory gestures toward Beijing.[8]

But great expectations soon soured. Chen Shui-bian's governing capacity was circumscribed by the fact that he had been elected without a majority of the popular vote as well as by his party's minority status in the parliament. The standoff between a combative president and a hostile parliament escalated from competition over control of the legislative agenda to a crippling deadlock. Together, the KMT and another sizeable party that had broken off from it, the People First Party (PFP), blocked many major legislations introduced by the DPP government. In return, the DPP cabinet refused to implement some of the laws passed by the legislature, accusing it of transgressing executive power. The KMT-PFP coalition then blocked more bills and froze the government budget, and the vicious cycle went on. Both sides exhausted all possible legal means to strangle one another. These endless political battles appalled and alienated the electorate.

At the most fundamental level, the power struggle between the two camps involved the cultural survival of their die-hard supporters. The conflict was about who has the power to decide who we are and what to teach children in school, with the state becoming the arena of an identity struggle. As zealots of the two camps competed to gain control of the state apparatus and use its power to steer cross-strait relations, erect a cultural hegemony, and impose their vision of nation-building, they paid little attention to civility, compromise, tolerance, due process, and rule of law, all essential elements to make a liberal democracy work. This race to the political bottom eroded the contending political elites' commitment to due process and shook the faith of both sides in the openness and fairness of the political game.

The electorate also experienced deterioration in the quality of governance on other fronts. The most shocking experience came from a seemingly unlikely realm—the economy. Suddenly, in public eyes, Taiwan's political system seemed to lose much of its capacity to deliver material security and prosperity, which citizens had taken almost for granted. The year 2001 saw the beginning of the worst economic recession since the oil crisis of 1972 and 1973. From 2001 to 2003, the economy contracted by 2.2%, the currency depreciated about 12%, and the stock market plummeted by more than 40%. By March 2003, the effective unemployment rate climbed to 7.51%, which was a shocking experience for many. It was to stay above 7% for the rest of Chen Shui-bian's first term.[9]

Another major disappointment was the stalling of the most promising reform dividend that a historical power rotation should have brought: the elimination of both the structural corruption embedded in the island's electoral politics and the collusive ties between politicians and big business. Waves of new revelations damaged the credibility of the DPP leadership, who had long projected themselves as crusaders for clean politics. Tycoons with close ties to the president were awarded lucrative business deals and cushy appointments. State-owned assets were sold to well-connected conglomerates at fire-sale prices. The promise of clean government turned out to be an illusion.

In the summer of 2001, when the first-wave East Asia Barometer survey was implemented in Taiwan, the island's new democratic regime was under considerable strain. To most of the electorate, the gap between the promise and reality of democracy was glaring. It was at this juncture that we sought to examine to what extent Taiwan's new democracy had acquired a robust popular base of legitimation with both widespread and strongly felt attachments to the democratic regime and dwindling support for nondemocratic alternatives. An assessment of the extent of the public's normative commitment to democracy tells us much about how far Taiwan's political system had traveled toward democratic consolidation at this early stage of its evolution.

2. THE MEANING OF DEMOCRACY

Taiwan respondents' ideas about the meaning of democracy were generally similar to those elsewhere in Asia (see chapter 1, table 1.3). The overwhelming majority of views were positive. The largest proportion of respondents understood democracy as either (or both) "freedom and liberty" and "political rights, institutions, and processes"; that is, in ways consistent with the standard Western understanding of liberal democracy. The second strongest cluster of ideas associated democracy either with general and positive ideas like "popular sovereignty," "people's power," or "a government that cares what people think" (24.1%), or with the notion of "by and for the people" (17.1%). Such ideas look away from rights and institutions toward government's substantive representation of popular interests. Looking across Asia, the proportion of persons holding liberal-democratic ideas of democracy was lower in Taiwan than in most of the other new democracies in our survey, while the proportion of persons holding populist views was higher than any-where else in the region.

In Taiwan as elsewhere in the region, few people (6.3%) understood democracy in terms of social equality and justice, and even fewer (1.4%) in terms of the market economy. In most East Asian newly industrializing societies (with the exceptions of South Korea and Mongolia) democratic transition was not accompanied by a popular demand for economic reform or social redistribution. Social equity was not a salient issue in Taiwan be-cause economic prosperity had been widely distributed under the export-led development strategy of the old regime.

In short, when respondents from Taiwan evaluated their new democratic regime, they were likely to be applying either the standards of liberal de-mocracy or of populism. In the former case, people define democracy to be political liberty and democratic procedures. In the latter case, people define democracy as government that serves the public's interests. Some respon-dents see democracy as a combination of both.

Our historical review suggested that the new regime marked a distinct ad-vance over the old regime in the first of these two areas but was less clearly superior in the second. How did the public see it? First we will explore how far respondents believed the regime had changed in the direction of democ-racy, and then we will look at their perception of the democratic system's performance as a government.

3. EVALUATING THE TRANSITION

In asking respondents to compare the level of democracy of the old and the new regimes, we defined the old regime in Taiwan as the system prior to the abolition of martial law in 1988. The current regime was the one in place under Chen Shui-bian at the time of the survey in 2001. We grouped the scores that respondents gave the two regimes into four categories: 1–2 stands for very dictatorial, 3–5 somewhat dictatorial, 6–8 somewhat democratic, and 9–10 very democratic.

3.1. PERCEPTIONS OF PAST AND CURRENT REGIMES

Table 4.1 shows that a broad majority (72.7%) perceived the current regime as being somewhat or very democratic. This represented a substantial change, compared with the 62% who perceived the former regime as somewhat or very dictatorial. The mean rating of the two regimes shifted markedly, from 4.4 for the old regime—solidly in the dictatorial range—to 7.3 for the new regime, the second-highest mean rating for a new regime in our survey after Thailand. Figure 4.1 indicates that 73.9% of our respondents saw the magnitude of shift from the old to the new regime as two or more points in the direction of democracy on the scale of 1 to 10.

The view of an epochal change, however, was not unanimous. In a pattern found among the Asian new democracies also in Korea and the Philippines, a sizable minority of respondents from Taiwan (20.3%) believed that the system in the martial law era was already somewhat democratic. Seventeen point one percent saw no change, or change in a negative direction, including a small handful of highly disgruntled respondents who saw backsliding in the dictatorial direction of up to 9 points on the scale. This strong minority perception that the old system was already democratic probably reflects the fact that, according to some commentators, the KMT system was a "soft authoritarian regime," in the sense that it allowed for limited pluralism and local level electoral contestation (Winckler 1984). The

TABLE 4.1 **PERCEPTIONS OF PAST AND CURRENT REGIMES: TAIWAN**

(Percent of respondents)

REGIME TYPES	PAST REGIME	CURRENT REGIME
Very dictatorial (1–2)	12.6	1.3
Somewhat dictatorial (3–5)	49.4	13.0
Somewhat democratic (6–8)	18.2	53.0
Very democratic (9–10)	2.1	19.7
DK/NA	17.7	12.9
Total	100.0	100.0
Mean on a 10-point scale	4.4	7.3

Notes: Regime types are based on the respondent's ranking of the regime on a scale from 1, "complete dictatorship," to 10, "complete democracy." Scores of 5 and below are degrees of dictatorship and scores of 6 and above are degrees of democracy.

N = 1415.

DK/NA = Don't know/no answer.

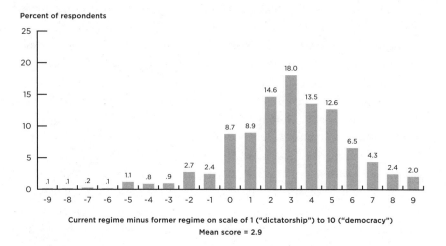

Percent of respondents

Current regime minus former regime on scale of 1 ("dictatorship") to 10 ("democracy")
Mean score = 2.9

FIGURE 4.1   **Perceived Regime Change: Taiwan**

highly negative views of a small number of respondents toward the new regime probably reflected the involvement of Taiwan's transition with the issue of identity. Some of the respondents holding strong Chinese identities probably thought of the DPP regime as having violated or as intending to violate their rights.

Based on respondents' ratings of past and current regimes, we identified six patterns of perceived regime change (see chapter 1, table 1.7). As in most countries in Asia, the largest proportion of respondents from Taiwan (48.4%) rated the old regime as somewhere in the dictatorial range and the new regime in the lower range of democratic scores (6, 7, or 8), the pattern we label "moderate change to democracy." There were also substantial proportions who held each of two contrasting views: one group saw both the old and the new regimes as democratic (19.2%, "continuing democracy") and another (16%) viewed the change to democracy as dramatic, meaning the old regime was dictatorial and the new regime scored 9 or 10 on the democracy scale. Such a range of opinion reminds us that holistic evaluations of regimes are subjective, with citizens perceiving varying intensities of repression and varying degrees of freedom in any given regime. Divergent perceptions about the magnitude of regime change were noticeable as well in the survey results from South Korea and the Philippines.

3.2. COMPARING REGIME PERFORMANCE

One way that a newly installed democratic regime can win the loyalty of citizens is by providing better government than the old regime. Conversely, poor performance may foster doubts about democracy as a whole or about some of the new regime's institutions. We asked respondents to compare the performance of the current and former regimes with respect to nine major areas of activity in two domains, democratic performance and policy performance (see table 4.2). On these nine indicators, we asked our respondents whether things have become worse, stayed the same, or become better.

Much as in Asia's other new democracies (except for Thailand), overall satisfaction with government is generally speaking not on the rise. As measured by both the mean ratings and the percentage difference indices, the curve starts from highly positive assessments of improvements in the two areas of political freedom that we asked about, descends to modestly positive judgments about equal treatment under the law, independence of the judiciary, and cracking down on corruption, and enters negative territory in assessments of the new regime's performance in the areas of income distribution, economic development, and, worst of all, law and order.

Most respondents saw large positive changes in the freedoms of speech and association. In this their perceptions were consistent with the judgment of such outside observers as Freedom House. Freedom House gave Taiwan an average score of 5 on political rights and 4.8 on civil liberties (on a seven-point scale with 7 as the lowest) for the five years from 1983 to 1988 and raised the score to an average of 1.8 on political rights and 2 on civil liberties for the five years from 1996 to 2001 (Freedom House 2005). The new regime was more democratic than the old, and respondents from Taiwan knew it.

But in other respects they were not so positive. Close to half of our respondents felt that there was no bottom-line change in popular influence over government despite the improvement in civil liberties. They considered themselves just as powerless as they had been under martial law, while another 15% felt even more disempowered than before. The same phenomenon of increased political liberties with stagnant political influence appears in the EAB results from Korea and the Philippines, and, according to Putnam, Pharr, and Dalton, is a common phenomenon in established

TABLE 4.2 PERCEIVED PERFORMANCE OF CURRENT AND PAST REGIMES: TAIWAN

	MEAN[a]	SD[a]	NEGATIVE CHANGE[b]	POSITIVE CHANGE[b]	NO CHANGE[b]	PDI[c]	VALID %[d]
Democratic performance							
Freedom of speech	1.11	0.99	9.0	81.3	9.8	72.3	93.8
Freedom of association	1.15	0.80	3.6	83.9	12.6	80.3	86.2
Equal treatment	0.55	0.96	14.4	59.3	26.3	44.9	92.2
Popular influence	0.25	0.93	15.0	37.9	47.1	22.8	85.2
Independent judiciary	0.31	1.01	20.4	49.9	29.7	29.4	77.0
Average	0.67	0.94	12.5	62.4	25.1	50.0	86.9
Policy performance							
Anticorruption	0.27	1.11	23.2	49.6	27.2	26.5	88.2
Law and order	-0.58	1.14	57.6	22.8	19.6	-34.8	94.1
Economic development	-0.37	1.26	54.7	31.7	13.6	-23.0	93.0
Economic equality	-0.29	1.12	39.9	26.7	33.4	-13.2	90.2
Average	-0.24	1.16	43.8	32.7	23.5	-11.1	91.4

Notes: N = 1415.

Past regime is defined as pre-1987.

[a] Scale ranges from -2 (much worse) to +2 (much better).
[b] Percent of valid sample.
[c] PDI (percentage difference index) = percent seeing positive change minus percent seeing negative change.
[d] Percent of sample giving a valid answer to this question.

democracies as well (2000). We explore some of the causes of this attitude in section 4.1.

Opinions were sharply divided on the new regime's anticorruption efforts. Although about half of the respondents thought the situation had become better, the other half was almost equally divided between those who said that the regime's anticorruption efforts were either no more effective (27.2%) or even less effective (23.2%) than those of the martial law regime. This divergent assessment suggests that the many revelations of political scandals implicating high-ranking officials in the period since the end of martial law had cut both ways with the public. Some people noticed that more and more corrupt officials and politicians were being brought to trial; others were shocked by revelations concerning the extent and magnitude of political corruption. This point is explored further in section 4.2.

In contrast, opinions on the new regime's inability to crack down on crime and maintain law and order were overwhelming negative, with 57.6% of the respondents believing that the situation had become worse than during the martial law regime. This popular perception is consistent with official statistics, which show that from 1992 and 2002 criminal offenses increased by a whopping 117%.[10] However, depending on one's occupation, domicile location, and other social variables, some people were more likely to be victims of crime than others. So, divergent assessments of the ability of the new regime in delivering law and order still existed, with 22.8% of respondents experiencing positive change and 19.6% no change.

The economic slowdown that started in the late years of Lee Teng-hui's presidency and turned into a recession in 2001 inevitably affected the public's assessment of the post–martial law regime's economic performance. Taiwan's GNP grew at an average annual rate of 8.73% between 1983 and 1988, but slowed to 3.32% between 1996 and 2001, and began to contract in 2001. A majority of respondents perceived a negative change in the government's economic performance since the transition. Nor did respondents give the post–transition regime high marks on whether "the gap between the rich and poor has narrowed." Nearly three-quarters saw either no change or negative change. By objective standards they were again right. Income distribution in Taiwan's economy scored a Gini coefficient of 0.295 in the last years of the martial law regime (from 1983 to 1988), a remarkable record among developing countries. But a few years after the transition, during the period from 1996 to 2001, the average annual score rose to 0.329, and it reached 0.35 in 2001. Although this was still impressive by world standards, it represented a worsening trend.[11]

4. APPRAISING DEMOCRATIC INSTITUTIONS

The effective functioning of democratic institutions depends on citizens' belief in their own capacity to perform as citizens and their confidence in various institutions of state and society. In this section we examine three of these attitudes.

4.1. POLITICAL EFFICACY

To estimate Taiwan citizens' perceived participatory capacity, respondents were asked about their self-perceived ability to understand the complexities of politics and government and their perceived capacity to participate in politics (see chapter 1, table 1.4).

Roughly half (60.8%) of respondents in Taiwan believed they could neither understand nor participate in politics, while those who felt capable of both amounted to only 10%. These findings are similar to those from other East Asian democracies. To assess further the perceived efficacy of popular participation, we asked respondents how strongly they agreed or disagreed with the following statements: "The nation is run by a powerful few and ordinary citizens cannot do much about it," and "People like me don't have any influence over what the government does." On both statements, 35% of our respondents disagreed. Taken together only one-sixth (16%) disagreed with both statements, while 44.5% agreed with both. These figures are once again similar to those from other East Asian democracies.

4.2. POLITICAL CORRUPTION

In most new East Asian democracies, the most troubling development under the new regime in the eyes of the citizens was the encroachment of money politics. As shown in table 4.3, in Taiwan almost twice as many (47.5%) of our respondents thought that most national officials were corrupt as believed that they were not (25.8%). Respondents thought things were even worse at the local level. There, as many as 56.5% of respondents thought that officials were corrupt, while only 23.9% believed that they were not.

The cross-tabulation in table 4.3 suggests that the two evaluations were correlated. If one believed that most officials were corrupt at the local level, one tended to believe that the same was true for the national government

TABLE 4.3 PERCEPTION OF POLITICAL CORRUPTION AT NATIONAL AND LOCAL LEVELS: TAIWAN

(Percent of total sample)

NATIONAL GOVERNMENT

LOCAL GOVERNMENT	Hardly anyone is involved	Not a lot of officials are involved	Most officials are corrupt	Almost everyone is corrupt	DK/NA	Total
Hardly anyone is involved	0.6	0.4	0.3	0.1	0.4	1.8
Not a lot of officials are involved	0.8	**14.7**	3.5	0.1	3.0	**22.1**
Most officials are corrupt	0.3	7.6	**35.2**	2.0	5.3	**50.4**
Almost everyone is corrupt	–	0.6	1.6	3.3	0.7	6.1
DK/NA	0.2	0.6	1.3	0.3	**17.3**	**19.7**
Total	1.9	**23.9**	**41.8**	5.7	**26.7**	**100.0**

Notes: N = 1415.

Blank cell means no cases.

Percentages above 10 are in boldface.

and vice versa. In China, by contrast, the perception of corruption was concentrated at the local level and in Japan, it was concentrated at the national level. Taiwan had the highest percentage of respondents who reported that most officials were corrupt at both levels.

Yet, surprisingly, only 23.5% of respondents from Taiwan said that they or their family members had personally witnessed corruption or bribe-taking in the past year. This percentage was lower than in Korea, Thailand, or Mongolia, even though in Korea and Thailand concern over corruption was less pronounced than in Taiwan. This suggests that the concern over corruption in Taiwan was produced as much by the dynamics of posttransition political and media competition as by the growth of corruption itself. After the transition, the political parties and the media associated with them produced a stream of revelations about scandalous behavior on the part of Lee Teng-hui's associates and Chen Shui-bian's confidants. These stories promoted the belief that once Taiwan became democratized, political corruption spread into national politics and reached the core of government. These findings remind us not to conflate perceived corruption with actual corruption. But they take away nothing from the damage that can be done to a regime's legitimacy by the perception, however created, that corruption is widespread.

4.3. TRUST IN INSTITUTIONS

If citizens think that the system is governing poorly, they tend to withdraw their confidence from the public institutions that they blame for these deficiencies. And their level of trust in specific institutions affects their support for the regime as a whole. Figure 4.2 reveals both the strengths and the weaknesses of Taiwan's emerging political system as seen by its citizens. On the positive side, respondents saw the new democracy as endowed with a trustworthy military, civil service, local governments, election commission, and courts (in that descending order), all key parts of an effective state. The public also respected the integrity of the key civil society actors, the NGOs, who can be expected to play a key role in the future deepening of Taiwan's democracy. But the public showed more distrust than trust for the television networks and national government. The island's four television networks were necessarily politicized, as they are tied to either the government or political parties. The first two are owned by the government, the third belongs to the KMT, and the fourth, which was licensed in 1997 as a concession

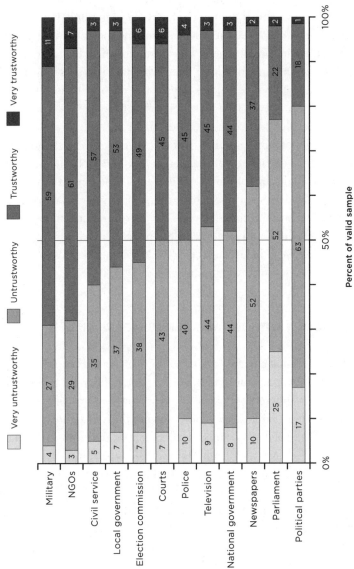

FIGURE 4.2 Trust in Institutions: Taiwan

to the opposition, is owned by a consortium of DPP political figures and donors. The privately-owned cable television stations, which arrived around the mid-1990s and steadily outperformed the networks in attracting viewers, have enjoyed more credibility than the networks. But it became increasingly difficult for any cable station not to take a partisan stand, because cutthroat competition compelled them to find a niche market in a highly polarized political environment. Newspapers were driven by the same market and political forces, and might appear to be more politicized as they usually gave more coverage to political news. This is the reason why in our survey newspapers suffered an even lower level of trustworthiness.

Most respondents dismissed the trustworthiness of what are arguably the two key institutions of representative democracy: political parties and parliament. Their distrust of these institutions stemmed from both the long-term trend of the encroachment of money politics and, more apparently, the effect of Taiwan's divided government under its semipresidential constitution after Chen Shui-bian's election. After only a year of endless, nasty battles between political parties and gridlock on the parliamentary floor, egged on by the partisan media, citizens' respect for these core institutions had apparently worn thin when our survey was taken.

4.4. SATISFACTION WITH THE WAY DEMOCRACY WORKS

So far we have seen that citizens formed sophisticated and complex views of the degree of democratization from the old regime to the new, governmental performance in different domains, and trustworthiness of different institutions. The question, "How satisfied are you with the way democracy works in our country?" allowed us to compare affect toward the regime in general across the eight East Asian cases. In Taiwan, the question had the added advantage of having been used in one of our previous surveys. This allowed us to compare citizens' evaluation of the system's overall performance in 1996 (after Taiwan's first popular election for president, when Lee Teng-hui won) with 2001 (the time of our survey and one year after the island's first power rotation).

Table 4.4 shows that in 1996 more than two-thirds of the citizens were largely satisfied with the way democracy worked in Taiwan (including 4.4% who were very satisfied and 62.8% who were fairly satisfied), while close to one-third were dissatisfied. Five years later, the level of satisfaction had

TABLE 4.4 **SATISFACTION WITH THE WAY DEMOCRACY WORKS IN TAIWAN**

	1996	2001
Very satisfied	4.4%	4.4%
Fairly satisfied	**62.8%**	**49.0%**
Not very satisfied	**30.2%**	**41.6%**
Not at all satisfied	2.6%	5.0%
Mean	2.31	2.47
SD	0.6	0.66
Valid Cases	1256	1270

Source: Comparative Studies of Electoral System in Taiwan (1996); East Asia Barometer Survey in Taiwan (2001).

Note: Percentages above 30 are in boldface.

dropped considerably. Only 54.4% of respondents were satisfied (including 4.4% very satisfied and 49% fairly satisfied). The percentage of dissatisfied citizens increased to 46.6%. As with other attitudes reported above, this surely reflected the escalation of partisan conflict after the 2000 power rotation and the fact that Chen Shui-bian had come to office without a majority of the popular vote.

A correlation analysis confirms that the measure of satisfaction with how democracy works determines people's attitudes toward various aspects of incumbent and government performance. After controlling for education, age, and income, satisfaction with the way democracy works in Taiwan was associated, at the $p<.05$ or higher level of statistical significance, with the following attitudes: evaluation of the economy today, evaluation of the economic trend over the past five years, sum score of perceived changes in democratic performance (from table 4.2), sum score of perceived changes in policy performance (also from table 4.2), sum score of perceived corruption at local and national levels (from table 4.3), and satisfaction with the performance of the incumbent Chen Shui-bian. Satisfaction with how democracy works is thus a reflection of attitudes toward both the incumbent and government policy performance (Bratton, Mattes, and Gyimah-Boadi 2005).

TABLE 4.5 **SATISFACTION WITH THE WAY DEMOCRACY WORKS: CORRELATION ANALYSIS**

	SATISFACTION WITH THE WAY DEMOCRACY WORKS
Years of formal education	-0.142**
Age -0.031	
Income -0.061*	
Evaluation of the economy today	0.125**
Evaluation of the economy over the past five years	0.110**
Satisfaction with the performance of the incumbent	0.323**
Sum score of the perceived changes on political dimension	0.276**
Sum score of the perceived changes on policy output dimension	0.223**
Sum score of the perceived corruption at local and national level	-0.148**

*Correlation is significant at the 0.05 level (2-tailed).

**Correlation is significant at the 0.01 level (2-tailed).

5. POPULAR COMMITMENT TO DEMOCRATIC LEGITIMACY

When political and economic problems shake the public's faith in the performance of a particular regime and their trust in its institutions, this may or may not call into question their commitment to democratic principles of legitimacy. For example, chapter 7 shows that Japanese citizens remain committed to democracy as the only legitimate of government despite feeling alienated from many aspects of Japan's political system. In Taiwan, to what extent was citizens' commitment to democratic politics undermined by the problems the nation faced at the start of its experiment with democracy?

Over the years, political scientists have grappled with the concept of democratic legitimacy, trying different measurement strategies with mixed successes. We conceive of democratic legitimacy as a multifaceted phenomenon with no single indicator up to the task. We therefore devised a dual-cluster battery to assess the level of popular commitment to democratic legitimacy. The first cluster focuses on people's belief in the desirability, suitability, superiority, priority, and efficacy of democracy.[12] The second cluster assesses popular attitudes toward four authoritarian alternatives: rule by a strong leader, military rule, one-party rule, and rule by experts. Democracy is consolidated—it is "the only game in town"—when citizens not only believe in it, but consider alternatives to it unacceptable.

5.1. SUPPORT FOR DEMOCRACY

Table 1.8 in chapter 1 shows the extent to which respondents from Taiwan supported democracy (in the five dimensions that we asked about) in comparison with samples elsewhere in Asia. A majority of respondents from Taiwan considered democracy both desirable and suitable. But in both cases the majorities were the smallest among the eight regimes studied.

Moreover, as shown in figure 4.3, of the 72.2% who said that they desired democracy, close to a third only wanted democracy in the 6–7 range of our scale, that is, a moderate level of democracy rather than full democracy. The mean level given by all respondents for the democracy they desired was 7.7, less than a half point above the average level respondents gave for where

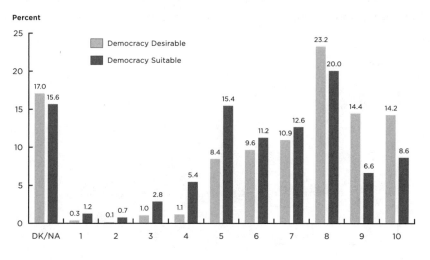

Notes: Desirability and suitability are based on the respondent's ranking of the regime on a scale from 1 to 10.

FIGURE 4.3 **Desirability and Suitability of Democracy: Taiwan**

they thought the political system already was. On suitability, 25.5% of our respondents gave a score between 1 and 5, and 23.8% gave a score between 6 and 7, registering negative views or lukewarm affirmation of democracy's suitability for Taiwan. Together they outnumber the fewer than 40% who gave a score of 8 or above. Apparently, the way democracy had worked in Taiwan had not yet convinced a large number of people about democracy's suitability. A modest mean of 6.75 and a large standard deviation (2.02) also underscore the divergence of people's views on this issue.

On the other three variables (effectiveness, preferability, and priority), respondents from Taiwan are clustered with Hong Kong respondents in giving the lowest percentages of support for democracy among countries in the region. While 40% of Taiwan respondents said that "democratic government is always preferable under all circumstances," nearly a quarter (23.2%) said that under some circumstances an authoritarian government can be preferable to a democratic one. A substantial proportion of our respondents (25.9%) said they "don't care whether we have democratic or nondemocratic regime." In a nutshell, there are more people in Taiwan who are skeptical about democracy's superiority than people who believe in it. When respondents were forced to choose between democracy and economic development, the twin aspirations of most developing societies, democracy lost favor to development by a ratio of more than 5 to 1, with only 10.5% of respondents believing that democracy is more important. In contrast, almost two-thirds supported the view that economic development is more important.

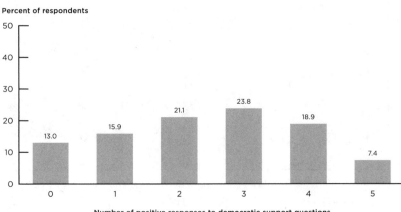

FIGURE 4.4 **Democratic Support: Taiwan**

On our 6-point index of overall attachment to democracy, as shown in figure 4.4, only about 7.4% of Taiwan's electorate responded affirmatively to all five questions, with an additional 18.9% responding affirmatively to four out of five questions. Nowhere else in the region did such a high proportion of respondents (28.9%) give only zero or one prodemocracy response, and nowhere except in Hong Kong were there so few respondents (26.3%) who gave four or five prodemocracy responses. In short, positive support for democratic legitimacy had not yet taken hold in Taiwan.

5.2. REJECTION OF AUTHORITARIAN ALTERNATIVES

Even where positive support for democracy is weak, the system can survive because the public sees no viable alternatives. Table 1.9 in chapter 1 shows that respondents from Taiwan differed little from other Asian populations in their rejection of authoritarian options. They stood close to the middle of the pack both in the mean number of items rejected and in the percentages that rejected each specific item. The lowest level of rejection was addressed to the item we labeled "strong leader." This question asked respondents to agree or disagree with the statement, "We should get rid of parliament and elections and have a strong leader decide things." The nearly one-third who agreed with this idea were expressing a combination of exasperation with Taiwan's parties and elections and nostalgia for the effectiveness of rule under Chiang Ching-kuo.

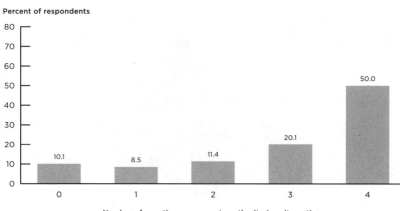

Percent of respondents

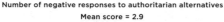

Number of negative responses to authoritarian alternatives
Mean score = 2.9

FIGURE 4.5 **Authoritarian Detachment: Taiwan**

The intensity of detachment from authoritarianism is shown in figure 4.5, which counts the total number of antiauthoritarian responses per respondent. The contrast with figure 4.4 is striking, in that a full 50% of the sample rejected all four nondemocratic alternatives, the third-highest percentage among our eight Asian countries. On the other hand, this means that in Taiwan, as elsewhere in the region, half the respondents were willing to consider at least one authoritarian alternative and many of them more than one. In sum, authoritarianism remains a formidable potential competitor to democracy.

5.3. OVERALL SUPPORT FOR DEMOCRACY

Figure 4.6 combines the information on democratic support and authoritarian detachment to identify constituencies ranging from the strongest supporters to the strongest opponents of democracy (see the notes to table 1.11, chapter 1, for a description of how these categories are defined). Judging from this measure, the cultural foundation of Taiwan's new democracy is not robust. However, supporters of one kind or another made up half the population, the second-lowest proportion among the seven countries for which these data were compiled (we did not include China in this part of the study). There were also significant numbers of "skeptical supporters" (18.96%), who rejected most authoritarian alternatives but harbored many

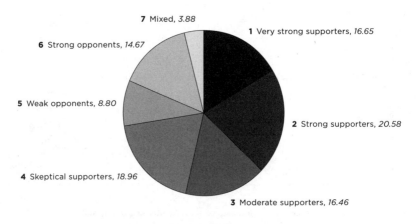

Percent of respondents

FIGURE 4.6 **Patterns of Commitment to Democracy: Taiwan**

reservations about democracy. Including the opponents, the mixed, and the skeptical supporters, nearly half of the public does not accept democracy as "the only game in town."

6. EXPECTATIONS ABOUT THE FUTURE OF DEMOCRACY

Even if citizens retain doubts about democratic principles, a new democracy may generate such a sense of momentum that it makes other forms of government appear irrelevant. To assess whether this bandwagon effect might be occurring, we asked respondents where they expected Taiwan to be in five years on a 10-point scale from complete dictatorship to complete democracy. The results are displayed in table 4.6. Fewer than one-third of respondents thought the regime would be "very democratic" in five years. An even larger number (32.3%) said that they didn't know, or declined to answer, which was a 19.4% jump from the percent of current nonresponses. Apparently, this question is not an easy one to answer for many respondents from Taiwan. For those who did answer, the average expectation for the size of the advance over the present level was a modest

TABLE 4.6 **CURRENT AND EXPECTED FUTURE REGIME TYPE: TAIWAN**

(Percent of respondents)

RATING	CURRENT REGIME	FUTURE REGIME	CHANGE[a]
Very dictatorial (1–2)	1.3	0.6	-0.8
Somewhat dictatorial (3–5)	13.0	7.9	-5.0
Somewhat democratic (6–8)	53.0	29.6	-23.4
Very democratic (9–10)	19.7	29.6	9.8
DK/NA	12.9	32.3	19.4
Total	100.0	100.0	
Mean on a 10-point scale	7.3	7.9	0.6

*Notes:*N = 1415.

Future regime is five years from time of survey.

Scale runs from 1, "complete dictatorship," to 10, "complete democracy."

[a] Change in percent of respondents rating the regime at the given level when the object of evaluation shifts from the current to the future regime.

six-tenths of a point on the scale of ten, the second lowest in the region after Japan. Also, a relatively large standard deviation (1.90) suggested that people held widely differing expectations for Taiwan's political future. This high level of uncertainty reflects people's anxiety about Taiwan's long-term political future, in particular its future relationship with mainland China.

We combined respondents' views of the current and future state of affairs to describe seven types of views about change in Taiwan and elsewhere in the region (see chapter 1, table 1.12). This shows that close to one-third of respondents in all three Chinese political systems—China, Hong Kong, and Taiwan—were unsure about what the future would hold. Among those who gave level-of-democracy scores for both the current and future regimes, it was the Hong Kong respondents who were most pessimistic (39% expecting authoritarian persistence), the mainlanders who were most optimistic (43% expecting developing democracy, defined as moving from a lower to a higher level of democracy), and the Taiwan sample who were most divided, with 80% split among the three categories of struggling democracy, developing democracy, and consolidating democracy. By the metric of this table, the Taiwan sample was not markedly more pessimistic than those of other new democracies such as Korea, Mongolia, or the Philippines, where many respondents expected limited democratic transition or struggling or developing democracy.

7. CONCLUSION

Our findings do not suggest that democracy in Taiwan is in imminent danger of reversal, but they show that public support for the new order is fragile. On the one hand, a majority of Taiwan citizens at the time of our survey recognized the changes that had taken place in the areas of political freedom, rule of law, and opportunities for citizen participation. A substantial percentage thought that democratization had brought more effective control of political corruption. A majority reported guarded optimism about the island's democratic future.

On the other hand, just as Taiwan experienced its first transfer of power after democratic transition, many saw the transition from a one-party authoritarian regime to a competitive democratic system as an incremental political change rather than a quantum leap. A large majority saw deterioration in the capacity of the political system to deliver economic growth, social equity, and law and order. A sizable minority considered the current political system to be more corrupt and less responsive to their voices and concerns than the old regime. The proportion of people who said they were dissatisfied with the way democracy works rose to almost equal the proportion who said they were satisfied. Because Taiwan's citizens experienced a variant of soft authoritarianism that was seemingly less corrupt and more efficacious than democracy in delivering social stability and economic development, democracy faces a demanding standard to prove its worth.

A large majority of Taiwan citizens expressed distrust for the key institutions of representative democracy, in particular parliament and political parties. This distrust is fed by the perception of corruption at both national and local levels of government, and by the perceived deteriorating state of some aspects of governance. Unfortunately, there has been no quick fix for the institutional deficiencies built into the constitution since our survey was taken. Constitutional amendments have been discussed, but to be implemented they must first gain the support of a three-quarters majority in the Legislative Yuan, something that would require precisely the political cooperation that the current institutional setup militates against.

If the new democratic regime has not gained points for performance, neither could it count for legitimacy on deep reserves of normative commitment to democracy among the public. The proportion of citizens who harbored either professed reservations about democracy or lingering attachments to authoritarianism remained substantial. Indeed, by some measures citizens in Taiwan demonstrated the lowest level of commitment to democracy among the new East Asian democracies at the time of our survey. Only about half of the population rejected all authoritarian alternatives. This might have something to do with the political upheaval surrounding the historical power rotation following the 2000 presidential election. But the level of popular skepticism toward democracy has been lessened only slightly since then.[13] In the years after our survey, Taiwan continued to experience political traumas, including protracted gridlock between the president and the legislature, intense polarization over the twin issues of state and national identity, the bitterly disputed 2004 presidential election (which led the opposition to challenge the legitimacy of the incumbent president, Chen Shui-bian), and grave charges of corruption against the presidential family that generated calls for President Chen's resignation.

Taiwan's electorate does not share a common vision of the democratic future. Their uncertainty and division on this and other issues flows in large part from Taiwan's unique contested status in the international system and

the domestic clash between two irreconcilable claims about national identity. As long as the island's status as a state remains unresolved, Taiwan's new
democracy will have a hard time consolidating.

NOTES

1. For the concept of the party-state see Giovanni Sartori, *Parties and Party Systems* (New York: Cambridge University Press, 1976), 47. Sartori's definition of a party-state system corresponds to what Samuel Huntington and Clement Moore termed "a single-party authoritarian system." See Samuel Huntington and Clement Moore, eds., *Authoritarian Politics in Modern Society* (New York: Basic Books, 1970). A one-party dominant regime refers to a democracy characterized by a ruling party with large and seemingly permanent majority. See T. J. Pemple, "Introduction," in *Uncommon Democracies: The One-Party Dominant Regimes*, ed. T. J. Pemple (Ithaca: Cornell University Press, 1990).

2. For more on the historical background, see Thomas Gold, *State and Society in the Taiwan Miracle* (Armonk, NY: M. E. Sharpe, 1986).

3. This is the average GNP growth rate between 1950 and 1988 calculated from *Taiwan Statistical Data Book 2005* (Taipei: Council of Economic Planning and Development, 2005).

4. The old KMT resembled Leninist regimes as far as the symbiosis between the party and the state and the way the party-state organized and penetrated the society are concerned. For the quasi-Leninist features of the KMT, see Tun-jen Cheng. "Democratizing the Quasi-Leninist Regime in Taiwan," *World Politics* 42 (July 1989): 471–499. However, it is also important to point out that on many important scores the KMT regime was quite different from the Leninist regimes of the former Soviet bloc. Unlike the communist regime, the KMT was long associated with the West; it had ample experience with private property rights, markets, and the rule of law; and it enjoyed the support of a distinctive development coalition. For a full treatment of the Leninist legacy in the Eastern European context, see Beverley Crawford and Arend Lijphart, eds., *Liberalization and Leninist Legacies: Comparative Perspectives on Democratic Transitions* (Berkeley: University of California International and Area Studies, 1996).

5. For the controversies over constitutional reform, see Yun-han Chu, "Consolidating Democracy in Taiwan: From *Guoshi* to *Guofa* Conference," in *Democratization in Taiwan: Implications for China*, ed. Hung-mao Tien and Steve Yui-sang Tsang (New York: St. Martins Press, 1998).

6. The postelection survey was carried out in June 2002 and organized by a research team led by Fu Hu and Yun-han Chu of National Taiwan University under the auspices of the Comparative Study of Electoral System (CSES) Project. Please visit the CSES website (www.cses.org) for details.

7. Based on the TVBS Poll of June 19, 2000, available at: http://www.tvbs.com.tw/news/poll_center/default.asp.

8. To dispel the widely held apprehension that his presidency might cause rupture to cross-strait relations, in his inaugural address Chen made his "Four No's pledge": no to declaring independence, no to changing Taiwan's formal name from the Republic of China, no to enshrining Lee Teng-hui's controversial idea of "special state-to-state relations" in the Constitution, and no to holding a referendum on formal independence.

9. *The United Daily News*, March 22, 2003. In the case of Taiwan, the effective unemployment rate, the so-called broad measure, is on average 2.3% higher than the official unemployment rate (the so-called narrow measure), which excludes laid-off people who have stopped looking for jobs.

10. The figure is computed from *TaiMin diqu xingshi anjian tongji 1973–2003* [Statistics of criminal cases in the Taiwan-Fujian region, 1997–2003], published by Taiwan's Criminal Investigation Bureau.

11. The income distribution statistics were calculated from various issues of the annual Household Income Survey Report published by Taiwan's Directorate-General of Budget, Accounting and Statistics.

12. Please refer to chapter 1 for elaboration on measuring support for democracy. The exact wording of these questions can be found in appendix 4.

13. Two follow-up surveys have found a similar pattern of fragile popular support for democracy, although the level of normative commitment among Taiwan's electorate has slightly recovered from the depression observed in 2001. For instance, we found that the percentage of respondents believing that "democracy is always preferable to any other kind of government" has increased from the low of 40.4% (2001) to 42.2% (2003) and 47.5% (2006). But it has not yet climbed over the 50% threshold. Please refer to Yun-han Chu, "Taiwan's Year of Stress," *Journal of Democracy* 16, no. 2 (April 2005): 43–57, and Yu-tzung Chang, Yun-han Chu, and Chong-Min Park, "Authoritarian Nostalgia in Asia," *Journal of Democracy* 18, no. 3 (July 2007): 70.

5

DEVELOPING DEMOCRACY UNDER A
NEW CONSTITUTION IN THAILAND

Robert B. Albritton and Thawilwadee Bureekul

FEW EMERGING DEMOCRACIES OFFER a better laboratory for exploring democratic consolidation than Thailand. The evolution of Thailand's political system was so dramatic that even one of the most severe critics of Thai democracy acknowledged, "Thailand has been shifting incrementally away from semidemocracy toward democracy" (Samudavanija 1995:340). However, the establishment of truly democratic institutions and practices has been a relatively recent phenomenon. There remains, therefore, much room for a discussion of the extent of Thai democracy's degree of consolidation (Linz and Stepan 2001; O'Donnell 2001).

Thailand's history of parliamentarism dates back to the fall of the absolute monarchy in 1932. But in the period up to 1985, only about six of those years can be characterized as truly democratic. Regardless of the actual form of government, however, a commitment to democracy—even an ideology of democracy—maintained itself through periods of one-party rule, personalistic autocracy, and military despotism. The transition to genuine democracy, beginning in the mid-1980s, built upon this latent democratic commitment in the mass public, and established itself in the events of "Bloody May" in 1992, when mass demonstrations forced a military junta to relinquish its power, permit new elections, and institute a transition toward democracy that was interrupted by a military coup in 2006. This study examines mass attitudes toward democracy in 2001, five years after a new constitution introduced significant structural revisions to the political system. Data for the chapter come from one of the first probability sample surveys of political attitudes in Thailand. A total of 1,546 valid responses were gathered from a nationwide sample of eligible voters.

The 2001 survey caught the Thai public in an optimistic and supportive frame of mind. Yet signs of trouble could be discerned as well. A key issue was the split between Bangkok and the rural hinterland. With each voter in the rural areas counting as much as each voter in Bangkok, it was only a matter of time before political power would shift to the politics and priorities of rural Thailand, resulting in policies and practices Bangkok elites viewed as corrupt. Corruption indeed was the chief reason given by the military leaders who ousted the Prime Minister Thaksin Shinawatra in a bloodless coup on September 19, 2006.

The lesson to be learned from our data and the ensuing events is that even high levels of support for democracy among mass publics do not guarantee democratic persistence when faced with a determined, antidemocratic elite that controls instruments of power such as the military. While the leaders of the 2006 coup promised a rapid return to democracy, as long as such coups are possible, democracy cannot be considered consolidated no matter how supportive mass publics may be.

1. HISTORICAL DEVELOPMENT OF DEMOCRATIC GOVERNANCE IN THAILAND

A palace coup at dawn on June 24, 1932, brought the Thai absolute monarchy to an end. When he finally abdicated in 1935, King Prajadhipok (Rama VII) specifically criticized the regime that had replaced him and, in a brief public message, transferred sovereignty to the people of Thailand. In his message of abdication, the king emphasized that he was turning power over to the people, rather than to the incumbent government. He stated, "I am willing to surrender the powers I formerly exercised to the people as a whole, but I am not willing to turn them over to any individual or any group to use in an autocratic manner without heeding the voice of the people" (Wyatt 1982:249).

Although the abdication marked the final dissolution of royal powers, it is also clear that what followed was not a genuine participatory democracy.

Political power was monopolized by an exclusive elite in a one-party state (the People's Party), which promised full electoral democracy only when at least half the population had completed primary education or ten years had passed, whichever came first.

Thailand held its first direct elections in November 1937, when 26% of the electorate chose half of the National Assembly. Another round of elections was held in November 1938, but the National Assembly remained half-appointed. Because of World War II no new elections were held until 1946. Prime Minister Phibun Songkram took advantage of his extended tenure to undertake a program of economic and social nation-building, which was carried out in a highly authoritarian manner.

During the postwar period, prospects for democracy brightened temporarily with the creation of four political parties (at least in name) and a new constitution providing for a fully elected House of Representatives and a Senate chosen by the House. In November 1947, however, the military seized the government, supporting a series of authoritarian governments for the next twenty-six years. Throughout the postwar era, however, the ideology of democracy persisted, reinforced in part by a growing consciousness, especially among the rural population, of oppression by the military, the police, and the bureaucracy. This disaffection from authoritarianism served to bolster an equally antiauthoritarian sentiment among the educated middle classes. By 1973, a coalition of workers, farmers, students, and members of the middle classes began to mobilize for democracy and repeatedly clashed with the police in street demonstrations. In order to prevent mass bloodshed, the king intervened to end the authoritarian regime.

The ensuing period was one of political and economic instability. Although leftist parties had benefited from the revolution initially, they lost power in the 1976 parliamentary elections, ushering in a period of organized atrocities by right-wing vigilantes against figures advocating radical democracy. The bloodshed culminated in an infamous massacre at Thammasat University, where protesting students were shot, lynched, burned alive, or imprisoned. Not long after, the military reasserted itself with the support of the ruling establishment, including much of the middle class, bringing this experiment in democracy to an end.

By 1978, disaffection with the excesses of the authoritarian right had again revived the demand for democracy among the Thai public. There followed a period of political stability and, arguably, steady progression toward democratic governance under the leadership of General Prem Tinsulanonda. Modern Thai democracy can be dated to the parliamentary elections of 1983, which provided the mandate for the consolidation of Prem's leadership. In 1986, when economic conditions created social unrest, Prem rebuffed demands from the military for another seizure of power, choosing instead to step aside and hold new elections. In 1988, fully democratic elections were finally held and a full-fledged coalition government assumed office under Chatichai Choonhaven.

By the 1990s, support for democracy was robust and growing. Although perceived corruption of the Chatichai cabinet led to another coup in 1991, popular pressure forced the junta to promise new elections within a year and appoint a highly regarded bureaucrat, Anand Panyarachun, as prime minister. When the leader of the junta reneged on a promise not to seek the premiership following the 1992 elections, mass demonstrations again resulted in the monarch's intervention, who tilted the balance in favor of restoring democracy. In the opinions of many analysts, this episode represented an affirmation of democratic politics rather than a failure of democratic persistence, for it made clear that continuation of authoritarian rule, even if benign in nature, was no longer compatible with public sentiment.

The 1997 Constitution radically revised the electoral system and created new institutions of governance that parallel elections as major instruments of democratic politics. Three institutions were of special relevance for understanding how Thailand's political system worked after 1997. The first was the Constitutional Court, a body of fifteen judges appointed by the king on the advice of the Senate, which in turn worked from a list submitted by a committee composed primarily of academics in law and political science. The court was composed of five members from the Supreme Court of Justice, two members of the Supreme Administrative Court, five qualified lawyers, and three political scientists. These persons were supposed to be removed from any association with politics or government and were charged with interpretation of the Constitution as issues arose.

The second new institution was the Election Commission. The process of selection for this body was similar to that for the Constitutional Court, and members of the commission were banned from holding political office or joining political parties. The commission had the power to invalidate elections, disqualify candidates, and call new elections when balloting was suspect. The exercise of this power led to microscopic examinations of the integrity of election processes, leading to the most open, corruption-free elections in Thai history.[1]

The third important new institution was the National Anti-Corruption Commission, composed of nine members chosen in a manner similar to the Constitutional Court and the Election Commission. This body had sweeping constitutional authority to investigate officials' assets and determine whether corruption had occurred. Anyone with a petition endorsed by fifty thousand citizens could bring any government official before the commission, which could impose a five-year ban from political office or initiate criminal proceedings. It remains to be seen how these instruments designed to control the government will be carried over in future constitutional constructions.

The 1997 Constitution, however, never solved the problem of how these bodies were to be constituted. The solution was to have members of these agencies appointed by a theoretically nonpartisan Senate. Because these bodies often ruled in favor of the government, criticism of the Thaksin administration, which took power in 2001, began to spill over onto these independent bodies.

As in 1991, a military coup in September 2006 overturned a democratically elected government on the pretext of corruption. Whether corruption truly existed at the highest levels has yet to be proven, but what is clear is that Thai elites were still willing to sacrifice democracy when they found control of government slipping from their grasp. For many Thai traditional elites who rationalized the coup, there appeared to be a sentiment that "we had to destroy democracy in order to save it."

Clearly, Thailand failed a major test of democratic government—that winners of authoritative elections exercise a monopoly over legitimate force (Linz and Stepan 1996a:93). Even among supporters of the coup, however, the ideology of democracy continued, and polls taken only weeks prior to the coup showed overwhelming support for democracy. Both supporters and opponents of the Thaksin regime claimed to view democratic procedures and institutions as most appropriate for governing collective life. The strong support for democracy, even in the midst of deep political cleavages over the Thaksin government, made Thailand an "attitudinally" consolidated democracy (Linz and Stepan 1996a:94).

2. CONCEPTIONS OF DEMOCRACY

Since 1932, the ideology of democracy has been so often invoked by democratic, authoritarian, and even despotic regimes that popular conceptions of this form of government are highly ambiguous. Wyatt (1984) suggests that during the early days of constitutional governance, enthusiasm for "constitution" and "democracy" was not dampened by the fact that people had no clear idea of either of the terms' meanings.[2]

Some interpreters argue that democracy is understood differently in Thailand than in Europe and North America, because of cultural traditions (e.g., the so-called Asian values) that place a greater emphasis on communal rather than individualistic values. According to this view, Thai respondents should express values markedly different from those of Europeans and Americans, if not for the fixed choices offered in survey instruments.

Our survey addressed these issues by posting the following open-ended question: "What does democracy mean to you?" Respondents were encouraged to supply up to three answers. The responses are displayed in chapter 1, table 1.3. Only about 80% of respondents could formulate a clear interpretation of democracy, and those who offered a second or a third response amounted to only 25% and 7% respectively. However, among those who responded, their understandings of democracy do not appear to differ substantially from those of European and American respondents. Over one-third (35%) of Thai respondents understood democracy in terms of freedom and liberties, such as the freedoms of speech, press, and expression. Another 27% understood democracy in terms of political rights and democratic procedures. Yet another 26% offered interpretations in general positive terms.

Most surprising was the infrequent mention of traditional Asian values, e.g., good governance, social equality, or duties to society. Fewer than 11% of respondents mentioned social equality and justice. Only one person mentioned "openness or government transparency," and no one mentioned job creation or welfare provisions. Nor did anyone mention fighting corruption. Equally noteworthy is the fact that few respondents mentioned the development of institutions traditionally associated with democratic governance. There were no mentions of political parties or even the parliament as a component of democracy. In fact, as we will see in section 4, for many Thais, political parties and the parliament seem to be part of the problem rather than part of the solution.

These findings do not necessarily conform to elite views of what less-educated individuals believe about democracy. The data show that the Thai public was equipped with clear interpretations of democracy even by the standards of the mature democracies, and suggest that Thai views of democracy do not differ substantially from the general meanings of liberal democracy in international discourse. Furthermore, these views appear consistent throughout the country and are not restricted to Bangkok residents or the elite urban middle class. In short, our data suggest that Thai citizens understood democracy consistently as "liberal democracy."

3. EVALUATING THE TRANSITION

At the time of the survey, the dramatic regime change of the early 1990s was still fresh in the memories of most Thais. Almost a decade after that change, how did the Thai people evaluate their new regime? We found that in every aspect of government performance—be it political, economic, or social—our respondents perceived sweeping improvements from the previous regimes, in particular in comparison to the military junta that controlled the Thai government in 1991 and 1992. Not only was there a significant advance in the level of democracy, but Thailand is also one of the few instances where democratization was perceived to have resulted in significant improvements in policy output. Compared to their East Asian neighbors, Thai respondents were by far the most affirmative about tangible impacts of the transition. Similar findings based upon polls in 2005 and 2006 replicate these highly positive evaluations of government.[3] Clearly, popular evaluations of government performance had little to do with grounds for the 2006 military coup.

3.1. PERCEPTIONS OF REGIME CHANGE

As reported in table 5.1, the Thai people perceived a dramatic transformation of their political system since 1992. Whereas nearly four out of five Thais (78%) judged their past regime to be dictatorial, an even larger number (88%) perceived their current regime to be at least somewhat democratic, with some 43% giving it the highest ratings on the 10-point scale. Whereas the previous regime received an average rating of 3.0, the current regime received a rating of 8.2, the largest increase and the highest democratic self-rating among the countries surveyed.

This perception of dramatic changes becomes particularly important when considered in the context of the reception enjoyed by the military regime in the early 1990s. Although there was significant opposition to military domination of the government, many Thais were supportive of the administration of the appointed prime minister, Anand Panyarachun, during

TABLE 5.1 **PERCEPTIONS OF PAST AND CURRENT REGIMES: THAILAND**

(Percent of respondents)

REGIME TYPES	PAST REGIME	CURRENT REGIME
Very dictatorial (1–2)	41.3	0.6
Somewhat dictatorial (3–5)	36.3	6.1
Somewhat democratic (6–8)	5.3	44.9
Very democratic (9–10)	2.4	43.4
DK/NA	14.7	4.9
Total	100.0	100.0
Mean on a 10-point scale	3.0	8.2

Notes: Regime types are based on the respondent's ranking of the regime on a scale from 1, "complete dictatorship," to 10, "complete democracy." Scores of 5 and below are degrees of dictatorship and scores of 6 and above are degrees of democracy.

N = 1544.

DK/NA = Don't know/no answer.

this period. The data show, however, that in retrospect, Thais viewed the Suchinda-Anand regime as highly authoritarian compared to the regime in place at the turn of the twenty-first century.

3.2. COMPARING PAST AND PRESENT REGIMES

The positive overall impression of regime transformation is confirmed by specific comparisons of the two regimes in nine areas of political and economic performance. Table 5.2 presents the average rating for each of these domains, the percentages of positive and negative ratings, and the percentage differential index (PDI) between positive and negative ratings. All mean and PDI scores reported in table 5.2 are substantially in excess of 0, suggesting that in all areas of politics and policy, the performance of the new regime was evaluated positively by Thai citizens. Particularly dramatic improvements were reported in freedom of speech, equal treatment of citizens, and popular influence in the political process. Overall the new regime

TABLE 5.2 PERCEIVED PERFORMANCE OF CURRENT AND PAST REGIMES: THAILAND

	MEAN[a]	SD[a]	NEGATIVE CHANGE[b]	POSITIVE CHANGE[b]	NO CHANGE[b]	PDI[c]	VALID %[d]
Democratic performance							
Freedom of speech	1.10	0.68	1.9	85.8	12.2	83.9	97.2
Freedom of association	0.83	0.74	3.1	70.1	26.7	67.0	97.1
Equal treatment	0.99	0.73	2.6	78.8	18.6	76.2	97.2
Popular influence	0.96	0.76	3.9	78.3	17.7	74.4	96.9
Independent judiciary	0.55	0.81	8.0	55.1	36.9	47.0	97.0
Average	0.88	0.74	3.9	73.6	22.4	69.7	97.1
Policy performance							
Anticorruption	0.86	0.81	5.6	72.9	21.5	67.3	97.2
Law and order	0.85	0.80	6.2	74.3	19.6	68.1	97.0
Economic development	0.65	0.87	10.7	64.9	24.4	54.1	97.2
Economic equality	0.47	0.83	9.4	49.2	41.4	39.8	97.1
Average	0.71	0.83	8.0	65.3	26.7	57.3	97.1

Notes: N = 1546.

Past regime is defined as pre-1992.

[a] Scale ranges from −2 (much worse) to +2 (much better).

[b] Percent of valid sample.

[c] PDI (percentage difference index) = percent seeing positive change minus percent seeing negative change.

[d] Percent of sample giving a valid answer to this question.

received an average PDI score of 69.7 in its democratic performance and 57.3 in its policy performance. Compared to its neighbors in the region, Thailand experienced by far the most improvement in perceived government performance as a result of democratization, and was the only country to report substantial advances in every major performance domain.

4. APPRAISING DEMOCRATIC INSTITUTIONS

Our data reveal that although Thais are distinguished by an extraordinary level of confidence in their active participatory capacities, they are less optimistic about their political efficacy. Although they place great faith in their public institutions, by and large they are mistrustful of their fellow citizens. On the whole, however, Thai citizens expressed a remarkable level of satisfaction with the functioning of their political system. Nearly nine out of ten of our respondents reported being "very satisfied" (34%) or at least "fairly satisfied" (55%) with the state of Thai democracy.

4.1. POLITICAL EFFICACY

Respondents were asked to evaluate their abilities to understand as well as to participate actively in the political process (see chapter 1, table 1.4). Fewer than 13% of the respondents expressed confidence in their ability both to understand and to participate in politics. Adding another 3% who said they could understand but not participate, only about 16% indicated that they could understand politics. These numbers are unremarkable compared to Thailand's neighbors in the region. What distinguished Thai respondents was their self-perceived capacity for active participation. An overwhelming majority of 84.2% expressed confidence in their ability to participate in politics, and included among these were a striking 71.7% who said they could participate even though they could not understand politics. This was by far the highest level of self-confidence about participation among all countries in the survey, and may reflect the distinctively antielitist character of Thai democracy, as we will discuss shortly.

Nonetheless, when it comes to the perceived efficacy of popular participation, Thais were little different from their neighbors. When asked to evaluate the statement, "The nation is run by a powerful few and ordinary citizens cannot do much about it," only 40% disagreed. And for the statement, "People like me don't have any influence over what the government does," only 42% disagreed. These figures are similar to those from other new democracies in the region. In this sense, the citizenship culture in Thailand bears a striking resemblance to that of Mongolia as revealed in the present survey, or Mexico as famously described by Almond and Verba (1963). In each case, a sense of pride in the power of the mass public is coupled with cynicism regarding the public's actual influence in the day-to-day operations of government. Borrowing from Almond and Verba, such a pattern may be labeled an "aspirational" political culture, characterized by a frustrated desire for influence.

4.2. PERCEPTIONS OF CORRUPTION

While glowing popular evaluations of the performance of the current government undoubtedly contributed to its legitimacy, allegations of widespread corruption—especially electoral corruption—continued to dog the democratic regime (Bowie 1996; Neher 1996; Chantornvong 2002). Thus we sought to determine the degree that the Thai public perceived corruption to be a problem.

The EAB survey included a pair of items probing the respondent's perception of corruption at local and national levels of government (see table 5.3). When asked about corruption and bribe-taking at the national level of government, two-thirds (65%) of our respondents believed that hardly anyone or only a few officials were involved. When asked about corruption and bribe-taking in local government, nearly four-fifths (79%) believed hardly any or only a few local officials were involved. Taken together, only 15% believed that most national and local government officials were corrupt, whereas a clear majority (60%) believed that most officials at all levels of government were honest. Except for China, the level of perceived corruption in Thailand was the lowest in any of the countries included in the EAB survey. The level of corruption reported as having been experienced by our respondents was even lower than the perceptions. Of the respondents in the current survey, only 17% indicated that they had personally witnessed corruption or bribery.

These findings are broadly compatible with those from other surveys conducted in Thailand. A 1999 survey led by Professor Pasuk Phongpaichit of the Chulalongkorn Political Economy Center found that fewer than 31% of respondents reported being offered a bribe in the preceding

.TABLE 5.3 **PERCEPTION OF POLITICAL CORRUPTION AT NATIONAL AND LOCAL LEVELS: THAILAND**

(Percent of total sample)

LOCAL GOVERNMENT	NATIONAL GOVERNMENT					
	Hardly anyone is involved	Not a lot of officials are involved	Most officials are corrupt	Almost everyone is corrupt	DK/NA	Total
Hardly anyone is involved	6.3	**17.2**	4.3	0.6	0.3	**28.7**
Not a lot of officials are involved	0.6	**35.6**	**11.9**	2.2	-	**50.3**
Most officials are corrupt	0.1	3.3	8.5	2.8	-	**14.8**
Almost everyone is corrupt	0.1	1.3	1.6	2.5	-	5.4
DK/NA	-	0.2	0.1	-	0.6	0.8
Total	7.1	**57.6**	**26.3**	8.1	0.8	**100.0**

Notes: N = 1546.

Blank cell means no cases.

Percentages above 10 are in boldface.

general election (Phongpaichit et al. 2000:198), which took place before the implementation of the new constitution. A survey conducted by the National Statistical Office of Thailand around the same time as the EAB survey reported that roughly 40% of respondents perceived a great deal of corruption in government (National Statistical Office 2003:5). This is a higher number than we found—perhaps because of differences in question wording—but still a lower number than the prevalent discourse on Thailand would lead one to expect.

In both the NSO and EAB surveys, residents of the Bangkok area were more likely to report direct experiences of bribery and corruption than persons from other parts of Thailand, particularly those in rural areas. According to the NSO, over half (51%) of Bangkok respondents perceived a great deal of corruption, while percentages for other regions of the country ranged from 35% to 43% (National Statistical Office 2003:5). The EAB findings are presented in table 5.4.

It is important to note the gap between perceptions of corruption and personal experiences of corruption. This is primarily a result of the fact that in most polls roughly 80% of respondents indicated that they learned about corruption through the media. Disparities between perceptions of corruption and actual experiences of corruption are thus attributable to a free press and crusading media. The September 19, 2006 coup was preceded by mass rallies accusing the government of corruption, duly reported in the media. As noted earlier, whether any of the charges had substance remains to be seen.

4.3. INSTITUTIONAL TRUST

Trust in the institutions of the body politic constitutes a major factor contributing to democratic consolidation. Alone among the countries surveyed, over 50% of Thai respondents who answered our questions about trust in institutions said that they trusted every institution we named (see figure 5.1). Since all of the institutions examined in the survey garnered majority support from the Thai population, the interesting question becomes the relative levels of trust Thais bestowed on the various institutions.

As figure 5.1 indicates, Thais expressed a great deal of trust in three of the new institutions created by the current constitution: the Constitutional Court, the National Anti-Corruption Commission, and the Election Commission. Trust in the last of these three institutions was probably dampened

TABLE 5.4 **PERSONAL EXPERIENCES OF CORRUPTION BY SETTING (RURAL/URBAN)**

(Percent of respondents)

	RURAL	SUBURBS	PROVINCIAL CAPITALS	SUBURBAN BANGKOK	BANGKOK	TOTAL
Never witnessed corruption personally	84.5	83.1	79.9	78.2	76.1	83.1
Have witnessed corruption personally	15.5	16.9	20.1	21.8	23.9	16.9

N = 1536.

by the controversies surrounding many of its rulings, such as the seventy-eight disqualifications it issued in the 2000 Senate elections. Even so, the Election Commission received substantial trust from 70% of the population and the other two institutions even more, suggesting that the foundational institutions of Thai democracy command a large measure of confidence and respect among Thai citizens.

The fact that the military was one of the most trusted instruments of the state, tied with television at 80%, indicates that years of military rule, which included massacres of civilians in 1976 and 1991, did not undermine the public's confidence in the armed forces. In the same vein, the fact that the civil service was more trusted than Parliament may also be a legacy of Thailand's recent history, in which the deeply entrenched bureaucratic state played such a prominent role (Riggs 1966).

At the other end of the spectrum stood the political parties. Yet over half of Thai respondents expressed trust in these important components of democracy, by far the highest level of trust expressed in political parties in any country in the EAB survey. Newspapers received the second-lowest level of trust. What some observers might regard as a wonderfully open and critical press may be looked upon by citizens as a rancorous intrusion into an otherwise complacent society. Placing this finding in perspective is the high level of trust enjoyed by television. It should be noted that some of the most prominent Thai television stations were controlled by the government, helping to facilitate trust in government institutions and apparently reaping the confidence of the public in return. This finding points to the need for more examination of the impact of the media on Thai society.[4]

In contrast to the high levels of institutional trust, we found trust in fellow citizens to be exceptionally low. When asked whether "most people can be trusted" or "you cannot be too careful in dealing with other people," 81% agreed with the latter. Contrary to images of Asian societies as communal, Thais tend to be disconnected from other members of their society. In fact, the low level of trust in "others" is deeply rooted in Thai society and culture, inculcated in successive generations from early childhood. A popular children's story teaches that the lesson of life should be "don't trust anyone."[5] The indoctrination of mistrust has serious repercussions for Thai society, creating problems for the accumulation of social capital. As Danny Unger (1998) observed, based on a variety of other studies (Ayal 1963; Embree 1950; Narthsupha 1970), the ability of Thais to engage in associational relationships is remarkably low.

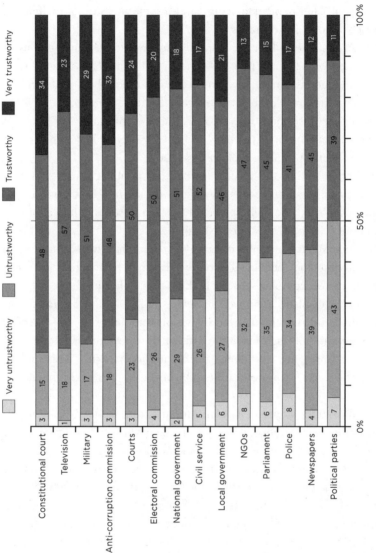

FIGURE 5.1 Trust in Institutions: Thailand

Legend (top): Very untrustworthy | Untrustworthy | Trustworthy | Very trustworthy

Institution	Very untrustworthy	Untrustworthy	Trustworthy	Very trustworthy
Constitutional court	3	15	48	34
Television	1	18	57	23
Military	3	17	51	29
Anti-corruption commission	3	18	48	32
Courts	3	23	50	24
Electoral commission	4	26	50	20
National government	2	29	51	18
Civil service	5	26	52	17
Local government	6	27	46	21
NGOs	8	32	47	13
Parliament	6	35	45	15
Police	8	34	41	17
Newspapers	4	39	45	12
Political parties	7	43	39	11

Percent of valid sample

5. COMMITMENT TO DEMOCRACY

To assess commitment to democracy we turn to the clusters of questions from the EAB survey tapping attachment to democratic politics and detachment from authoritarianism. We found a robust level of commitment to democracy and rejection of authoritarianism, although like their neighbors across East Asia, Thai citizens were more supportive of democracy in principle than in practice. Moreover, we found poorer, less-educated Thais to be more supportive of democracy than their wealthier, better-educated compatriots, and residents of rural areas to be more supportive than urbanites from Bangkok.

5.1. ATTACHMENT TO DEMOCRATIC POLITICS

The EAB survey found a very high level of attachment to democratic politics among the Thai electorate, as shown in chapter 1, table 1.8. When asked to indicate on a 10-point scale how democratic they would like their political system to be, 93% of our respondents expressed a desire for democracy by choosing a score of 6 or above. Similarly, when asked to evaluate the suitability of democracy for Thailand, 88% believed democracy to be suitable. Furthermore, Thais were as supportive of the practice of democracy as they were of the idea of democracy. Close to 90% expressed confidence in the ability of democracy to solve problems of the nation and nearly 83% believed that democracy is preferable to all other forms of government. These numbers are especially remarkable considering that nearly two-fifths (39%) of our respondents rated the economy as "bad" or "very bad" and only 14% rated it as "good" or "very good."

When forced to choose between democracy and economic development, however, the commitment to democracy was more ambivalent, as elsewhere in Asia. Nearly half (49%) indicated a preference for economic development, while only 17% considered democracy more important than economic development. The question, however, asked respondents to choose between an abstract concept (democracy) and a concrete improvement in one's personal livelihood; therefore, one should be cautious in interpreting these results.

On a 6-point index that aggregates the responses regarding desirability, suitability, efficacy, preference, and priority, the Thai sample averaged 4.0, with nearly three-quarters (79%) of respondents receiving a score of 4 or

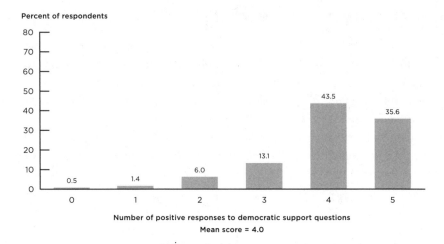

Percent of respondents

Number of positive responses to democratic support questions
Mean score = 4.0

FIGURE 5.2 **Democratic Support: Thailand**

above (see figure 5.2). These numbers reflect a higher level of democratic support than any other society in our survey.

5.2. DETACHMENT FROM AUTHORITARIANISM

Thai respondents rejected all four authoritarian alternatives by large margins (see chapter 1, table 1.9). More than three-quarters (77%) rejected the dictatorship of a strong leader, 61% rejected a single-party dictatorship, and 78% rejected the dictatorship of technocratic experts. Given Thailand's history of military dictatorships, detachment from military rule was the firmest, with over 81% rejecting this alternative.

Together, rejection of these four alternatives measures the general level of opposition to authoritarianism at the regime level. On a 5-point index of the number of authoritarian alternatives rejected by the respondent, the Thai sample averaged 3.0, indicating that the average Thai was detached from three of the four types of dictatorships mentioned (see figure 5.3). Over 43% were fully detached from authoritarianism, expressing opposition to all four types, with an additional 29% rejecting three out of four authoritarian options, a pattern of authoritarian detachment typical of the countries in our study.

Roughly two-thirds of those accepting one authoritarian alternative accepted the abolition of opposition parties. This finding should be interpreted to reflect the Thai aversion to political parties, rather than as a rejection of democracy in principle. There are many examples of Thai mistrust of political parties, ranging from the ban on party affiliation for candidates for the Senate, to the exclusion of party figures from governmental watchdog commissions and courts. In the opinion of many, behind party labels lurks the shadowy presence of powerful patrons, who purchase political support with their wealth and dispense patronage to produce distorted outcomes in the political process. Many see political parties as part of the problem, not part of the solution, for the construction of democratic governance.

Although no significant differences were found between rural and urban populations in overall detachment from authoritarianism, urban residents were significantly ($p<.05$) more willing to abolish political parties. The banning of opposition parties drew significantly higher support as well among the better-educated and persons of higher socioeconomic status, probably because parties are seen as instruments for mass mobilization against elite dominance of the political arena. These findings thus reflect a fear of popular democracy on the part of the elites, who exercised great influence over the drafting of the 1997 Constitution. When the question concerning political parties is eliminated, roughly two-thirds of respondents rejected all remaining authoritarian alternatives. Support for the abolition of opposition parties must therefore be interpreted in its proper social context, as a desire for "nonpartisan" rather than "one-party" government in Thai democracy.

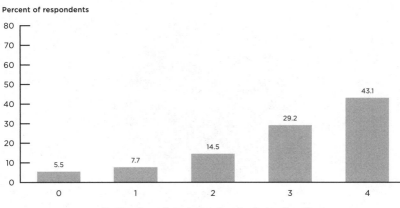

Percent of respondents

Number of negative responses to authoritarian alternatives
Mean score = 3.0

FIGURE 5.3 **Authoritarian Detachment: Thailand**

5.3. OVERALL COMMITMENT TO DEMOCRACY

Figure 5.4 presents seven patterns of regime orientation, calculated by taking into account the levels of democratic attachment and authoritarian detachment in a formula explained in the notes to table 1.11, chapter 1. The figure confirms the strong Thai commitment to democracy reported throughout this chapter. The country has 36% of "very strong supporters," second in Asia only to Japan, and the highest number of overall supporters (the top three categories, not including skeptical supporters) in the region (80%).

5.4. THE SOCIAL CONTEXT OF DEMOCRATIC SUPPORT AND
THE TWO DEMOCRACIES THESIS

The data gathered in this study provided an opportunity to test the argument that there are significant differences in support for democracy between Bangkok elites and ordinary citizens living in the *changwats* (provinces) outside Bangkok. A number of Thai scholars have argued that Thailand is a tale of two democracies: that of the sophisticated urban elites with origins or current residency in Bangkok, and that of parochial rural interests that view the democratic process, especially elections, as a vehicle for the advance-

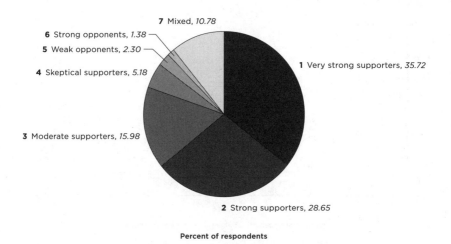

7 Mixed, *10.78*
6 Strong opponents, *1.38*
5 Weak opponents, *2.30*
4 Skeptical supporters, *5.18*
1 Very strong supporters, *35.72*
3 Moderate supporters, *15.98*
2 Strong supporters, *28.65*

Percent of respondents

FIGURE 5.4 **Patterns of Commitment to Democracy: Thailand**

ment of personal or community benefits (Laothamatas 1996; Phongpaichit and Baker 2001).

Anek Laothamatas describes the "urban view" as holding that

> voting in farming areas is not guided by political principles, policy issues, or what is perceived to be in the national interest, all of which are regarded as the only legitimate rationale for citizens casting their ballots in a democratic election. The ideal candidates for rural voters are those who visit them often, address their immediate grievances effectively, and bring numerous public works to their communities.
>
> (Laothamatas 1996:202)

As a result, the ability of rural constituencies to acquire substantial power in parliament often raises doubts among the urban middle class, the mass media, and some academics as to the efficacy of the democratic processes. For many members of these groups, "democracy turns out to be the rule of the corrupt and incompetent" (Laothamatas 1996:208). Urban, educated, and cosmopolitan candidates, who may also be skilled policy experts, are often held in equal contempt by villagers, regarded as being alien to rural electorates in tastes, culture, and outlook.

This cleavage is important because historically the stance of the Bangkok elites determined the fates of experiments with democracy. While the middle class opposes authoritarian rule when it restricts individual freedoms and intervenes in commerce, the possibility that the reins of government may be seized by politicians with a populist agenda can pose an even more direct threat than the dangers of authoritarian retrogression. Laothamatas (1996) thus argues that the 1991 coup could not have been sustained if not for support from the urban middle class. The same can be said for the 2006 coup. Samudavanija notes that the role of the middle class in Thailand vis-à-vis democracy has been "reactive rather than proactive" (1998:156).

Some studies (Albritton and Prabudhanitisarn 1997; Albritton et al. 1995) indicate that the differences between urban and rural constituencies disappear when education is controlled for. However, secondary analysis of the data gathered by Logerfo (1996) indicates that even after controlling for education, significant differences between Bangkok and rural areas remain. More recent research (Albritton and Bureekul 2001; Albritton and Bureekul 2002) supports the latter view. Respondents from Bangkok and rural areas were found to differ markedly in a variety of measures, such as support for democracy, criteria for choosing candidates in elections, and tolerance of corruption.

Using the data from the EAB survey, we conducted an analysis of variance in support for democracy, using as the independent variable five categories of location of the respondent. The results were consistent with previous findings showing Bangkok residents to be significantly lower in their levels of democratic support. Indeed, residents of "downtown" (central) Bangkok exhibited the lowest level of democratic support, while rural residents registered the highest.

We also conducted an OLS regression to estimate the relative effects of socioeconomic status (SES) and Bangkok residency on political participation as well as on support for democracy.[6] We found socioeconomic status to be negatively correlated with both democratic support and participation.[7] Bangkok respondents were significantly less supportive of democracy, even when controlling for SES. The results were virtually identical when support for democracy was analyzed by Bangkok residency controlling for educational status alone.

As democracy spreads, the influence of Bangkok (and specifically the Bangkok elites) inevitably diminishes relative to the rest of the nation, which is still roughly 80% rural. Nonetheless, as the seat of government, Bangkok will continue to exert disproportionate influence over the formulation of national policies. This analysis provides a context for interpreting the 2006 coup as the result of the persistent conflict between the metropole and the rural hinterland. The division between the capital and the hinterlands is likely to remain a critical problem in the security and sustainability of democratic governance in Thailand.

6. EXPECTATIONS OF THAI DEMOCRACY

Our last target of analysis is Thai expectations about the future of democracy in their country. In the EAB survey we asked respondents to indicate their expectations about the state of Thai democracy in five years' time. On a 10-point scale, they expected their system to progress toward greater democracy by a margin of 0.8 in the next five years, from 8.2 to 9.0 (see table 5.5). Compared to other East Asian countries in our survey, Thai respondents assigned the highest level of democracy to their current regime and were likewise the most optimistic in their expectations for the future. Nearly nine out of ten (88%) Thai respondents believed that five years into the future their country would be at least somewhat democratic, with 66% expecting to attain near-complete democracy. In contrast, those who expected their government to be dictatorial amounted to only 3.5%.

Based on respondents' current regime ratings and expected future ratings, we identified seven patterns of expected regime transformation (see chapter 1, table 1.12). Forty-two percent of Thai respondents considered the current regime to be an advanced democracy and expected its consolidation as such. Another 28% regarded the current regime as a limited democracy and expected continuing democratic development toward complete democracy. Even among the handful of respondents who regarded the current regime as dictatorial, most expected the transition to be at least a partial democracy. Once again, these patterns confirm the extraordinary optimism of the Thai people regarding the future of their democracy.

7. SUMMARY AND CONCLUSIONS

Our study demonstrates that Thai conceptions of democracy are not fundamentally different from those of citizens of the advanced Western democracies. As in other societies throughout East Asia, those views of democracy typically labeled "Asian values" were rejected by a majority of Thai respondents.

TABLE 5.5 CURRENT AND EXPECTED FUTURE REGIME TYPE: THAILAND

(Percent of respondents)

RATING	CURRENT REGIME	FUTURE REGIME	CHANGE[a]
Very dictatorial (1–2)	0.6	0.6	0.0
Somewhat dictatorial (3–5)	6.1	2.9	-3.1
Somewhat democratic (6–8)	44.9	21.7	-23.3
Very democratic (9–10)	43.4	66.4	23.0
DK/NA	4.9	8.4	3.5
Total	100.0	100.0	
Mean on a 10-point scale	8.2	9.0	0.8

Notes: N = 1308.

Scale runs from 1, "complete dictatorship," to 10, "complete democracy."

Future regime is five years from time of survey.

[a] Change in percent of respondents rating the regime at the given level when the object of evaluation shifts from the current to the future regime.

One of the most important findings of the study, perhaps, is that in discussions of democracy, Asians and Westerners are talking about the same thing. Nonetheless, many Thais who constitute the academic and social elites often refer to "Thai democracy" as though it contained unique elements distinct from the experiences of other nations. Our research failed to unearth any such concepts that would distinguish perceptions of democracy in Thailand from those of liberal democracy adherents throughout the world.

Our respondents were clear about what democracy is not. It is not benign authoritarianism, and there is no substitute for the key institutions of democratic politics. All alternatives to democratic government were soundly rejected by our respondents. Thailand thus meets all of Linz and Stepan's criteria for attitudinal support of a "consolidated democracy" (2001:95).

Theories of democracy hold that trust in the key institutions of state and society is a key ingredient in the sustainability of democracy. In this respect as well, the underpinnings of democratic support in Thailand appear strong. The relatively high levels of trust in the military, the police, and the civil service may reflect Thailand's vulnerability to its often harsh natural environment as well as various domestic political threats. Such attitudes often characterize rural societies in which the population is heavily dependent upon the coercive organs of the state to maintain basic order and security. Nevertheless, the relatively low level of trust in other Thais is a cause for concern.

As in previous studies (Albritton and Bureekul 2002), we found deep cleavages between urban and rural Thailand with regard to support for democracy. Our analysis suggests that, far from being the vanguard of the democratic transition, Bangkok and its middle-class residents lag behind. For the middle class, the outcomes of democratic politics appear far less predictable than those of bureaucratic-authoritarian rule, and the special relationships with the government assiduously cultivated over the years also become less secure in a democratic polity. Although we found no significant differences between Thais of different social backgrounds in terms of their conceptions of democracy, rural Thais displayed greater commitment to democratic governance as a countervailing power against the dominance of Bangkok elites. In this sense, Thailand at the turn of the century was truly a tale of two democracies.

The conflict over the Thaksin regime that developed after our survey was conducted exposed other significant differences between "traditional elites" and the masses in their understandings of popular democracy. Publicly expressed views of academics and supporters of traditional society indicated that the "reformers" expected voters to support traditional elites, that is, those who were "supposed" to lead the nation. The capture of the government by mass (as opposed to elite-led) democracy brought about a corresponding disillusionment with democratic elections among intellectual and urban elites. The conflict between an emerging, mass-based democracy and traditions embedded in a hierarchical society posed a major obstacle to further consolidation of Thai democracy.

The ideology of democracy is rooted solidly in the consciousness of the Thai people. To the extent that support for democracy in the mass public is an important measure of democratic consolidation, Thailand has the potential to become a beacon of democracy in Southeast Asia. But the Thai case also shows that while popular support for democracy may be a necessary condition for democratic consolidation, it is not a sufficient condition. As Linz and Stepan (1996a:93) note, free and contested elections are not sufficient for democratic consolidation. As in Myanmar (Burma), a small, determined elite can suppress prodemocratic masses by virtue of its control over the military. Although the 2006 coup used corruption in government as a pretext, poll data, even a few weeks before, indicated that the belief in high levels of corruption was not shared among mass publics.[8] Rather, the coup was perpetrated (as in 1991) by elements among traditional elites who saw political power shifting from an elite-led democracy to new classes of people oriented to business and rural masses. Whether the Bangkok intellectual and social elites will ever cede political authority to the hinterland remains the major issue for Thai democratic governance.

NOTES

1. News media reports of widespread corruption are often based on *charges* of corruption, which are often used as a political ploy to invalidate elections. In addition, reports of corruption are themselves made possible by the heightened transparency afforded by the Election Commission and the new election laws. Much is always made of the distribution of money during elections. There is, however, no hard, empirical evidence that such practices bias or determine election *outcomes*.

2. According to Wyatt (1984:250), some thought that the word for democracy (*prachathipatai*) referred to King Prajadhipok's brother and that the word for the constitution (*ratthathammanun*) was a relative of the prime minister.

3. For example, a poll taken by the present authors in April 2006 indicated that roughly 80% of respondents were satisfied or highly satisfied with the performance of the Thaksin government.

4. For a thorough examination of the Thai press, see McCargo 2001.

5. *Phra Apai Mani* (The Guru Teaches Sudsakorn) by Sunthorn Phu.

6. We created our measure of socioeconomic status through a principal components factor analysis of income, education, and occupational status. All of these variables loaded onto the same factor, with factor loadings at 0.8 or above.

7. This is consistent with findings by Suchit Bungbongkarn (1996), who argued that Thais with higher levels of education are more cynical about politics and therefore less likely to participate in the democratic process. He based his argument upon substantially lower voter turnouts in Bangkok.

8. This was a survey conducted by the present authors in April 2006 for the Asian Barometer project.

6

THE MASS PUBLIC AND DEMOCRATIC POLITICS IN MONGOLIA

Damba Ganbat, Rollin F. Tusalem, and David D. Yang

1. MONGOLIAN DEMOCRACY IN HISTORICAL CONTEXT

ON OCTOBER 20, 1999, three members of the Mongolian parliament were convicted on corruption charges related to a casino bribery scandal and given prison sentences ranging from three to five years. The trio, all members of the ruling Democratic Coalition and one of them a former justice minister, had been part of the crop of young reformers who swept into office three years earlier, dislodging the Communist Party from power for the first time since 1924.[1] For many, the guilty verdicts confirmed what was already suspected—that corruption in postcommunist Mongolia was rampant, and the biggest culprits were the high-living young democrats whose dramatic victory in the 1996 elections had been heralded as the dawn of a new era. Around the same time, as part of the celebrations for the 360th anniversary of the founding of Ulaanbaatar, workmen were refurbishing a statue of Marshal Choibalsan, one of the leaders of the communist regime, whose brutal sixteen-year rule (1936–1952) had earned him a reputation as "Mongolia's Stalin" (Severinghaus 2000). A newspaper took an informal poll of public opinion regarding the refurbishment and found a fair amount of support among men in the street. Despite his cruelty, the marshal was regarded as a genuine nationalist hero. It was a fitting portent of things to come. One year later, the reconstituted Mongolian People's Revolutionary Party (MPRP)—the party of the former communist regime—succeeded in refurbishing its political dominance as well, capturing seventy-two of seventy-six seats in the 2000 parliamentary elections.

The dramatic reversal of fortunes was in many ways emblematic of Mongolian politics in the transition era. Mongolia is often considered the only country outside of Eastern Europe to have made a successful transition to democracy from communist rule. It consistently receives high marks from international watchdog groups in areas such as political rights, civil liberties, and press freedoms. But unlike most other countries in the Soviet bloc, Mongolia remains a predominantly rural society, with nearly one-third of the population engaged in nomadic herding. In 2002, at the time of our survey, the country had a per capita purchasing power parity GDP of a mere $1,770 (compared to $4,600 for China and $4,000 for the Philippines), a UN Human Development Index ranking of 117, and a population with an average life expectancy of 64.5 years (UNDP 2002; CIA 2002).

Given its economic backwardness, Mongolia is often regarded as one of the most improbable cases to have undergone a successful transition among the family of third-wave democracies (Fish 1998:128). And democratization made its problems worse: the country has suffered from skyrocketing unemployment, rising poverty (36% of population lived below the poverty line in 2002), disintegration of the social service infrastructure, and a breakdown in law and order.

Prior to the fall of the communist dictatorship, Mongolia had been a client state of the Soviet Union, which dictated Mongolia's domestic and foreign policies with large amounts of economic aid and sixty-five thousand troops stationed in the country (Batbayar 2003). For more than six decades, beginning in 1924 when the communist state replaced a monarchy, Mongolia was ruled by the one-party dictatorship of the MPRP. Any criticism of the ruling party or its communist ideology and centrally planned economy was swiftly suppressed.

Democratic transition occurred in the wake of the upheavals that took place in the Soviet Union in the late 1980s (Batbayar 2003; Boone 1994). The collapse of Marxism-Leninism as the Soviet Union's guiding ideology led to communism's demise in Mongolia, testimony to the extent to which the political histories of the two nations had become intertwined despite their cultural, ethnic, and religious disparities.

Samuel Huntington (1991:113) characterized Mongolia's transition to democracy as a process of "transplacement," meaning that democratization resulted from joint action by groups both in and out of power. In early 1990, the democratic opposition led by the Mongolian Democratic Union (MDU) began staging hunger strikes in front of the government compound to demand political freedom and human rights. The communist leadership initially ignored these demands; however, when they intensified, the ruling MPRP agreed to a roundtable meeting with the MDU. This process led to Mongolia's first-ever democratic elections in the summer of 1990. Under the new constitution of 1992, Mongolia became a parliamentary democracy with a directly-elected president endowed with certain key veto powers. In the 1993 presidential election, P. Ochirbat, the candidate of the Democratic Forces, became the country's first democratically elected president with 58% of the popular vote.

After the heady days of those founding elections, however, Mongolia's young democracy lost much of its political innocence. The reconstituted MPRP reestablished itself as the dominant political player. In the period leading up to our survey, the party won two out of three elections, capturing seventy-one out of seventy-six seats in 1992, and seventy-two out of seventy-six seats in 2000, thanks to a fractious opposition and a first-past-the-post electoral system (Severinghaus 1995, 2001).

The period from 1996 to 2000 was an exception to the pattern of MPRP dominance. An opposition coalition achieved a landmark upset in the 1996 parliamentary elections, capturing fifty out of seventy-six seats. This victory was touted as the first peaceful transfer of power between a Leninist party and the democratic opposition in Asia. But it was soon tarnished by infighting, corruption scandals, and the self-serving antics of some coalition MPs. The four years of coalition rule witnessed the rise and fall of four governments, the aforementioned conviction of three parliamentarians on corruption charges, and the unsolved murder of S. Zorig, a leading light of the democratic revolution who was poised to become the country's next prime minister.

Meanwhile the MPRP proved a quick study in parliamentary maneuvering, paralyzing the government by boycotting legislative sessions for weeks at a time. The party's obstructionist powers were amplified after it recaptured the presidency in 1997.[2] By 2000 the reversal of fortune was complete. The Democratic Coalition was defeated at the polls and the MPRP recovered its ascendancy.

In light of such developments it was not surprising that our survey, conducted in 2002, revealed strong popular concern over issues of corruption and governance. These problems have persisted in the years following. In the fifth parliamentary elections, held in 2004, no party won sufficient seats to form a cabinet, leading again to the formation of a coalition cabinet. The formation of the cabinet involved the electoral commission in behind-the-scenes negotiations that were widely criticized as nontransparent. In early 2006 the coalition collapsed and the cabinet resigned. Several members of parliament changed their party affiliations, bringing the MPRP back to power without a new election. These developments deepened public distrust of political institutions and popular concern with corruption.

Despite such problems, scholars have generally classified Mongolia as a successful case of democratic transition from communist dictatorship (Batbayar 2003; Ginsburg 1998; Finch 2002; Fish 1998). Its democratization was bloodless and no violent attempts were made subsequently to overthrow the elected government. Unlike many Eastern European and Central Asian examples, Mongolia's democratic system has been stable. The opposition parties remained viable and energetic. And even if the MPRP enjoyed a near monopoly of power at all levels of government much of the time, it remained bound by democratic principles and committed to free and regular elections, if only because of the government's dependence on foreign aid (Batbayar 2003:57).

International lending agencies have stipulated that any regression toward authoritarianism can result in a substantial decrease in loan guarantees. In 1996, advisors from the International Republican Institute helped draft a "Contract with Mongolia" as the centerpiece of the opposition campaign that led to victory in the parliamentary elections.[3] Cooperation between domestic and international prodemocratic forces has thus helped Mongolia remain politically free, even if effective governance proved more elusive (Freedom House 2004). Internationally, therefore, the country is often regarded as a third-wave democracy that has outperformed its East European and Central Asian counterparts, many of which Freedom House has rated as either partly-free or unfree (Fritz 2002; Sabloff 2002). Likewise, civil society in Mongolia has been rated as more active than those of its Central Asian counterparts (Clearly 1995).

However, constitutional reforms and economic liberalization based on the advice of international organizations have not yet produced a sizeable middle class, nor have these reforms narrowed the chasm between rich and poor that widened dramatically in the postcommunist era (Brooks 1998; Nixson, Suvd, and Walters 2000). In the long run, no system of government can be sustained by international donors alone. The ultimate guarantor of Mongolian democracy will have to be the Mongolian people. To appraise the state of Mongolia's democratic consolidation, we need to

understand how the new regime is perceived through the eyes of its ordinary citizens, who experienced the transition on a daily basis. We need to
understand how much support the new regime enjoys from the public,
how it fares when judged against the former regime, how much citizens
trust institutions, how satisfied citizens are with existing channels of participation, and the extent to which they are committed to a democratic
political culture, questions that have seldom been broached by Mongolia-
watchers in the West.

This chapter offers initial answers to these questions. Data for this chapter come from the first-ever national random sample survey of political attitudes in Mongolia, conducted from October to December in 2002. Valid
responses were collected from 1,144 randomly selected voting-age citizens
across the country.

We found that although most Mongolians in 2002 acknowledged some
genuine progress toward democracy, many appeared frustrated by the new
regime's failure to deliver effective governance. Corruption was perceived
to be rife, although most institutions of the body politic still retained the
public's confidence. Although support for democratic rule was widespread,
commitment to democratic principles was more moderate, not least because
many citizens were cynical about their say in the system. On the whole,
however, the vast majority of Mongolians were confident that the flaws of
the system could be overcome, and by a margin of six to one envisioned a
more democratic future for their country.

2. CONCEPTIONS OF DEMOCRACY

We begin our analysis with a basic question: How do ordinary Mongolians understand democracy? As shown in chapter 1, table 1.3, Mongolians
stood out among the countries surveyed for their strong identification of
democracy with classic liberal democratic values. Fifty-nine percent associated democracy with freedom and liberty, and 25% associated it with
political rights, institutions, and processes. Taken together, 71% of respondents selected one or both of these two categories, more than in any other
country surveyed.

The second-largest category of responses in Mongolia associated democracy with social equality and justice. At 33%, the Mongolians were the
second-most-likely nationality after the South Koreans to define democracy
in this way. Although the two countries entered democracy from different

historical trajectories—Korea from a developmentalist capitalist state and Mongolia from a socialist background—their citizens seemed to expect the new regime to alleviate perceived inequities inherited from the past. As shown in our discussion of table 6.2 (see section 3.2), thus far Mongolians are far from satisfied with their new regime's performance in promoting economic equality.

Finally, like others in Asia, Mongolians who did not have very specific associations with democracy nonetheless viewed it favorably. Thirty-nine percent of respondents gave one or more responses that we coded either as "good government," "by and for the people," or "in general positive terms."

3. EVALUATING THE TRANSITION

Given the continuing dominance of the former ruling party, one may wonder whether the democratic transition of the 1990s—lauded by democracy-watchers in the West—was perceived as such by ordinary citizens. Our data suggest that ordinary Mongolians did recognize the transi-

TABLE 6.1 **PERCEPTIONS OF PAST AND CURRENT REGIMES: MONGOLIA**

(Percent of respondents)

REGIME TYPES	PAST REGIME	CURRENT REGIME
Very dictatorial (1–2)	30.9	3.4
Somewhat dictatorial (3–5)	49.1	23.5
Somewhat democratic (6–8)	13.9	58.8
Very democratic (9–10)	1.7	11.8
DK/NA	4.4	2.6
Total	100.0	100.0
Mean on a 10-point scale	3.6	6.4

Notes: Regime types are based on the respondent's ranking of the regime on a scale from 1, "complete dictatorship," to 10, "complete democracy." Scores of 5 and below are degrees of dictatorship and scores of 6 and above are degrees of democracy.

N = 1144.

DK/NA = Don't know/no answer.

tion, although they perceived it to be limited. Democratization's impact on the quality of governmental performance and the nation's political life were perceived as uneven.

3.1. PERCEPTIONS OF REGIME CHANGE

Respondents were asked to rate both the current and the past (in Mongolia, identified as pre-1990) regimes on a 10 point scale of democracy. As table 6.1 shows, the mean rating of the past regime was 3.6 and the mean score of the present regime was 6.4, which represents an increase of almost three points on the 10-point scale. While 80% of our respondents perceived the past regime as undemocratic, nearly as many (71%) perceived the current regime (even if it is controlled by the MPRP, the reformed Communist Party) as democratic. Yet in the eyes of our respondents, the new democracy remains of a limited nature, having yet to evolve into an advanced form.

The distribution of regime change scores is presented in figure 6.1. The distribution follows a normal bell-shaped curve centered around 3, the average score differential between past and current regimes. Just under 85% of the scores are positive, indicating that the vast majority of Mongolian citizens perceived at least some progress toward greater democracy. However, approximately 60% of the sample is clustered between 1 and 4, suggesting that most Mongolians saw the progress to be modest in extent. Overall this

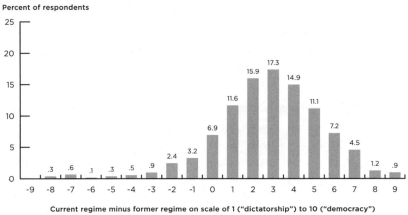

Percent of respondents

Current regime minus former regime on scale of 1 ("dictatorship") to 10 ("democracy")
Mean score = 2.8

FIGURE 6.1 Perceived Regime Change: Mongolia

score distribution is fairly similar to those of other third-wave democracies in the survey, except for the Thais, who assigned noticeably higher scores to their transition.

3.2. COMPARING PAST AND PRESENT REGIMES

Respondents were asked to compare current circumstances with those under the former regime in nine major government performance domains. Table 6.2 shows that respondents perceived significant improvement in the area of democratic performance, but saw much to be improved in the area of socioeconomic policy performance.

The greatest improvements were felt in freedom of speech (+86%) and freedom of association (+85%). The remaining three areas of democratic performance also exhibited significant improvements. In fact the PDI scores for the five democratic performance domains average +52, indicating that Mongolians perceived substantial increases in their political freedoms as well as their ability to influence the political process. Mongolians registered the highest improvements in freedom of speech and freedom of association among all new democracies in the survey, perhaps reflecting the severe restrictions on civil liberties in the country's totalitarian past.

Despite progress in the political sphere, the current regime's policy performance drew negative evaluations, a problem common to many democratizing nations. In three of the four policy performance domains—corruption control, law and order, and economic equality—more Mongolians reported experiencing negative than positive consequences from the transition to democracy. Only in the domain of economic development did Mongolians report marked improvements in the wake of the shift to private ownership and a market economy. Despite a PDI score of +44 on economic development, the average PDI score of the socioeconomic policy domains is –17, one of the lowest among the countries surveyed. In fact, Mongolia's PDI scores in the areas of economic equality and law and order are the lowest among the third-wave democracies in the study. Because of the regimented nature of Mongolia's Soviet-era socioeconomic system, the impact of liberalization on these areas appears to have been severe.

Our finding of public concern over the deterioration of law and order is consistent with other evidence. The courts are the least trusted branch of government in contemporary Mongolia (see figure 6.2). In surveys conducted by the Mongolian National Chamber of Commerce and Industry

TABLE 6.2 PERCEIVED PERFORMANCE OF CURRENT AND PAST REGIMES: MONGOLIA

	MEAN[a]	SD[a]	NEGATIVE CHANGE[b]	POSITIVE CHANGE[b]	NO CHANGE[b]	PDI[c]	VALID %[d]
Democratic performance							
Freedom of speech	1.29	0.78	3.7	89.7	6.6	85.94	99.4
Freedom of association	1.34	0.77	3.1	88.5	8.3	85.42	98.3
Equal treatment	0.27	1.03	25.2	48.0	26.8	22.78	98.5
Popular influence	0.38	1.01	19.9	53.3	26.8	33.42	98.2
Independent judiciary	0.36	0.98	19.1	50.6	30.3	31.52	94.9
Average	0.73	0.92	14.2	66.0	19.7	51.81	97.9
Policy performance							
Anticorruption	-0.06	1.06	33.3	32.6	34.1	-0.63	97.2
Law and order	-0.72	1.03	66.5	13.8	19.7	-52.71	99.2
Economic development	0.50	0.96	18.4	62.2	19.4	43.83	99.3
Economic equality	-0.89	1.11	72.0	14.3	13.7	-57.69	99.2
Average	-0.29	1.04	47.5	30.7	21.7	-16.80	99.7

Notes: N = 1144.

Past regime is defined as pre-1990.

[a] Scale ranges from -2 (much worse) to +2 (much better).

[b] Percent of valid sample.

[c] PDI (percentage difference index) = percent seeing positive change minus percent seeing negative change.

[d] Percent of sample giving a valid answer to this question.

(MCCI) as well as the Mongolian Judicial Reform Project (JRP), judicial corruption was perceived to be widespread. Forty-two percent of the respondents in the MCCI survey regard judicial institutions as the "most corrupt" institution of the government.[4] In the JRP survey, 56% of respondents claim that legal institutions cannot be trusted because of corruption.[5]

Finally, it should be noted that Mongolians give economic equality the highest negative PDI rating at -58, an indication of the widening gap between rich and poor in the postcommunist era. This is a price Mongolians have paid for the privatization of property ownership associated with the transition to democracy.

4. APPRAISING DEMOCRATIC INSTITUTIONS

Considering the tangle of economic troubles inherited from the Soviet era, it is hardly surprising that the most tangible achievements of the new regime are perceived to have come in the political sphere.

Our data reveal that although Mongolians were relatively confident in their own participatory capabilities, they were generally pessimistic about their political efficacy. Several key institutions of the new regime were deeply mistrusted, and perceptions of corruption remained prevalent. However, Mongolians appeared content with the functioning of the current regime, with more than two-thirds (67%) expressing satisfaction with "the way democracy works in our country."

4.1. POLITICAL EFFICACY

Respondents were asked about their self-perceived ability to understand the complexities of politics and government and their perceived capacity to participate in politics. As shown in chapter 1, table 1.4, less than one-third of Mongolian respondents (30%) expressed confidence in their ability both to understand and to participate in politics. Another 33% found politics too complex for their comprehension but were confident in their ability to participate. A total of 63%, therefore, were confident in their participatory capacity.

How can this be explained, given Mongolia's heavily rural population, modest level of development, and lack of a vibrant civil society tradition? Some scholars point to the rigors of the nomadic lifestyle: Mongolians are the "Marlboro Men" of the steppes—rugged, self-reliant, resourceful, and confident—but thoroughly embedded within their communities. Modern Mongolians are also said to draw inspiration from the great Genghis Khan's teachings about participatory government (he convened the first Great Huraldai [assembly] of all Mongols) and meritocratic equality—he promoted commanders without regard to birth and knew them all personally (Sabloff 2001). Another factor may be Mongolia's communist legacy. The mobilizational nature of communist regimes demands high levels of participation and politicization from their subjects. Voting was compulsory, as was membership in various youth groups. While not democratic, such participation familiarized the citizenry with the political domain and imbued them with an egalitarian ideology.

Paradoxically, when it comes to the perceived efficacy of popular participation, Mongolians proved no more optimistic than their neighbors. When asked to evaluate the statement, "The nation is run by a powerful few and ordinary citizens cannot do much about it," only 38% disagreed. For the statement, "People like me don't have any influence over what the government does," only 42% disagreed. Less than a quarter (23%) disagreed with both statements, whereas nearly half (45%) agreed with both. These figures are almost identical to those from other third-wave democracies in the region. If an extraordinary level of self-confidence in participatory abilities is coupled with a significantly more pedestrian level of perceived efficacy, Mongolia's political system may be characterized by a frustrated desire for popular political influence.[6]

4.2. PERCEPTIONS OF CORRUPTION

Political corruption is widely regarded as the most serious obstacle to the consolidation of new democracies. Cooter (1997) claims that a democratic state must not only provide for the protection of civil liberties and individual rights, but must also ensure that market forces are able to operate unhindered by cronyism and nepotism in order to uphold some notion of moral equity.

Corruption is a pervasive feature of political life in today's Mongolia. In April 2002, about six thousand Mongolians protested outside the national government's headquarters in Ulaanbaatar, demanding the resignation of several government ministers. These "corruption rallies" were organized by the opposition Democratic Party, which accused the ruling party of giving the Russians more ownership rights to Mongolia's copper industry (Erdenet Mining Corporation) than had been publicly revealed. Protest rallies proliferated as the opposition hammered the government for cronyism and lack of transparency in the allocation of government contracts. The ruling party was accused of rewarding business deals to close associates and personal relatives of governmental ministers. Despite these accusations, national radio and television outlets rarely reported on corruption at the local and national levels, because they remained state owned and subject to tight government controls.[7]

The EAB survey included a number of items probing the respondent's perception of corruption (see table 6.3). When asked about the extent of corruption among officials at the national level, 57% believed "almost everyone" or "most officials" were corrupt. Officials at the local level did not fare much better—43% of the respondents believed either "almost everyone" or "most officials" were corrupt. Taken together, more than a third (35%) believed most national and local government officials to be corrupt, whereas those who did not believe most local or national officials to be corrupt amounted to only 28%.

A notable feature of political corruption in Mongolia is that citizens perceive national officials to be more corrupt than local officials. As noted, respondents were more likely to classify national level officials as almost all or mostly corrupt than to classify local level officials as such. The perception that hardly anyone is corrupt was significantly more common at the local level than at the national level (18% versus 4%). This contrasts with our findings from other countries in the EAB surveys, which typically show that national governments enjoy more popular confidence than local governments (see also Wang 2005).

Media coverage of major national corruption cases may have influenced this perception—and citizen perceptions may be correct. Whether due to narrower opportunities for corruption or to the bonds of local solidarity, local corruption may in fact be less pervasive in Mongolia than corruption at the national level.

4.3. INSTITUTIONAL TRUST

The EAB survey asked respondents how much trust they had in twelve governmental and political institutions. The results are presented in figure 6.2. Eight of the twelve institutions were trusted by at least half of our respondents. Those highly trusted included both national and local governments,

TABLE 6.3 PERCEPTION OF POLITICAL CORRUPTION AT NATIONAL AND LOCAL LEVELS: MONGOLIA

(Percent of total sample)

NATIONAL GOVERNMENT

LOCAL GOVERNMENT	Hardly anyone is involved	Not a lot of officials are involved	Most officials are corrupt	Almost everyone is corrupt	DK/NA	Total
Hardly anyone is involved	2.8	7.1	4.7	1.4	2.4	**18.3**
Not a lot of officials are involved	0.5	**17.1**	**11.9**	3.3	0.6	**33.4**
Most officials are corrupt	0.5	5.1	**15.9**	5.9	0.4	**27.9**
Almost everyone is corrupt	0.2	1.7	4.6	8.2	—	**14.7**
DK/NA	-	1.0	0.9	0.4	3.4	5.7
Total	4.0	31.9	38.0	19.3	6.8	100.0

Notes: N = 1144.

Blank cell means no cases.

Percentages above 10 are in boldface.

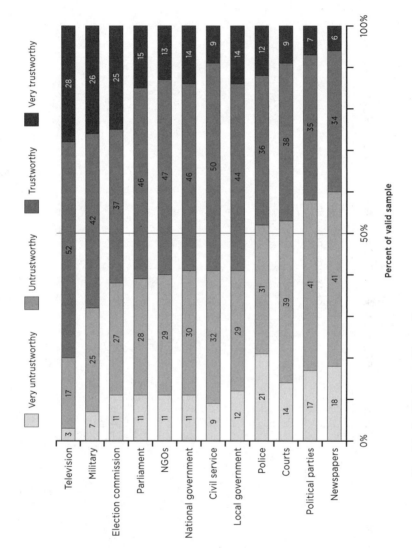

FIGURE 6.2 Trust in Institutions: Mongolia

despite widely held perceptions of corruption in both. However, political parties were regarded by a majority as untrustworthy, hardly unexpected considering that the country's first experience with multiparty politics was marked by four years of petty bickering that repeatedly brought governmental functions to a halt. Yet, the Great Hural (parliament)—scene of many unsightly squabbles—commanded an impressive amount of popular confidence.

Among the organs of the state, the military and the election commission were regarded as the two most trustworthy institutions. The positive rating of the election commission is noteworthy because opposition party legislators have accused the commission of being biased toward the ruling MPRP. While the civil service received reasonably good marks, the performance of the police and the courts failed to inspire confidence, again confirming the judiciary's disrepute among the citizenry.

In general, Mongolians placed greater faith in their societal institutions than in their government. Television was especially well regarded, earning the trust of nearly four out of five Mongolians, whereas only about half as many expressed faith in the print media. This was ironic, because the print media had begun to steer an independent course away from government monopoly, while the broadcast media remained state-owned at the time of our survey (in 2005, the parliament passed a law to privatize Mongolian National Radio and Television).

Over one hundred newspapers representing a wide array of political ideologies are freely circulated on a national basis, although the opposition still complains of lack of full access, especially to the major outlets. Meanwhile, the ruling parties have not hesitated to exercise their influence over television program content, sometimes denying access to the opposition. Even the Democratic Coalition lost its reformist zeal on the issue during its four years in power, an attitude it would later regret.[8]

Overall, Mongolian citizens exhibit a middling level of institutional trust compared to other countries in our survey. Like most of their neighbors, Mongolians place faith in the media and the military, and are suspicious of their government and contemptuous of political parties. While most East Asians hold their courts in high esteem, however, the legal system is one of the least trusted institutions in Mongolia; and while parliaments are seldom trusted across East Asia, most Mongolians cherish their Great Hural. Perhaps the public has not forgotten the heroic days of 1990, when tens of thousands demonstrated to demand multiparty elections and made the Great Hural the symbol of Mongolia's struggle for democracy.

5. COMMITMENT TO DEMOCRACY

The consolidation of new democracies hinges critically on the development of a culture that embraces democratic legitimacy and rejects antidemocratic alternatives. The Mongolian public's attitude toward democracy and its alternatives will be the focus of this section.

5.1. ATTACHMENT TO DEMOCRATIC POLITICS

We used five questions to estimate Mongolians' level of support for democracy in principle as well as in action. These questions addressed the desirability of democracy, the suitability of democracy, the preference for democracy, the efficacy of democracy, and the priority of democracy. The findings are summarized in chapter 1, table 1.8.

Respondents were asked to indicate on a 10-point scale how democratic they want their current political regime to be. Ninety-two percent of Mongolians articulated a clear desire for democracy, choosing a score of 6 or above. A plurality of one-third (30%) expressed the desire for complete democracy, choosing 10 on the scale. At least in principle, most Mongolians wanted to live in a democracy as opposed to other alternatives.

Another 10-point scale was employed to gauge the respondent's evaluation of democratic suitability. As with desirability, a large majority (86%) believed democracy to be suitable for their nation, with more than one-quarter believing that complete democracy was suitable, choosing 10 on the scale. The EAB survey also asked respondents whether or not they believed that "democracy is capable of solving the problems of our society." A majority (78%) again replied affirmatively, although the figure was somewhat lower than the percentages expressing desirability and suitability.

The EAB survey asked respondents if they would always prefer democracy to authoritarian rule. Fifty-seven percent preferred democratic rule to authoritarian rule, while about a quarter expressed feelings of communist nostalgia, and about 20% did not believe that regime type matters. These results reveal a substantial reservoir of nostalgia for the former regime, which had been firmly rejected a decade ago. The economic dislocation created by the marketization of the economy is a contributing factor to this nostalgia. When asked to indicate their priority between economic development and democratic governance, a majority (54%) replied that economic development is far more or somewhat more important than democracy.

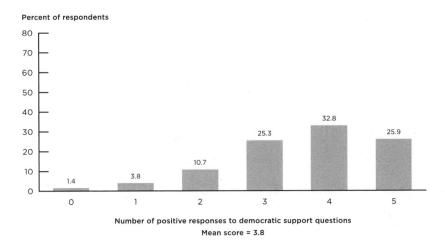

FIGURE 6.3 **Democratic Support: Mongolia**

Only about a quarter (26%) believed that democracy is somewhat more or far more important than development. A fifth of respondents considered economic and democratic development to be of equal importance. In all, fewer than half of Mongolians (45%) valued democracy at least as much as economic development.

On our 6-point summary measure of support for democracy Mongolians average 3.8, indicating a fairly robust level of democratic support (see figure 6.3). Like most of their neighbors in East Asia, Mongolians tend to be more supportive of democracy as a political ideal than as a political practice. Even among those who embrace democracy as the best method of governance, it is not always regarded as a higher priority than economic development.

5.2. DETACHMENT FROM AUTHORITARIANISM

The hardships of transition may foster rose-tinted memories of life during the communist past. The EAB survey asked respondents if they would support the return to some form of authoritarian rule. The results are displayed in chapter 1, table 1.9. Seventy-two percent of Mongolians rejected a return to one-party dictatorship. An even larger majority (86%) rejected military rule, which is remarkable considering the high level of trust enjoyed by the army. Some 66% of respondents rejected rule by technocratic experts and

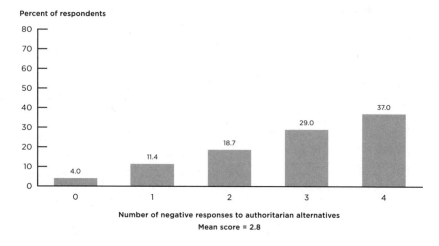

Percent of respondents

Number of negative responses to authoritarian alternatives
Mean score = 2.8

FIGURE 6.4 Authoritarian Detachment: Mongolia

59% turned down dictatorship by a strong leader. Yet only 37% of respondents rejected all four types of dictatorships, which suggested that economic collapse, deterioration in law and order, or failure to bridge class cleavages could lead to the rise of antidemocratic forces in the political arena.

We constructed a summary measure of authoritarian detachment by counting the number of authoritarian alternatives rejected by each respondent. On this index, the mean for the Mongolian sample stands at 2.8. As figure 6.4 shows, nearly over one-third (34%) remain open to two or more authoritarian possibilities. A significant number of Mongolians have yet to reject authoritarianism fully after more than a decade of democratic experience.

5.3. OVERALL COMMITMENT TO DEMOCRACY

When all our measures of democratic attachment and authoritarian detachment are combined, Mongolians' strong support for democracy comes into view. Figure 6.5 presents seven patterns of regime orientation (for definitions of the categories, see the notes to table 1.11, chapter 1). Roughly 69% of Mongolian respondents were clear supporters of democracy (not including skeptical supporters). Relatively small groups had mixed attitudes (11%) or attitudes of opposition (8%). By this criterion, Mongolia has to be viewed as one of the more consolidated democracies in our study.

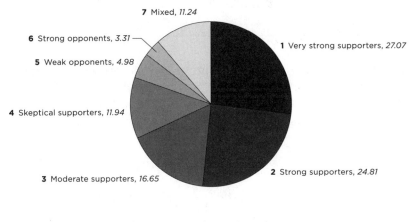

7 Mixed, *11.24*

6 Strong opponents, *3.31*

5 Weak opponents, *4.98*

4 Skeptical supporters, *11.94*

3 Moderate supporters, *16.65*

1 Very strong supporters, *27.07*

2 Strong supporters, *24.81*

Percent of respondents

FIGURE 6.5   **Patterns of Commitment to Democracy: Mongolia**

6. EXPECTATIONS OF MONGOLIAN DEMOCRACY

As we have seen, Mongolia's experiment with democracy to date has been marked by uneven accomplishments. It has delivered on promises of freedom but fallen short in effective governance. The citizenry is skeptical of political leaders and institutions, and public support for democracy is shallow. Under these circumstances, popular optimism for the future of democracy might prove decisive for the prospects of consolidation. To assess these expectations, the EAB survey compared each respondent's current and future regime ratings on the 10-point scale.

The results are displayed in table 6.4. On the whole, Mongolians anticipated significant improvements in the development of their new democracy. On the 10-point scale, they expected the system to progress toward democracy by 1.6 points from 6.4 to 8.0 in the next five years. Nearly 40% thought that five years from the time of the survey they would live in a complete democracy, despite the fact that only 12% placed the current regime in the same category. Even most of the 27% who also considered the current regime to be of a dictatorial variety were optimistic about the future, as only 7% expected to live in an authoritarian regime in five years. In fact, close to 85% of Mongolians believed that in five years, they would live in at least a limited democracy.

TABLE 6.4 **CURRENT AND EXPECTED FUTURE REGIME TYPE: MONGOLIA**

(Percent of respondents)

RATING	CURRENT REGIME	FUTURE REGIME	CHANGE[a]
Very dictatorial (1–2)	3.4	0.8	-2.6
Somewhat dictatorial (3–5)	23.5	6.5	-17.0
Somewhat democratic (6–8)	58.8	44.9	-13.9
Very democratic (9–10)	11.8	39.9	28.1
DK/NA	2.6	8.0	5.5
Total	100.0	100.0	
Mean on a 10-point scale	6.4	8.0	1.6

Notes: N = 1308.

Scale runs from 1, "complete dictatorship," to 10, "complete democracy."

Future regime is five years from time of survey.

[a] Change in percent of respondents rating the regime at the given level when the object of evaluation shifts from the current to the future regime.

We classified our respondents' current and future regime ratings into seven patterns of expected regime change (see chapter 1, table 1.12). Only 7.9% of respondents expected the future regime to be authoritarian (either through persistence or reversal); 22.5% who viewed the current regime as not yet truly democratic expected a limited or advanced democratic transition; and a large majority of about 70% expected democracy either to struggle ahead slowly, to develop markedly, or to achieve consolidation.

By these measures, Mongolians were among the more optimistic citizens of the region. Their doubts about the achievements of the new democratic regime are tempered by optimism for the future.

7. CONCLUSION

Mongolia represents an East Asian case of double transition: unlike other third-wave democracies in the region, the country has undergone the democratization of communist one-party rule into a multiparty competitive system and the simultaneous transformation of a planned economy into a free market economy. As many scholars (Linz and Stepan 1996a; Rose, Mishler, and Haerpfer 1998) point out, the totalitarian nature of the communist past and the economic costs of market reform in former communist countries pose special obstacles to democratic consolidation.

Unlike South Korea and Taiwan, Mongolia lacks the cultural legacy of a vibrant civil society (Clearly 1995). Nor does it have an institutional legacy of checks and balances to safeguard constitutional rule. Democracy was introduced without the crucial institutions of civil society and the rule of law, a phenomenon termed "backward democratization" by Richard Rose and Doh Chull Shin (2001). As Rose and Shin point out, transitions of this sort may be haunted by the specter of electoral authoritarianism, bedecked in the institutional trappings of democratic governance yet falling short of the standards of established democracies.

The EAB survey reveals that Mongolian democracy in 2002 was still some distance from consolidation as defined in chapter 1. Discontent over the perceived breakdown in law and order and economic equality simmered, and the public's distrust for their political leaders remained high. After more than a decade of democratic experience, a sizeable minority was not yet fully detached from authoritarian rule.

Yet, despite widespread perceptions of corruption among the country's leaders and a pervasive feeling of political impotence, large majorities of the public expressed themselves as satisfied with the performance of the current system, committed to democracy, and optimistic that the regime would become more democratic in the near future. Such positive attitudes carry a risk of complacency. If the sanguine attitudes of the citizenry are translated into a low level of public demand for greater democracy, there will be little pressure on the power elite to increase its supply.

NOTES

1. "Mongolia: Casino trial ends in sentences for legislators," *BBC Monitoring Asia Pacific—Political*, October 21, 1999. See also, "Mongolia corruption," *Agence France Presse—English*, May 6, 1999. Available online from LexisNexis.
2. The MPRP controlled just enough seats to prevent parliamentary overrule of a presidential veto. On one occasion, the MPRP president rejected the same coalition nominee for prime minister seven times in a row.
3. Calum MacLeod, "The Politics of the Zud," *Newsweek*, August 21, 2000.
4. Mongolian National Chamber of Commerce and Industry, "Corruption in Business Sector," Ulaanbaatar, 2000, annex 4, question 11. The report is available through the chamber, whose Web site is www.mongolchamber.mn/en.

5. Robert La Mont, "Some Means of Addressing Judicial Corruption in Mongolia," August 1, 2002, at http://www.forum.mn/res_mat/Judicial%20Corruption%20in%20Mongolia:pdf.

6. Compare Mexico's "aspirational" political culture as characterized by Almond and Verba (1963:416).

7. Irja Halasz, "Thousands Protest Corruption in Mongolian Capital," *Global Policy Forum*, April 15, 2002. Accessed from: http://www.globalpolicy.org/nations/corrupt/2002/0415mongolia.htm.

8. Morris Rossabi, "Mongolia in the 1990s: From Commissars to Capitalists?" Accessed from http://www.eurasianet.org/resource/mongolia/links/rossabi.html. See also Severinghaus (2000).

7

JAPANESE ATTITUDES AND VALUES TOWARD DEMOCRACY

Ken'ichi Ikeda and Masaru Kohno

JAPAN OFFERS AN INTRIGUING CASE for comparing the experiences of democracy and value change across East Asia. Japan has a longer history of sovereign independence than most other countries in the region. The roots of its democracy are deeper because even before World War II, Japan enjoyed a period of democratic experiment known as Taishō-era democracy. And Japan began its industrialization earlier than other Asian nations. Consequently, changes in values and attitudes in Japanese society associated with economic growth, urbanization, and the introduction of Western lifestyles are likely to be more complex and widespread. Findings from the Japanese case can serve as a benchmark against which findings from newer democracies in Asia can be compared.

The findings reported in this chapter come from a nationwide sample of eligible voters conducted in January and February 2003. We found that the Japanese people almost universally recognize the fundamental transition of political regime that occurred after World War II and see the present regime as democratic. There are, nevertheless, some variations, especially across age groups, in conceptions of democracy as well as in perceptions of the current regime's performance. Trust in democratic institutions is low and seems to be in decline.

The Japanese public is among the most dissatisfied with the government's performance of all the publics surveyed by the East Asian Barometer. Yet the Japanese support democracy as a system and show little interest in authoritarian alternatives. Democracy is consolidated in Japan, not because it is perceived as doing well, but because it is the default position for most Japanese citizens.

1. HISTORICAL BACKGROUND OF JAPANESE DEMOCRACY

It is customary to view the development of postwar Japanese politics as having gone through three stages: 1945 to 1955, 1955 to 1993, and 1993 to the present. In the first stage, Japan's parliamentary democracy was a typical multiparty system under which several major parties, from both conservative and progressive camps, competed for legislative seats and took turns forming the government. Most of the governments formed during this period were either coalition or minority governments, and only one out of a total of nine was based on a single-party legislative majority. This early period also witnessed constant party switching by individual politicians and a series of mergers and breakups of political parties, and was generally characterized by fluid partisan alignment.

A new party system emerged in 1955, when the Liberal Democratic Party (LDP) was established following the amalgamation of the conservative forces. For the next thirty-eight years, the LDP held uninterrupted power. The Japan Socialist Party (JSP), also created in 1955, never became a viable alternative to the LDP. The LDP suffered a long-term decline in its vote share during the 1960s, when two centrist parties—namely the Democratic Socialist Party (DSP) and the Komei Party—entered the race for the House of Representatives, the more important lower house of the Diet. From 1983 to 1986 the LDP was in coalition with the New Liberal Club (NLC), a small conservative group that had broken away from the LDP in 1976. But for this exception, the LDP was able to maintain a series of single-party governments throughout these years.

The third and current phase began in the early 1990s, when the LDP's grip on power weakened because of increasing public discontent born of a series of political scandals. In 1993, the largest LDP faction broke into two groups, one of which eventually joined the opposition in passing a no-confidence bill against the LDP government. In the next election, the LDP failed to obtain a majority and was forced to hand over power to a non-LDP coalition government. The non-LDP government collapsed in less than a year, and the LDP returned to power in coalition with its long-time rival, the former JSP. The LDP survived the next three general elections as the plurality party and remained in power by alternating coalition partners. The non-LDP camp, meanwhile, proved unable to consolidate and remained in opposition up to the time of our survey in 2003.

The dominance of a single conservative party over such a long period is remarkable, considering that over this period Japan underwent radical and continuous transformations in its social and economic conditions, including its industrial structures, occupational distribution, and living standards. The LDP has often been compared to other dominant parties, such as the Social Democrats in Sweden and the Christian Democrats in Italy, but its record is truly exceptional in terms of both longevity and the degree of its dominance. The LDP's monopoly of power has also provoked much criticism, especially in the late 1980s and early 1990s.

Many observers argued that the LDP's problems—chronic factionalism, preoccupation with money politics, and lack of policy innovations—could be traced to the peculiar electoral system that had been used for the House of Representatives since 1947, a system of single nontransferable votes coupled with multimember districts. The non-LDP coalition government that came to power in 1993 made revisions of the electoral law a priority. With the introduction of some single-member districts into the system, there was hope that a viable two-party system would finally emerge. The consolidation of the anti-LDP camp into the New Frontier Party (NFP) in December 1994 encouraged such hopes. But the new party proved to be short lived. At the time of our survey, the only serious challenge to the LDP came from the newly-formed Democratic Party of Japan (DPJ). Although the DPJ came close to besting the LDP in the general elections of 2003 and maintained its vote strength in the 2005 election, the LDP managed to win back many seats in the 2005 election by increasing the turnout rate of its voter base. Thus it was unclear whether or when a two-party system would emerge as the designers of the electoral system reform had anticipated.

2. CONCEPTIONS OF DEMOCRACY

Japan returned the highest number of don't know/no answer (DK/NA) responses to the question, "What does democracy mean to you?" in the EAB survey. This is not unusual for surveys in Japan, where respondents often have difficulty responding to open-ended questions related to politics. It may also reflect the fact that democracy has been so long established in Japan that many people do not think very specifically about what it is.

Roughly two-thirds of Japanese respondents gave at least one interpretation. One-third gave two answers, and one-ninth gave three answers. The responses are displayed in chapter 1, table 1.3.

As the table shows, Japanese respondents who gave valid answers (N = 933) offered a range of fairly evenly divided understandings of the term rather than focusing on one or two concepts as in some other countries in the EAB survey. Almost half understood democracy in terms of freedom and liberty (30%), particularly in terms of freedom in general and freedom of expression. The next-largest group (18%) understood democracy in general positive terms, including answers such as "taking into account all parties concerned," "fair treatment," or "self-responsibility." The third-largest group understood democracy in terms of social equality and justice, numbering 17.5% of the sample, with five out of six responses in this category being related to equality rather than justice. The fourth-largest category (9%) understood democracy in terms of political rights, institutions, and processes. In this category, the typical response was "majority rule." Only 3.4% of the respondents who answered the question thought of democracy in negative terms, such as "focusing too much on individual interests."

Within the EAB survey, the Japanese pattern of responses most closely resembled that of the Koreans, who identified the same top four categories of meanings of democracy, and did so in close to the same order. Where Japanese differed from Koreans was, first, in the greater percentage of DK/NA answers, and second, in the smaller emphasis given by Japanese respondents to the relationship of democracy to the market economy.

The relatively small proportion of answers mentioning institutions and processes suggests that Japanese citizens tend to conceptualize democracy statically rather than dynamically as a regime to be attained through the assertion of citizenship rights. This may reflect the historical character of Japanese democracy as a system imposed after defeat in war rather than the product of indigenous political movements with broad grassroots involvement. Arguably, such an interpretation is consistent with findings reported elsewhere regarding low levels of active and challenging political participation in Japan, such as demonstrations, boycotts, strikes, and other unconventional forms of protest (Dalton 2002:62–63).

As "freedom and liberty"

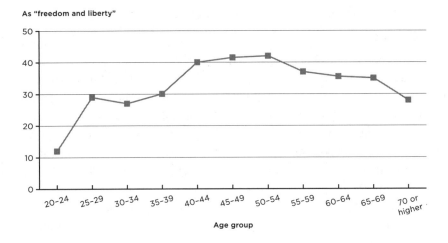

FIGURE 7.1   **Meaning of Democracy by Age Group**

As shown in figure 7.1, people above the age of forty—those most affected by the early stages of Japan's postwar political development—were most likely to define democracy in terms of freedom and liberty. Younger respondents were more like to define democracy in general positive terms, offering few specific ideas. This suggests that democracy has become a background condition of life in the course of sixty years of practice since World War II. Since it is no longer the subject of debate or aspiration, younger people do not think carefully about what it is.

3. EVALUATING DEMOCRATIC PROGRESS AND ITS CONSEQUENCES

In this section, we explore the extent of Japan's democratic consolidation by examining public perceptions of the current regime in comparison to the prewar military regime. We found that the overwhelming majority of Japanese perceived a fundamental regime change to have taken place at the end of World War II, and considered the new regime vastly more democratic than the military dictatorship of the prewar era. We also find that while the democratic performance of the current regime is evaluated highly, many Japanese have reservations about its performance, especially in promoting social and economic equality.

3.1. PERCEPTIONS OF REGIME CHANGE

The EAB survey asked respondents to rate their current and past regimes on a 10-point scale of democracy. The results for Japan are reported in table 7.1. Less than one-sixth of respondents had difficulty evaluating the prewar regime. The perceived contrast between the prewar and postwar regimes was stark. More than three-quarters of Japanese (77%) rated the current regime as democratic by placing it at 6 or above on the scale, while an almost equal proportion (75.4%) rated the prewar regime as dictatorial by placing it at 5 or below. While the current regime received a mean rating of 7.0, the prewar regime received a 3.1. However, it should also be noted that even after more than five decades of democratic rule, the rating of 7 out of a possible 10 means that Japan remains a partial or limited democracy in the eyes of its citizens.

The perception of regime change was somewhat affected by age. As the wartime regime fades further into the past, younger generations have less strong feelings that there is something historically special about the current political system. Views of "equally dictatorial" and "less dictatorial" were more frequently found among younger people (the average age for

TABLE 7.1 **PERCEPTIONS OF PAST AND CURRENT REGIMES: JAPAN**

(Percent of respondents)		
REGIME TYPES	PAST REGIME	CURRENT REGIME
Very dictatorial (1–2)	35.0	0.5
Somewhat dictatorial (3–5)	40.4	13.5
Somewhat democratic (6–8)	7.6	65.6
Very democratic (9–10)	0.6	11.3
DK/NA	16.4	9.1
Total	100.0	100.0
Mean on the 10-point scale	3.1	7.0

Notes: Regime types are based on the respondent's ranking of the regime on a scale from 1, "complete dictatorship," to 10, "complete democracy." Scores of 5 and below are degrees of dictatorship and scores of 6 and above are degrees of democracy.

N = 1419.

DK/NA = Don't know/no answer.

respondents holding these views were forty-six and forty-three respectively), whereas views of moderate or dramatic democratic transition were more likely to be held by older people (the average age was fifty-two and fifty-three respectively). Those under the age of thirty-five were least likely to perceive regime change. Nonetheless, most Japanese still have enough indirect knowledge of the prewar regime to recognize the dramatic democratization of the country's political system in the postwar era, and except for age these assessments vary little with demographic categories.

Based on the ratings of past and current regimes we identified six patterns of perceived regime change (see chapter 1, table 1.7). Consistent with the Japanese respondents' reserved assessment of their current regime, the majority of those able to answer these two questions (64%) assessed the regime change as a shift from dictatorship to a moderate level of democracy. In the eight countries surveyed by the EAB, Japan recorded the highest percentage who selected this pattern. A much smaller proportion (12%) saw a dramatic democratic transition, while another 11% only considered the current regime to be less dictatorial than the prewar regime rather than truly democratic. Interestingly, nearly 9% of respondents considered the current regime to be a continuation of prewar democracy, perhaps referring to the brief democratic experiment of the Taishō era. Overall, an overwhelming majority (84.5%) of the Japanese public perceived at least some progress toward greater democracy since the end of World War II.

Individual perceptions of the regime change are affected by demographic factors. We found that male respondents were 5% more likely than females to perceive a regime change and that university graduates were more likely than those with lower degrees to perceive a regime change (72% versus 58%). These differences suggest that groups who participate relatively actively in politics in Japan are more cognizant than other groups of the differences between the former and the new regimes.

3.2. COMPARING PAST AND PRESENT REGIMES

The EAB survey asked respondents to rate each of nine major government performance domains on a 5-point scale. The findings for Japan are presented in table 7.2. Japanese citizens perceived significant improvements in their political and personal freedoms. The greatest improvements were felt in the areas of freedom of speech (+93%) and freedom of association

TABLE 7.2 PERCEIVED PERFORMANCE OF CURRENT AND PAST REGIMES: JAPAN

	MEAN[a]	SD[a]	NEGATIVE CHANGE[b]	POSITIVE CHANGE[b]	NO CHANGE[b]	PDI[c]	VALID %[d]
Democratic performance							
Freedom of speech	1.45	0.67	1.7	94.3	4.0	92.6	95.5
Freedom of association	1.22	0.71	2.1	88.1	9.8	86.0	89.3
Equal treatment	0.54	1.03	18.9	63.3	17.8	44.4	91.7
Popular influence	0.38	0.95	14.9	48.1	37.0	33.2	88.5
Independent judiciary	0.64	1.00	14.5	62.4	23.1	47.9	76.7
Average	0.84	0.87	10.4	71.2	18.3	60.8	9.0
Policy performance							
Anticorruption	−0.33	1.17	45.7	28.1	26.3	−17.6	89.3
Law and order	0.10	1.12	34.3	46.2	19.6	11.9	92.4
Economic development	0.57	1.23	23.6	66.4	10.0	42.8	94.3
Economic equality	0.25	1.10	26.0	49.9	24.2	23.9	92.3
Average	0.15	1.15	32.4	47.6	20.0	15.2	92.1

Notes: N = 1418.

Past regime is defined as pre-1945.

[a] Scale ranges from −2 (much worse) to +2 (much better).

[b] Percent of valid sample.

[c] PDI (percentage difference index) = percent seeing positive change minus percent seeing negative change.

[d] Percent of sample giving a valid answer to this question.

(+86%), although significant improvements were also registered in the other three areas of democratic performance. The PDI scores for the five democratic performance areas averaged +60.8, second only to Thailand among the countries surveyed. Japan registered the greatest improvements in the freedom of speech and freedom of association of all countries in the survey, as befits its status as the oldest liberal democracy in East Asia. This suggests that the regime has what Tanaka (2002, 2003) calls "system support," and is well consolidated.

However, at the level of policy performance, there has been a persistent sense of crisis over many years which is reflected in our EAB data. A substantial number of our respondents evaluated the policy performance of the democratic regime negatively or as unchanged, and the PDI scores in the policy areas are unimpressive. In the dimension of corruption control, for instance, almost half (46%) of respondents evaluated the current regime's performance negatively, and the PDI score is nearly -18. While this particular area may be heavily affected by the media's persistent focus on political corruption in Japan's postwar history (Pharr 2000), the current regime did not fare as well as one may expect even in the economic areas, despite the remarkable successes of the Japanese economy from the 1950s to the 1980s.

Although more respondents approved of the present regime's performance in economic development, almost a quarter (24%) evaluated the same area negatively, despite the fact that Japan's GNP multiplied more than twenty thousand times between 1935 and the early 2000s. In the area of economic equality, a quarter of the respondents perceived negative changes, and the PDI score is only 23.9. This is despite the fact that, although there was a slight increase in inequality between 1970 and the late 1990s, Japan's performance in this area is relatively stable compared to other OECD (Organization for Economic Cooperation and Development) countries (OECD 1997). The lack of reliable data going back to the 1930s makes it impossible to offer any conclusive analysis, but there are some indications that inequality was more pronounced before the war. Japan's Gini coefficient stood at 0.451 in 1930 and 0.641 in 1940, suggesting far higher levels of inequality than, for instance, in 1980 when the coefficient was 0.334 (Tachibanaki 1998). Many of the postwar reforms undertaken by the occupation forces were targeted to address distributional problems, including land, tax, and administrative reforms. In light of these facts, the reservations expressed by many respondents about the economic performance of the postwar regime may be puzzling, but perhaps that is because few have specific knowledge of the previous regime and most evaluate the current system on its recent performance.

In any case, the overall ratings remain positive except for anticorruption, suggesting that even on the policy side, public dissatisfaction is not strong enough to lead to disillusionment with democracy as a type of regime,

We investigated the relationship between perceptions of regime performance and several standard demographic variables. The only significant factor was age. Respondents over the age of forty-five tended to evaluate the democratic performance of the current regime more highly than those in younger age groups, further supporting the idea that those whose life experience was closer to the era of military rule are more sensitive to the distinctive aspects of democratic governance. Other than this, demographic subgroups of the population differed little in their evaluations of regime performance, suggesting a broad national consensus on what citizens want from government and on what they perceive it as delivering.

4. APPRAISING DEMOCRATIC INSTITUTIONS

Not only were Japanese citizens dissatisfied with the policy performance of the regime, but as we will explain in this section, they also exhibited low levels of confidence in their participatory capacity, and compared with the publics in younger democracies in the region, were exceptionally distrustful of the key institutions of representative democracy. Yet we will argue that these findings do not mean that Japanese democracy is not consolidated—it remains the only thinkable form of regime, with no authoritarian alternative drawing significant public support.

4.1. OVERALL SATISFACTION WITH DEMOCRACY AND THE CURRENT GOVERNMENT

The EAB survey assessed satisfaction with the current regime by asking, "On the whole, how satisfied or dissatisfied are you with the way democracy works in our country?" On this question the public appeared evenly divided. Only 4% were "very satisfied," but likewise only 7% were "not at all satisfied." Forty-two percent were "fairly satisfied," while 39% were "not very satisfied." Demographic analyses showed that males were slightly more dissatisfied than females and people over sixty were more

TABLE 7.3 **TIME-SERIES DATA ON CABINET EVALUATION: 1979–2003**

	FROM	TO	AVERAGE SUPPORT (%)	AVERAGE NONSUPPORT (%)
Ōhira	Jan 79	Apr 80	34.2	42.8
Suzuki	Aug 80	Sep 82	38.5	38.3
Nakasone	Dec 82	Oct 87	47.5	34.1
Takeshita	Nov 87	Apr 89	39.1	40.1
Uno	Jun 89	—	22.8	56.5
Kaifu	Aug 89	Sep 91	50.2	33.5
Miyazawa	Nov 91	Jun 93	30.4	55.3
Hosokawa	Sep 93	Mar 94	67.2	20.9
Hata	Apr 94	Jun 94	49.9	35.6
Murayama	Jul 94	Dec 95	39.1	44.8
Hashimoto	Jan 96	Jun 98	45.1	41.0
Obuchi	Sep 98	Mar 00	40.4	44.6
Mori	Apr 00	Sep 01	24.9	62.2
Koizumi	May 01	Dec 03	60.1	29.7

Source: Yomiuri newspaper, ed., *Nidai-seitō jidai no akebono* [The dawn of the two-party system in Japan] (Tokyo: Bokutaku-sha, 2004).

dissatisfied than the younger generations. No clear variations existed for level of education.

In a related question, respondents were asked about their general satisfaction with the then current government (the Junichirō Koizumi cabinet) based on a 4-point scale ranging from 1 (very satisfied) to 4 (very dissatisfied). Only 3% indicated that they were "very satisfied" and another 32% "somewhat satisfied," whereas 41% were "somewhat dissatisfied" and 19% "very dissatisfied." The mean score was 2.8 (SD = .79), indicating that the majority of respondents were not satisfied. Less than two years earlier, however, this cabinet had enjoyed an exceptional level of popularity at its inauguration. In its first year, it enjoyed a 63.8% average approval rating.

These low levels of satisfaction are not exceptional in the recent history of Japan. We can compare them to a quarter-century's worth of monthly approval ratings in which respondents were asked whether they supported the current cabinet, as shown in table 7.3. It is evident that in the past twenty-five years, only half of the cabinets enjoyed more support than nonsupport. Such low evaluations of incumbents' performance no doubt had an impact on citizens' satisfaction with the democratic system as a whole, yet, as we will show later, did not lead to support for authoritarian alternatives to democracy.

4.2. PERCEPTIONS OF CORRUPTION

The EAB included a pair of items probing whether corruption is perceived to be more serious at the national or local level of government. The results are presented in table 7.4. Over half (51.8%) of the respondents believed that almost all or most officials in the national government were corrupt. Corruption at the local level was perceived to be less widespread, with 37.7% believing that almost all or most officials were corrupt. Considered together, less than one-third (31%) of respondents believed that most officials at both national and local levels were honest, whereas a slightly larger number (32%) believed most officials at both levels to be corrupt.

These results may reflect the extensive and lengthy media coverage of corruption among national politicians (Pharr 2000). As revealed in the results to a follow-up question, few of those who perceived widespread corruption had actually witnessed it either directly or indirectly (1% and 4% respectively).

4.3. INSTITUTIONAL TRUST

Trust in public institutions is an important aspect of social capital and hence an important ingredient of effective democratic governance (Putnam et al. 1993). In the EAB survey, respondents were asked to indicate their levels of trust in twelve state and societal institutions. The results are presented in figure 7.2. Among the countries we surveyed, trust in public institutions is relatively low in Japan. Five of the twelve institutions listed were trusted by fewer than half of our respondents, and these included the key institutions of Japanese democracy such as the parliament, national and local governments, and political parties. Although parliaments and political parties are rarely popular among the countries in our survey, the Japanese figures are by far the lowest, with roughly nine out of ten respondents expressing distrust. Trust in the national government is the lowest as well, with some 76% of the public expressing distrust.

TABLE 7.4   **PERCEPTION OF POLITICAL CORRUPTION AT NATIONAL AND LOCAL LEVELS: JAPAN**

(Percent of total sample)

LOCAL GOVERN-MENT	NATIONAL GOVERNMENT					
	Hardly anyone is involved	Not a lot of officials are involved	Most officials are corrupt	Almost everyone is corrupt	DK/NA	Total
Hardly anyone is involved	0.8	2.0	0.5	0.2	0.5	3.9
Not a lot of officials are involved	0.3	**28.3**	**15.4**	2.0	1.3	**47.2**
Most officials are corrupt	0.2	3.9	**19.3**	3.9	0.6	**28.0**
Almost everyone is corrupt	0.1	0.5	1.6	7.5	-	9.7
DK/NA	-	1.3	1.0	0.4	8.5	**11.1**
Total	1.3	**36.0**	**37.8**	**14.0**	**10.9**	100.0

Notes: N = 1418.

Blank cell means no cases.

Percentages above 10 are in boldface.

By comparison, the administrative organs of the state enjoyed higher levels of public confidence. The military and the police were trusted by roughly half of our respondents, while the courts (68%) and the electoral commission (65%) enjoyed even higher levels of trust, perhaps because of their perceived political neutrality (although some scandals have recently been revealed in these sectors as well). The one notable exception is the civil service, which, along with political parties, is one of the least-trusted institutions in Japan, a pattern contrary to most expectations. Perhaps this is due to the extraordinary amounts of power wielded by the bureaucracy in the Japanese system. In the eyes of the public, since the bureaucrats actually make policies, they are deeply enmeshed in the political process and must therefore shoulder responsibility for the troubles, economic and otherwise, that beset the country in recent years.

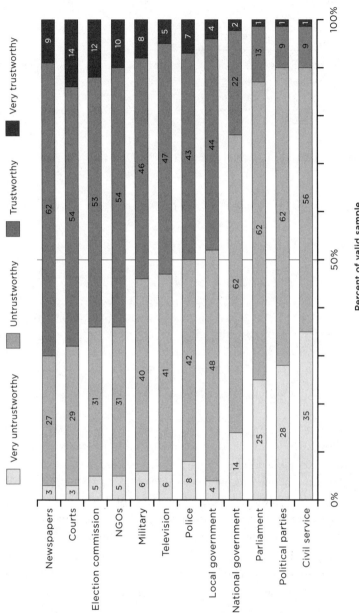

Very untrustworthy　　**Untrustworthy**　　**Trustworthy**　　**Very trustworthy**

	Very untrustworthy	Untrustworthy	Trustworthy	Very trustworthy
Newspapers	3	27	62	9
Courts	3	29	54	14
Election commission	5	31	53	12
NGOs	5	31	54	10
Military	6	40	46	8
Television	6	41	47	5
Police	8	42	43	7
Local government	4	48	44	4
National government	14	62	22	2
Parliament	25	62	13	1
Political parties	28	62	9	1
Civil service	35	56	9	1

0%　　　　　50%　　　　　100%

Percent of valid sample

FIGURE 7.2 Trust in Institutions: Japan

The most-trusted institutions were those of a societal nature. The mass media were well trusted, with newspapers judged to be the most trustworthy among all the institutions listed in the survey. Television was likewise highly regarded.[1] Although nongovernmental organizations (NGOs) have a relatively brief history in Japan, they were also thought to be highly trustworthy precisely because of their nongovernmental nature.

Trust in institutions seems to be correlated with the perceived distance from political corruption. The pattern is consistent across multiple surveys from 1990 to our survey in 2003 (see table 7.5). Newspapers, television, and the courts scored high in trust; political parties and parliament low. This is probably as a result of the stream of corruption scandals as well as the perceived responsibility of these institutions for the stagnation of Japanese society.

TABLE 7.5 **TIME-SERIES DATA ON TRUST IN INSTITUTIONS, 1990–2003**

(Percentage of respondents expressing trust)			
	WORLD VALUES SURVEY[a]	**WORLD VALUES SURVEY**[a]	**JGSS**[b]	**EAB SURVEY**
	1990	1995	2000	2003
Courts	61.4	74.1	69.0	68
The national government	—	30.0	—	24
Political parties	—	17.2	—	10
Parliament	28.3	24.2	28.8	14
Civil service	33.0	35.0	43.1	10
The military	24.0	59.5	61.6	54
The police	57.8	76.3	67.3	50
Newspapers	54.6	71.6	89.4	71
Television	—	68.1	76.9	52
N=	1011	1054	2893	1418
Scale	4-point scale	4-point scale	3-point scale	4-point scale

[a] World Values Survey data are from http://www.worldvaluessurvey.org.

[b] The Japanese General Social Survey; see http://jgss.daishodai.ac.jp/english/eframe/englishtop.html.

TABLE 7.6 **"POLITICS ARE TOO COMPLICATED TO UNDERSTAND"**

(Percent of total sample)

	AGREE	CAN'T SAY	DISAGREE	DK/NA	TOTAL
1976[a]	56.8	17.3	12.6	13.3	100.0
1983[b]	62.7	14.7	18.3	4.3	100.0
1993[c]	66.8	9.7	20.8	2.7	100.0
1995[c]	70.6	10.0	17.3	2.1	100.0
1996[c]	68.2	10.6	18.5	2.8	100.0
Average	65.6	12.0	17.8	4.5	100.0

Sources: Japanese Election Studies (JABISS 1976, JES 1983, JES2 1993–1996).

[a] 1976 data are from the JABISS study (Flanagan et al. 1991); N = 1921.

[b] 1983 data are from the JES study (Watanuki et al. 1986); N = 1769.

[c] 1993 to 1996 data are from the JES2 study (Kabashima et al. 1998); N = 2320, 2076, 2299 respectively.

4.4. POLITICAL EFFICACY

We asked respondents about their self-perceived political empowerment, as defined by the ability to understand politics and the capacity to participate in politics (sometimes referred to as "internal efficacy"; see chapter 1, table 1.4). Only 16.9% of our respondents believed they could understand politics, and an even smaller number (13.8%) felt capable of active engagement. Overall, more than half (59.2%) of respondents believed they could neither understand nor participate in politics, while those who felt capable of both amounted to only 10.2%.

A lengthy set of time-series data is available on the perceived ability to understand politics from the Japanese election studies between 1976 and 1996 (see table 7.6). It is surprising to find that, on this item, there has been virtually no change over the past twenty-five years.[2]

With regard to the perceived responsiveness of the political system to citizens' participation (sometimes called "external efficacy"), we turn to another pair of items in the EAB survey. When asked to evaluate the statement, "The nation is run by a powerful few and ordinary citizens cannot do much about it," only 36% disagreed, suggesting a deep cleavage between the governing elite and the overwhelming majority of the citizenry. Only 46%

disagreed with the statement, "People like me don't have any influence over what the government does."

For this item, too, we are fortunate to have a good set of time-series data (table 7.7), which again shows no significant changes over the years.[3]

We investigated the relationship between respondents' demographic characteristics and their evaluations of their own political empowerment and the system's responsiveness. The following findings are salient. First, as is true in most political systems, the level of education is positively correlated with the perception of both empowerment and system responsiveness (for empowerment, $r = .187$, $p < .001$; and for responsiveness, $r = .112$, $p < .001$)—the more highly educated are more involved and less alienated from the regime. Second, age is related to perceived system responsiveness (one-way variance; $p < .01$), but the relationship is not linear. It is a bell-shaped relationship peaking around the late fifties, defining the baby boomer generation born shortly after World War II who experienced the dramatic student movements of the late 1960s. As this student activist generation passes from the scene, we would expect a reversion toward the mean in overall levels of internal and external efficacy in the Japanese population.

We also looked at the interrelationships of several sets of attitudes. First, perceptions of citizen empowerment and system responsiveness are both

TABLE 7.7 "I HAVE NO SAY IN WHAT THE GOVERNMENT DOES"

(Percent of respondents)

	AGREE	CAN'T SAY	DISAGREE	DK/NA	TOTAL
1976[a]	56.8	17.3	12.6	13.3	100.0
1983[b]	58.6	13.6	21.9	5.9	100.0
1993[c]	58.8	9.7	28.5	3.0	100.0
1995[c]	59.4	14.8	23.9	1.8	100.0
1996[c]	58.4	11.5	27.4	2.7	100.0
Average	57.4	13.0	24.6	5.0	100.0

Sources: Japanese Election Studies (JABISS 1976, JES 1983, JES2 1993–1996).

[a] 1976 data are from JABISS study (Flanagan et al., 1991); N = 1921.

[b] 1983 data are from JES study (Watanuki at al., 1986); N = 1769.

[c] 1993 to 1996 data are from JES2 study (Kabashima at al., 1998); N = 2320, 2076, 2299 respectively.

positively correlated with the perception that the postwar regime is more democratic than the prewar regime (r = .119 and .187 respectively; p < .001 in both cases). This suggests that feelings of political efficacy strengthen support for and the perceived legitimacy of the current regime. Second, trust in democratic institutions is positively correlated with both perceived empowerment (r = .150, p < .001) and perceived system responsiveness (r = .166, p < .001). Though the correlation is not strong, the result reminds us of the power of trust in producing social capital (Putnam et al. 1993; Putnam 2000). If Japanese institutions were more highly trusted, perceptions of empowerment and system responsiveness might increase as well. Instead, however, Japan is caught in a vicious circle of mutually reinforcing negative attitudes; distrust lessens interactions between citizens and institutions, which in turn decreases political efficacy.

By cross-tabulating the two summary measures of efficacy, we produced table 7.8. Nearly six of ten respondents are situated in those cells where both citizen empowerment and system responsiveness are low or very low. In this sense, a majority of the Japanese public can be characterized as alienated from the political system. The second-largest group had a low sense of empowerment but a high sense of system responsiveness. For this category of people, the political system is perhaps perceived to be paternalistic. Only 9% were characterized by high or very high levels of citizen empowerment as well as perceived system responsiveness, representing an ideal type of democratic citizenship.

TABLE 7.8 **SYSTEM RESPONSIVENESS AND CITIZEN EMPOWERMENT**

(Percent of total sample)

PERCEIVED CITIZEN EMPOWERMENT	PERCEIVED SYSTEM RESPONSIVENESS				
	Very low	Low	High	Very high	Total
Very low	8.1	13.8	3.9	1.9	27.7
Low	4.7	33.4	12.4	5.6	56.1
High	0.8	4.9	3.9	2.8	12.4
Very high	0.2	1.2	0.4	2.0	3.8
Total	13.8	53.3	20.6	12.3	100.0

Note: N = 1418.

In conclusion, despite the venerability and stability of their democratic system, the Japanese are among the most dissatisfied citizens in Asia. They display—and have long displayed—lower trust in their political institutions and lower regard for their own capabilities as citizens than the citizens of most of Asia's newer democracies. Available trend data sets confirm that the public's low evaluations of various aspects of democratic governance have been consistent over the years. To what extent do these attitudes carry over into a lack of commitment to democracy as a regime?

5. COMMITMENT TO DEMOCRACY

The superiority of democracy over other political systems cannot be taken for granted. Rather, democratic consolidation is a product of constant choice making by those who actively desire, prefer, and support democracy over other political systems. Ultimately democratic legitimacy is established when no other system of governance is perceived as a viable alternative (Linz 1990; Linz and Stepan 1996b).

To assess democratic legitimacy, we turned to two clusters of questions from the EAB survey. The first cluster deals with values associated with democratic attachment; the second addresses detachment from authoritarian alternatives. We found a high level of commitment to democracy in Japan. Although the economy usually came first when respondents were forced to choose between the two, there was still widespread support for democracy except among those over the age of seventy. Despite relatively low levels of perceived political efficacy and pervasive distrust of key political institutions, the democratic regime of the postwar era was judged to be a positive experience after all.

5.1. ATTACHMENT TO DEMOCRATIC POLITICS

Even though the Japanese have long been dissatisfied with the incumbent authorities, they nonetheless remain relatively highly committed to democracy as an ideal or principle. Democracy is less an active choice than a habit; it has become the default position of Japanese citizens.

When asked to indicate on a 10-point scale how democratic they would like their political system to be, a convincing majority (87%) of Japanese respondents expressed a desire for democracy by choosing a score of 6 or above. A somewhat smaller number confirmed the suitability of democracy by selecting a score of 6 or above. The difference between desirability and suitability, of course, reflects the gap between the ideal and the reality, as enthusiasm for democracy is inevitably dampened by problems like corruption, political polarization, and inefficient public institutions, which the Japanese people have to face on a daily basis.

The desirability and suitability variables are correlated with some demographic variables, although the relationships are weak. Democratic desirability is positively correlated with education and income (r = .058 and .064 respectively), and suitability is positively correlated with age (r = .080). Otherwise, support for democracy is widely and evenly distributed in Japan.

Consistent with these findings, over two-thirds (67%) of our respondents agreed that democratic government is "preferable to all other kinds of government." With regard to efficacy, 61% believed that democracy is "capable of solving the problems facing society." Cross-tabulation of the preference and efficacy results revealed that 53% of our respondents considered democracy to be both preferable and also efficacious in solving societal problems. In this sense a majority of Japanese citizens can be considered core supporters of the democratic regime.

Finally, respondents were asked to prioritize between democracy and economic development. Nearly half (44%) believed that democracy is equally or more important than development, the third-highest percentage among countries surveyed. As Japan has the second-largest GDP in the world (at the time of publication), this finding is consistent with the prediction of postmaterialist theories that the citizens of wealthier countries will place greater priority on nonmaterial values (e.g., Inglehart 1997), although the same theory hardly explains the even higher priority accorded democracy in Thailand and Mongolia. Further supporting the postmaterialist thesis, the younger generations who have lived all their lives in prosperity were the most likely to value democracy over economic development.

As an overall measure of the depth of democratic attachment, we constructed a 6-point index ranging from 0 to 5 aggregating the responses regarding desirability, suitability, efficacy, preference, and priority. On this index, the Japanese average 4.0, indicating a level of attachment roughly comparable to those found in other East Asian democracies. Figure 7.3 shows that only about one in five Japanese (23.4%) provided prodemocratic responses to all five items, and only about a third (32.1%) supported four. Although Japan is the most mature democracy among the countries sur-

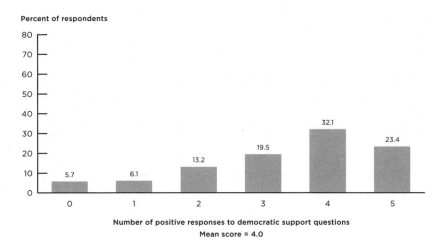

FIGURE 7.3 **Democratic Support: Japan**

veyed, skepticism of democratic politics remains prevalent and the public's level of democratic attachment is only average. Yet, as we will see in the next section, authoritarian alternatives do not command sufficient support to challenge the public's acceptance of democracy.

5.2. DETACHMENT FROM AUTHORITARIANISM

We asked respondents whether they would support various types of authoritarian regimes. The results are given in chapter 1, table 1.9. A compelling majority (79%) opposed the dictatorship of a strong leader, and an even larger majority (94%) rejected the return to military rule. Nearly as many (85%) rejected the option of rule by technocratic experts, but only about two-thirds (67%) opposed the banning of opposition parties. Compared to their neighbors across East Asia, Japanese citizens exhibited the highest levels of detachment from both military and technocratic rule, suggesting that Japan's wartime experiences and recent economic difficulties have thoroughly discredited these types of regimes. However, it is interesting to note that they were also among the most receptive of a single-party dictatorship, perhaps reflective of the public's profound mistrust of party politics and their prolonged experience with a dominant ruling party.

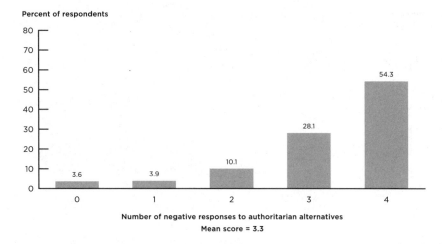

Percent of respondents

FIGURE 7.4 **Authoritarian Detachment: Japan**

Together, responses to these questions measure the general level of detachment from authoritarian politics. We constructed a 5-point index ranging from o to 4 by counting the number of authoritarian alternatives rejected by the respondent (see figure 7.4). On this index, Japan averaged a score of 3.3, one of the highest levels of authoritarian detachment in the EAB surveys. More than half (54%) of our respondents were fully detached, rejecting all four types of dictatorial rule. An additional 28% rejected three out of four options. It appears that more than five decades of democratic experience has discredited authoritarian politics in the eyes of the majority of Japanese citizens.

Cross-tabulation with several demographic variables showed two distinct results. Age is clearly related to authoritarian detachment. People over the age of seventy, who have direct experience of life under an authoritarian regime, exhibited the lowest level of detachment, perhaps reflecting a sense of nostalgia. Also notable is the effect of education. The higher the level of one's education, the more one rejects the authoritarian way of governing ($r = .205$, $p < .001$).

Although the Japanese are not happy with their government, they see no alternative type of regime that they can accept. The greater opposition to authoritarianism among the more highly educated is important for democratic consolidation, because this group is likely to have more political influence and thus be more able to resist a reversion to authoritarianism.

5.3. OVERALL COMMITMENT TO DEMOCRACY

To obtain an overall measure of popular commitment to democracy, we took into account levels of both democratic attachment and authoritarian detachment and identified seven patterns of regime orientation (see figure 7.5; the categories are explained in the notes to table 1.11, chapter 1). Nearly 10% of the public could be classified as opponents of democracy; another 15% were either ambivalent about democracy or offered only skeptical support. Most importantly, by this measure a majority (75.5%) of the Japanese people were moderate to strong supporters of democracy. Compared with other countries in the survey, Japan's long experience with democracy has created one of the widest bases of democratic support.

6. EXPECTATIONS OF JAPANESE DEMOCRACY

Respondents were asked to indicate their expectations about the state of Japanese democracy in five years' time. On a 10-point scale, they expected their system to progress toward greater democracy from 7.0 to 7.3 in the next five years (see table 7.9). Compared with their East Asian neighbors, Japanese respondents not only assigned a middling level of democracy to their current regime but were also less optimistic for the future. In fact, their expected

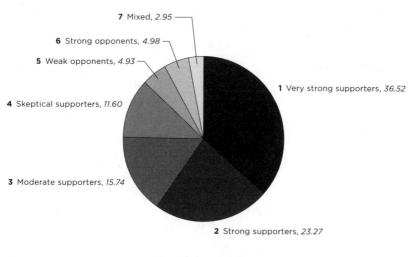

Percent of respondents

FIGURE 7.5 **Patterns of Commitment to Democracy: Japan**

TABLE 7.9 **CURRENT AND EXPECTED FUTURE REGIME TYPE: JAPAN**

(Percent of respondents)

RATING	CURRENT REGIME	FUTURE REGIME	CHANGE[a]
Very dictatorial (1–2)	0.5	0.4	0.0
Somewhat dictatorial (3–5)	13.5	11.8	-1.7
Somewhat democratic (6–8)	65.6	50.3	-15.4
Very democratic (9–10)	11.3	18.5	7.3
DK/NA	9.1	19.0	9.9
Total	100.0	100.0	
Mean on the 10-point scale	7.0	7.3	0.3

Notes: N = 1418.

Scale runs from 1, "complete dictatorship," to 10, "complete democracy."

Future regime is five years from time of survey.

[a] Change in percent of respondents rating the regime at the given level when the object of evaluation shifts from the current to the future regime.

level of democracy was the lowest among the countries surveyed. Although nearly 69% believed that five years into the future their government would be at least somewhat democratic, that percentage actually represents a decrease from the 77% who placed the current regime in the same category, as nearly 20% did not know what to expect for the future.

Based on respondents' current regime ratings and expected future ratings, we identified seven patterns of expected regime transformation (see chapter 1, table 1.12). The predominant expectation in Japan was for continuity. Nearly 58% expected the persistence of a limited democracy, while another 10% who considered the current regime an advanced democracy also expected continuing regime stability. Among the handful (15%) who considered the current regime to be somewhat dictatorial, the majority foresaw little democratic progress. Eleven percent expected authoritarian stagnation, while only 4.4% expected transition to a limited democracy. Those who predicted an advanced democratic transition amounted to a miniscule 0.2%. Cross-tabulation between expected regime ratings and demographic variables reveals that age is the only factor impacting expectations. Specifically, we found that expected regime change toward democracy increased with age (r = .166, p < .001).

7. CONCLUSION

Our findings confirm that the Japanese people regard their current political regime as a democracy. This may be at odds with some claims of Japanese "abnormality" that emphasize the conservative stranglehold on power and bureaucratic dominance in policymaking. But it is clear that Japan's democracy is firmly grounded in the Japanese people's perceptions and values, and that the Japanese people evaluate their democracy in a positive fashion.

To be sure, the Japanese understanding of democracy appears to be primarily static and system-oriented rather than dynamic and process-oriented. The origins of this static conception may be traced to the historical background of the current regime as a system created under the American occupation after World War II, a system for the Japanese citizen to adjust to with little participation and thus little sense of empowerment.

Age or generation emerged consistently throughout our analysis as a factor influencing popular values and perceptions of democracy. It is probably safe to posit that the salience of this factor also originates from the historical context in which the current regime evolved. For those with direct personal knowledge of the wartime regime, and for those who witnessed poverty and hardship in the immediate aftermath of the war, comparisons of the current democratic regime with the previous authoritarian one are inevitable in the conceptual formulation of democracy. Younger generations who only have direct experiences of the postwar period are more likely to gain their understanding of democracy through cross-national (and cross-cultural) comparisons between Japan and other countries.

Younger generations do not show positive leanings toward authoritarian alternatives. If anything, the threat they represent to the vitality of Japanese democracy is found in their tendency to be detached from public life—to show less interest, to participate less, and thus weaken the legitimacy of democratic governance. But as long as the country faces no threat from external powers and remains economically healthy, these trends need not portend any change in the prevailing Japanese commitment to a democratic form of government.

Our most striking comparative finding is that the citizens of Asia's oldest and apparently most-consolidated democracy are also the most negative about their system's performance and the most pessimistic about its future. It is possible that the Japanese numbers reflect a propensity to express oneself in a low-key or unassertive manner—a propensity that is built into the Japanese language—just as the high Thai numbers reflect an ebullient, assertive style of self-expression. It is also possible that the levels of support and optimism expressed by citizens in long-lived democracies are generally lower than those expressed in new democracies. We should not, however, use either of these speculations to dismiss the Japanese public's dissatisfaction with their political system. The time-series data we consulted show that the alienation is of long standing. It would be rash to argue that it is not real. While we do not think that Japanese democracy is unconsolidated or becoming deconsolidated—the rejection of all authoritarian alternatives is too strong for that—the troubles that the system faces are real, and the country's citizens are aware of them.

NOTES

The authors express their thanks to Taiwan National University, especially professors Fu Hu and Yun-han Chu, for arranging financial support for the face-to-face interviews in Japan.

1. In Japan, television stations are not seen as a homogeneous group. We can illustrate this with data from the Japanese Election and Democracy Study (JEDS) done in 2000. (This national sample survey conducted face-to-face interviews in April 2000, when there was no election going on. The response rate was 64.7% with N = 1,618. The data are available at http://ssjda.iss.u-tokyo.ac.jp/pages/ssjda-e/.) The data show that NHK (a semigovernmental organization) and private TV stations are perceived differently. The former enjoys a level of trust above that of the newspapers and the latter lags far behind both. On an 11-point scale of trust, 68% of respondents gave NHK a score of 6 or above, compared with 34% for commercial broadcasting stations and 67% for newspapers. Although NHK is not completely politically neutral, as shown in Krauss (2000), generally it is taken to be neutral and unaffected by the upheavals of politics and corruption, as are the national newspapers. Private TV stations are evaluated from a somewhat different perspective and are regarded as entertainment oriented.

2. Note that the choice of categories in our data is slightly different from these previous data sets in that we have excluded a neutral choice, "can't say."

3. In 1976, the number of DK/NA answers was particularly large. In both the "agree" and "disagree" categories, the percentages were smaller than in later years.

8

DEMOCRATIC TRANSITION FRUSTRATED

The Case of Hong Kong

Wai-man Lam and Hsin-chi Kuan

DESPITE FULFILLING THE PREREQUISITE socioeconomic conditions of democratization in the 1970s, Hong Kong has never had a full democracy. Initially, the United Kingdom—Hong Kong's colonial ruler—set the pace of Hong Kong's democratization. In 1997 sovereignty reverted to the People's Republic of China (PRC), and Hong Kong became a Special Administrative Region (SAR) of China, governed under a Basic Law promulgated by the National People's Congress in Beijing. Although the Basic Law guarantees the Hong Kong SAR "a high degree of autonomy" and anticipates direct democratic election of the chief executive and legislature "by universal suffrage," the extent of such autonomy and the timetable for political reform are determined by Beijing. At the time of our survey, election procedures were far from democratic and many citizens felt insecure in their enjoyment of political rights.

Yet our survey—conducted from September through December 2001—revealed a strong commitment to democratic values on the part of Hong Kong people. Most studies of Hong Kong political culture have focused on the low level of political participation and the rarity of large-scale collective mobilization. Scholars have experimented with various characterizations of Hong Kong's political culture: apathetic, utilitarian, alienated, cynical, depoliticized, and so on (for example, Lau and Kuan 1988, 1995; Lam 2003). By looking at popular understandings of democracy and commitment to its ideals, our study offers a different perspective. The lack of complete democracy in Hong Kong is not a sign of lack of commitment by its people.

We find that although there is some ambivalence about the possible conflict between democratization and economic efficiency, the people of Hong Kong have a passion for democracy, whether procedurally or substantively understood. Additionally, they have made strong demands on the government with regard to its democratic performance. Modernization has produced the readiness for democracy, but cannot by itself provide the institutions.

1. HONG KONG'S PARTIAL DEMOCRACY

Prior to the 1980s, the only government body with elected members under the British colonial system was the Urban Council, a local assembly with limited jurisdiction. In 1973, the maximum number of eligible voters was likely under six hundred thousand out of a population of around 4.2 million (Miners 1975:177). Universal suffrage was introduced in 1981, which was the colonial government's first step toward democratic reforms. A District Board (later renamed District Council) was established in each district, with members directly elected by all voting-age citizens in the district. But the territory's highest legislative body, the Legislative Council, did not have an elected component until 1985. At that time, an indirectly elected element was introduced by giving members of the District Boards, the Urban Council, the Regional Council,[1] and various functional constituencies the right to return twenty-four out of a total of fifty-seven seats (Hong Kong Government 1984).

In the 1980s Britain and China began negotiations over the future status of Hong Kong (Lo 1997; Kuan 1991). By the Sino-British Joint Declaration of 1984, Britain agreed to return the territory to Chinese sovereignty on July 1, 1997. China promised to preserve Hong Kong's capitalist system and grant the territory a high degree of autonomy for at least fifty years after the handover in an arrangement known as "one country, two systems." In 1990 China's National People's Congress enshrined the arrangement in the Basic Law of the Hong Kong Special Administrative Region (HKSAR), which was to become the constitutional document of the territory after the handover.

Meanwhile, democratization in Hong Kong proceeded slowly. It was not until 1991 that the colonial government allocated eighteen seats for direct election by geographical constituencies in the sixty-member Legislative Council. The number of indirectly elected functional constituency seats was increased to twenty-one, while the number of government officials sitting on the council was decreased to four. These reforms were in line with what the Basic Law promised, but they fell short of the people's aspirations.

With the arrival of Chris Patten as Hong Kong's last colonial governor in 1992, some significant political and administrative reforms resonating with the people's desire for greater democracy were introduced. Although Patten was limited in what he could do to speed up the democratization process, he managed to work within the boundaries of the Basic Law to give the people of Hong Kong a taste of a more democratic legislature. In the 1995 Legislative Council elections, apart from the twenty seats already allocated for direct election by geographical constituencies, the number of functional constituency seats was increased from twenty-one to thirty. Patten redefined the functional constituencies in such a way that more than 1.1 million voters became eligible to participate in functional constituency elections, a dramatic increase from the seventy thousand eligible just four years earlier. Furthermore, all official and appointed seats in the Legislative Council were abolished.

Beijing viewed these protodemocratic developments with suspicion. As tensions heightened in 1996 ahead of the handover, China announced that it intended to replace the partially elected legislature with an appointed Provisional Legislative Council at the time of the handover. To serve as the first chief executive of the HKSAR, Beijing selected Tung Chee-hwa, a local shipping tycoon.

The Basic Law envisages a "gradual and orderly" program of democratic transition. Universal suffrage (meaning in this context direct election of the legislature and chief executive) is proclaimed as the long-term goal. But no definite date is given for this to be realized. In the meantime, the Basic Law calls for the chief executive of the HKSAR to be indirectly elected by an election committee of delegates, who in turn are selected on the principle of functional representation. The sixty-member legislature is made up of three different constituencies: the election committee, functional constituencies, and geographical constituencies. To ensure an executive-led government and to prevent the popularly elected representatives from controlling a legislative majority, the proportion of seats directly elected from geographical constituencies was set to reach one-half of the total body only in 2007. Such were the institutions in place at the time of our survey.

The nature of elections in this partial democracy was not to form the government. Elections were not contests between the incumbent government and its challengers, and consequently could not serve to ensure political accountability. Apart from the denial of universal suffrage and the violation of the "one person, one vote" principle, the Basic Law also stipulated severe limitations on the legislature's constitutional competence. Legislators were not allowed to introduce bills related to public expenditure, constitutional structure, or the operation of the government. Nor could they introduce bills relating to government policies without the written consent of the chief executive. In addition, for an individual member's bill (called a private member's bill in Hong Kong) to pass, a majority vote in both the directly elected category as well as other indirectly elected categories was required.

This arrangement ensured that at the time of our survey the chief executive would control the legislature and thus the government as a whole—just as the governor did during the colonial era. While the appointed members of the Executive Council assist the chief executive in policymaking, the day-to-day operations of government are left to the discretion of the civil servants, supposedly politically neutral, who in theory function with optimum efficiency. However, under this system Tung Chee-hwa proved even more of a hands-on executive than his British predecessors. While the last British governors had been happy to leave domestic policies to the civil service, Tung initiated major reforms in many policy areas, catering to Beijing's preferences.

In 2005, Donald Yam-kuen Tsang, formerly chief secretary of the HK-SAR government, replaced Tung as the second chief executive (without competition). The fifth report of the Constitutional Development Task Force, one of his key policy initiatives, escalated the heat of debates on the political development of Hong Kong. Although it failed to provide a roadmap for democratic development, the report contained several significant reform initiatives that would have moved Hong Kong institutions in a more democratic direction. But the proposals failed to pass in the Legislative Council.

There has never been a mass democracy movement in Hong Kong. One reason may have been the deep divisions in the territory's robust civil society. Before the advent of political parties in the 1980s (a result of the introduction of partial elections), Hong Kong had numerous social organizations and an active mass media, most of which were popularly labeled as supporters of either Beijing (the Communist Party) or Taipei (the Nationalist Party). Popularly identified as the left and right respectively, the bitter struggle between these two groups provided the territory with many of its political intrigues. In the middle, civic groups such as the Reform Club of Hong Kong and the Hong Kong Civic Association took up the liberal banner. Such groups thrived under a colonial policy that exalted personal freedom and individuality even as they suppressed the development of any collective communist identity or communist affiliation (Lam 2004).

In the 1980s, a range of groups and parties emerged to compete in the limited elections that the colonial government and the Basic Law allowed. They represented various sections of the public and diverse political views, but were basically differentiated by the extent to which they were proestablishment or prodemocracy, although this is not the only political cleavage in Hong Kong (e.g., Li 2000). The Democratic Party was critical of both the Chinese and the Hong Kong governments and supported a quicker pace of democratization. The Democratic Alliance for the Betterment of Hong Kong (now the Democratic Alliance for the Betterment and Progress of Hong Kong), however, was made up of local supporters of Beijing and was consistently progovernment. The Liberal Party was composed mainly of businesspeople and also adopted a largely progovernment stance.

The political divisions in society rendered consolidation of a strong democratic force difficult. Also, given their limited role in government, all parties encountered difficulties in recruitment, and their limited social bases in turn made them weak leaders for democratization (e.g., Lau 1998). Support for the democrats tended to fluctuate with concerns over Beijing's interference in Hong Kong. As such concerns abated, support for the democrats eroded.

As a partial democracy, Hong Kong's major challenge was not democratic consolidation or the improvement of the quality of democracy, but the completion of democratic transition. Although the relations between economic development, political culture, and democracy are indeterminate (Inglehart 1997), the public's belief in democratic legitimacy matters. Democratic legitimacy, defined as citizens' belief in the legitimacy of, or their commitment to, democracy as the most preferred regime type, will serve as a critical condition of successful democratization if and when that opportunity comes (Montero et al. 1997; Kuan and Lau 2002:59, 65). In addition, Hong Kong, as a society of Chinese origin long under Western rule, serves as an interesting point of comparison for our other Asian cases. These reasons lead us to ask how Hong Kong people feel about their partial democracy. Do they want further democratization? As we will show, Hong

Kong's people, although politically frustrated, have not given up their aspiration for democracy.

2. HYBRIDITY IN CONCEPTIONS OF DEMOCRACY

As with other countries in the survey, we began our analysis with the question, "What does democracy mean to you?" (see chapter 1, table 1.3). In Hong Kong, the largest percentage (34%) of respondents understood democracy in terms of freedom and liberty, offering responses related to the freedoms of speech, press, association, belief, and individual choice. This liberal conception of democracy was the most popular in all but one of the countries surveyed. In the case of Hong Kong, its strength reflects the colony's liberal tradition, as the colonial government had always been more willing to offer individual freedoms than political rights. Hong Kong's legacy as an immigrant society probably also played a part—since so many residents were refugees from the Chinese mainland who came to Hong Kong in pursuit of a better life, the love of freedom has become a salient element of the local identity. The second-largest cluster (17%) of responses mentioned political institutions and procedures, which include items such as elections and competitive party systems.

Although liberal (freedom and liberty) and participatory (democratic institutions and processes) notions are tied to each other, they relate to distinct aspects of the democratization process. Scholars have pointed out that the differentiation between these two ideas is significant in that it delineates both the distinctiveness and the interconnectedness of the processes of liberalization and democratization. While liberalization encompasses the struggle for individual rights and liberties, democratization aims to create a system of government representative of the citizenry through popular participation in competitive elections. Without liberalization, democracy may exist only in form. Without democratization, liberalization may be manipulated and reversed (Lo 1997; O'Donnell and Schmitter 1986b). The processes of liberalization and democratization converge if popular rule is recognized to be the best guarantee of individual rights and liberties.

A third conception of democracy emphasizes social equality and justice, social entitlements, and government that is responsive to popular needs. We found that such understandings of democracy (constituting three lines in the table) are endorsed by a significant number (16.6%) of Hong Kong people. Such values may draw from the concept of *minben* (people as the basis) in traditional Chinese political culture. *Minben* emphasizes government *for* the people rather than *of* the people and is grounded in the substantive outcomes of governance. Thus a substantial proportion of Hong Kong citizens interpreted democracy as a political mechanism to create responsive and benevolent institutions capable of promoting social justice.

In short, Hong Kong people's notion of democracy is hybrid, incorporating liberal, institutional, and substantive values drawn from both Western notions of individualism and traditional Chinese understandings of good governance.

3. EVALUATING THE TRANSITION

At the time of our survey, Hong Kong had been under Chinese sovereignty for four years. The territory had been hit hard by the Asian financial crisis of 1997 and 1998, which exacerbated long-standing structural weaknesses in the economy. Between 1997 and 2001, the rate of GDP growth had slowed. In 2001 the rate of growth at constant (2000) market prices fell to 0.5%, while unemployment rose to 5.1%. During the same period, income for the lowest-earning quintile fell by 28%, while that of the top quintile rose by 4%.

However, Beijing's political restraint had been more conscientious than expected, and by most appearances little had changed in the human rights situation. Despite praise from international observers such as the European Commission and the UN Human Rights Commission, critics lamented that the mere possibility of intervention from Beijing was enough to inhibit the territory's political freedoms. There were signs of self-censorship in the media. And observers were startled by the January 2001 resignation of the head of the civil service, Anson Chan, after she was criticized by Beijing for insufficient loyalty to Chief Executive Tung Chee-hwa. Chan, a fiercely independent Chris Patten appointee, had been regarded as a symbol of the civil service's political neutrality.

Still, the changes in Hong Kong's political climate were gradual and subtle, and it remained to be seen how they were perceived by the general public. In this section, we will examine the Hong Kong public's evaluations of democratic progress and governmental performance in the Tung era.

3.1. PERCEPTIONS OF REGIME CHANGE

Respondents were asked to rate both the current and the past regimes on a 10-point scale, ranging from 1, "complete dictatorship" to 10, "complete

TABLE 8.1 **PERCEPTIONS OF PAST AND CURRENT REGIMES: HONG KONG**

(Percent of respondents)

REGIME TYPES	PAST REGIME	CURRENT REGIME
Very dictatorial	2.7	5.4
Somewhat dictatorial	20.5	47.1
Somewhat democratic	55.8	32.9
Very democratic	8.5	2.6
DK/NA[a]	12.5	12.1
Total	100.0	100.0
Mean on a 10-point scale	6.6	5.2

Notes: Regime types are based on the respondent's ranking of the regime on a scale from 1, "complete dictatorship," to 10, "complete democracy." Scores of 5 and below are degrees of dictatorship and scores of 6 and above are degrees of democracy.

N = 811.

[a] DK/NA = Don't know/no answer.

democracy." Although our respondents did not consider the Patten regime to be fully democratic, they judged Tung's government as being even less so. Table 8.1 shows that the majority of our respondents (64.3%) rated the colonial government under Chris Patten (the "past regime") either somewhat democratic or very democratic. Only about 35.5% placed the HK-SAR regime under Tung in these categories. While only 23% of Hong Kong people considered the Patten government to be somewhat or very dictatorial, nearly 53% gave those labels to the Tung regime. Overall, Tung's government received a mean score of 5.2, below the minimum threshold for being perceived as a democracy, whereas the Patten government, despite being a colonial regime, received a mean of 6.6, somewhat above that threshold.

Figure 8.1 displays the distribution of regime change scores. Sixty-seven percent of our respondents saw the change from the colonial regime to the SAR regime as a step backward toward dictatorship. Nineteen percent saw no change in the democratic character of the regime, while 14.3% saw the change as an advance in the democratic direction.

Percent of respondents

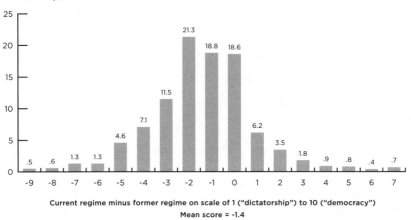

Current regime minus former regime on scale of 1 ("dictatorship") to 10 ("democracy")

Mean score = -1.4

FIGURE 8.1 **Perceived Regime Change: Hong Kong**

Table 1.7 in chapter 1 analyzes the same data in a different way and in comparative perspective. In the seven other Asian societies, a majority of citizens saw their country's change in regime as leading to greater democracy. The pattern in Hong Kong was the sole exception. About 40% of our respondents considered the change from the colonial to the SAR regime to be a move in the "more dictatorial" direction (defined as the previous regime having been democratic and the new regime nondemocratic), by far the highest percentage of respondents in any political system. Nearly 17% saw both regimes as dictatorial in nearly the same degree. Thirty-four percent classified both the colonial and the SAR regimes as being in some degree democratic, which was another category of response given more frequently by Hong Kong people than by residents of other regions on Asia.

3.2. COMPARING PAST AND PRESENT REGIMES

The EAB survey in Hong Kong contained a battery of questions asking respondents to compare the performance of the current and past regimes in six policy domains.[2] The results are presented in table 8.2, along with their Percentage Differential Indices (PDIs). Hong Kong citizens perceived a

TABLE 8.2 PERCEIVED PERFORMANCE OF CURRENT AND PAST REGIMES: HONG KONG

	MEAN[a]	SD[a]	NEGATIVE CHANGE[b]	POSITIVE CHANGE[b]	NO CHANGE[b]	PDI[c]	VALID %[d]
Democratic performance							
Freedom of speech	-0.16	0.77	34.1	18.3	47.6	-15.8	91.7
Freedom of association	-0.14	0.70	27.9	15.4	56.7	-12.5	86.6
Equal treatment	-0.46	0.79	52.8	12.2	35.0	-40.6	84.8
Popular influence	-0.26	0.69	31.4	10.0	58.6	-21.5	78.2
Independent judiciary	-0.34	0.80	44.1	13.7	42.2	-30.4	78.1
Average	-0.27	0.75	25.0	26.3	48.8	-24.1	83.88
Policy performance							
Anticorruption	0.00	0.81	25.0	26.3	48.8	1.3	86.4

Notes: N = 811.

Past regime is defined as pre-1997.

[a] Scale ranges from -2 (much worse) to +2 (much better).

[b] Percent of valid sample.

[c] PDI (percentage difference index) = percent seeing positive change minus percent seeing negative change.

[d] Percent of sample giving a valid answer to this question.

significant deterioration in the government's policy performance. Although there was virtually no net change in the perceived effectiveness of government action against corruption, the government's performance in all areas concerning democracy and the rule of law was perceived as worsening, with an average decline in the mean rating of 0.27 and an average PDI score of -24.1. Equal treatment, popular influence, and judicial independence all experienced dramatic declines.

Such perceived deterioration probably reflected the interruption of progress toward greater democracy with the transition to Chinese rule, as well as a series of policy missteps by the post-1997 government. For example, the SAR government abolished municipal councils. Because these councils contained significant directly elected elements, the move was interpreted as an attempt by the government to decrease the influence of prodemocratic grassroots forces and to centralize power. In addition, the government reintroduced appointed seats in the district councils after they had been abolished by the Patten administration, thus weakening the democratic function of the councils. The government invited the Standing Committee of China's National People's Congress to interpret the Basic Law, following a controversy regarding the right-of-abode stipulations in that document. The move was widely criticized as detrimental to Hong Kong's autonomy. The government was also frequently denounced for its perceived collusion with business elites. A 1999 decision granting development rights of the Cyberport project to Li Tzar-kai, the son of a leading real estate magnate, was criticized as a blatant act of cronyism. Even the government's macroeconomic policies, such as a series of attempts to shore up local property prices, were believed to favor well-placed real estate developers.

Despite these problems, the perceived decline of government performance with regard to civil liberties (freedom of speech and association) was relatively modest. Studies during the colonial era suggested that Hong Kong people were relatively satisfied with the government because it provided high levels of freedom even though it was not democratic.[3] The new regime was perceived as similarly undemocratic, and the extent of freedom as diminishing subtly. This was consistent with the outside rating by Freedom House. Freedom House's rating scale ranges from 1 to 7, with 7 being the least free. In the scale of political rights, Hong Kong received a rating of 4 for most of the years from 1980 to 1997, fell to 6 in 1997, and then recovered to 5 for 1998 and years following. On the scale of civil liberties, Hong Kong declined from a 2 to a 3 with the 1997 handover (Freedom House 1981–2006).[4]

4. APPRAISING INSTITUTIONS

This section examines popular assessments of various institutions of the body politic — specifically respondents' assessments of their own perceived capacities for democratic citizenship, perceptions of corruption in government, and popular trust in the territory's political institutions. We found that compared with their neighbors, Hong Kong people had especially low estimations of their participatory capacities and were the most alienated from the political process. However, the vaunted integrity of the civil service appeared largely intact and Hong Kong people continued to invest confidence in most institutions of the regime.

4.1. POLITICAL EFFICACY

Do Hong Kong people believe that they have the capacity to understand the political process and influence it? Some answers can be gleaned from a pair of items in the EAB survey probing the respondent's self-perceived ability to understand the complexities of politics and to participate actively. The findings are reported in chapter 1, table 1.4.

The Hong Kong people's self-perception of their participatory capacities was the lowest in Asia. Only 1.5% believed that they were capable of both understanding and participating in politics. Another 14% believed they could understand politics but lacked the ability to participate, and only 2% were confident of their ability to participate despite a professed inability to understand politics. The bulk of respondents (82.5%) believed that they had neither the ability to understand nor to participate in politics.

Accompanying the low level of perceived political efficacy was a pervasive sense of alienation from the political system. When asked to evaluate the statement, "The government is run by a powerful few and ordinary citizens cannot do much about it," 69% of Hong Kong people agreed. When asked to evaluate the statement, "People like me don't have any influence over what the government does," 79% agreed. These numbers were the highest of any political system in our survey, reflecting frustration over the public's thwarted democratic aspirations since the handover. Feelings of inefficacy are statistically linked to the perception of low system responsiveness. The more a respondent finds the system unresponsive, the more likely he or she is to feel disempowered. The correlation between these two factors is 0.31, significant at the .000 level.[5]

4.2. PERCEIVED CORRUPTION AND INSTITUTIONAL TRUST

One of the great policy successes of the colonial government came in the area of corruption control. Before the mid-1970s, Hong Kong had been plagued by endemic corruption in the civil service and police. In 1974 a high-profile scandal involving a senior police official spurred the government to take action, and it established the Independent Commission Against Corruption (ICAC) under the direct supervision of the governor. Pursuing a vigorous three-pronged strategy of punishment, prevention, and public education, the ICAC established its credibility among the public and perceptions of corruption quickly declined. The Hong Kong experience achieved international renown as a model of successful corruption control.

At the time of the handover there was concern about whether the new government would continue to control corruption effectively (Rose-Ackerman 1999:159–162). Five years into the new era, we found that the perceived level of corruption remained in check. As shown in table 8.3, only 19% of respondents believed that most or all officials were corrupt, the third-lowest level among the countries in the study after China and Thailand.

The perceived integrity of government officials must be a factor behind the high level of trust enjoyed by government institutions in Hong Kong. The EAB survey asked respondents how much trust they had in eight public institutions, and found that with the exception of political parties, all of them were trusted by more than half of the respondents (see figure 8.2). The

TABLE 8.3 **PERCEPTION OF POLITICAL CORRUPTION: HONG KONG**

(Percent of respondents)

	LOCAL GOVERNMENT
Hardly anyone is involved	6.6
Not a lot of officials are involved	**53.6**
Most officials are corrupt	**17.8**
Almost everyone is corrupt	1.0
Don't know/no answer	**21.0**
Total	**100.0**

Notes: N = 811.

Percentages above 10 are in boldface.

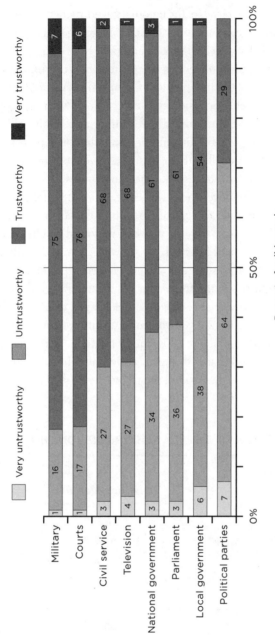

FIGURE 8.2 Trust in Institutions: Hong Kong

most highly trusted institutions were the professional organs of the state: the military, the courts, and the civil service. Television was also highly trusted, perhaps reflecting the media's long tradition of independence dating back to the colonial era. Relatively speaking, the political institutions of the regime were less trusted, although even the HKSAR government was trusted by 55% of respondents despite its perceived performance failures. The only institution distrusted by a majority of respondents was political parties. Their disrepute may be related to their perceived ineffectuality and hypocrisy—the progovernment DAB, for instance, had gained a reputation for grandstanding in front of the media while doing the government's bidding in the legislature. However, distrust for political parties is universal across East Asia, and overall Hong Kong citizens exhibited one of the highest levels of institutional trust compared to other countries in our survey.

As an overall measure of regime satisfaction, the EAB survey included an item asking, "On the whole, how satisfied or dissatisfied are you with the way democracy works in Hong Kong?" Fewer than half (48%) of Hong Kong people reported being satisfied with the performance of the current regime as a democracy, while 36% expressed dissatisfaction. These numbers represent one of the lowest levels of regime satisfaction in the EAB survey.

5. AMBIVALENCE IN COMMITMENT TO DEMOCRACY

Previous studies have found that in Hong Kong, political discontent strengthens rather than undermines the legitimacy of democracy as the best form of government under all circumstances (Kuan and Lau 2002:68). If that were the case, one would expect that popular discontent with the Tung administration would have reinforced Hong Kong people's commitment to democracy. Did that happen? Our data suggest that while hybridity is one salient characteristic of the political culture in Hong Kong, ambivalence is another. Although Hong Kong people desire democracy as an ideal, they do not always consider it suitable—mainly because of conflicting priorities between democratic participation and efficient governance.

5.1. ATTACHMENT TO DEMOCRATIC POLITICS

There is no doubt that the people of Hong Kong aspire to democracy in the abstract. When asked to indicate how much democracy they desired on a

10-point scale, 87.6% of Hong Kong people selected a value of 6 or above. Nearly 37% desired "complete democracy" (10 on the 10-point scale) and another 39.5% chose 8 or 9 on the scale (chapter 1, table 1.8). For 93.5% of our respondents, the level of democracy they said they desired was pegged at a higher level than the level of democracy they perceived the SAR as currently enjoying, reflecting a pervasive desire that the system move in a more democratic direction.[6]

But respondents' belief in the suitability of democracy for Hong Kong lagged behind their belief in its desirability. On a 10-point scale from 1 "total unsuitability" to 10 "total suitability," about two-thirds (66.8%) chose a score of 6 or above, with 42% selecting a score of 8 or above. While this is a solid vote of confidence for democracy, it is less robust than our respondents' belief in the desirability of democracy.

This seems to reflect Hong Kong people's commitments to certain values that compete with democracy. Hong Kong people placed great emphasis on the importance of economic development, with fewer than one-fifth according democracy equal or greater importance (chapter 1, table 1.8). Only 40% considered democracy always preferable to other forms of government and only 39% were confident that democracy could solve the problems facing society. Hong Kong had the lowest figures of all the Asian societies we surveyed on the variables of democratic efficacy, preferability, and priority.

Such findings may reflect the fact that Hong Kong people have been intensively exposed to a vision for a depoliticized Hong Kong, especially after 1997 when PRC leaders argued that Hong Kong should become an "economic city" instead of a "political city." Hong Kong's survival, some have argued, is dependent on the development of its economic prowess and the suppression of destabilizing political demands. In this view the people of Hong Kong are primarily economic animals, and the primary goal of Hong Kong society should be the flourishing of economic activities. Hong Kong people are often warned against an excess of democracy, and they are told time and again that too much democracy would achieve nothing but an inefficient government, and that there is no place within a democratic system for the resolution of the territory's increasing polarization (Lam 2004). Demands for a faster pace of democratization are often denounced for their "malicious" intent. Although the alleged contradictions between democracy, economic development, and efficiency may not exist, the dominance of the depoliticizing discourse has made them appear real to our respondents.

If democracy is not desired for its ability to deliver economic development and solve the problems of society, what do Hong Kong people find

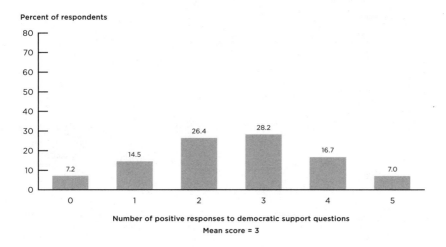

Percent of respondents

FIGURE 8.3 **Democratic Support: Hong Kong**

appealing about it? Since our respondents overwhelmingly associated democracy with freedom and rights, these values may be the chief attractions. Nonetheless, the public's commitment to democracy is conditional, maintained only if democracy, defined as freedom and rights, is not in conflict with economic development and efficiency concerns.

To measure the overall level of attachment to democracy, we constructed a 6-point index ranging from 0 to 5, aggregating the number of prodemocratic responses regarding desirability, suitability, efficacy, preference, and priority (see figure 8.3). Hong Kong averaged 3, one of the lowest scores among the societies surveyed. Only about 7% responded affirmatively to all five questions, with an additional 17% responding affirmatively to four out of five questions.

5.2. DETACHMENT FROM AUTHORITARIANISM

Considering their ambivalent attitude toward democracy, one might expect Hong Kong people to be receptive to some form of undemocratic rule as long as the system can deliver effective governance. After all, Hong Kong achieved its economic miracle without the benefit of democratic rule, and many might be loathe to jeopardize the political stability that has been the bedrock of the territory's economic prosperity. However, because of Hong Kong people's familiarity with life under authoritarian rule, one might also

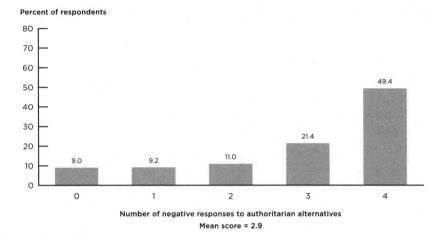

Percent of respondents

FIGURE 8.4 **Authoritarian Detachment: Hong Kong**

expect them to resist at least some types of nondemocratic regimes. Given these countervailing influences, how did Hong Kong people feel about various nondemocratic alternatives?

The EAB survey probed for support for four types of dictatorial alternatives (see chapter 1, table 1.9). The results were clear: A compelling majority in Hong Kong (72%) opposed the dictatorial rule of a strong leader, and an even larger number (86%) rejected rule by the military. A one-party dictatorship was likewise unwanted (62%), and close to three-quarters (74%) were opposed to the rule of technocratic experts.

To summarize the overall level of detachment from authoritarianism, we constructed a 5-point index based on the four questions just described. The mean score for Hong Kong was 2.9, with nearly half (49%) of our respondents rejecting all four authoritarian alternatives (see figure 8.4). Although a significant minority (9%) did not reject any of the alternatives, Hong Kong people overall were comparable to their East Asian neighbors in their level of authoritarian detachment.

5.3. OVERALL SUPPORT FOR DEMOCRACY

Taking into account both the depth of democratic attachment and the completeness of authoritarian detachment, we identified seven patterns of regime orientation for each of the eight EAB societies (defined in the notes to table 1.11, chapter 1). The results for Hong Kong are presented in figure 8.5. Hong Kong has the second largest proportion among our Asian societies of strong opponents of democracy, defined as respondents who give no more than two of the five possible answers in favor of democracy and who accept two or more of the four authoritarian alternatives. Although Hong Kong people in general desired democracy, for some the commitment to democracy is maintained only insofar as democracy is not seen to be in conflict with considerations of economic development and efficiency.

Yet in comparative perspective, Hong Kong exhibits a middling level of democratic support. As in Taiwan, the Philippines, and Mongolia, the segment made up of democratic opponents, skeptical democratic supporters, and those holding mixed views ranged from one-third to half of the population. However on the whole, democratic supporters considerably outnumbered opponents.

The robustness of democratic support in Hong Kong may reflect a dynamic by which discontent with democratic progress and dissatisfaction with the government's policy performance has reinforced the desire for fuller democracy, rather than weakened it as is the case elsewhere in Asia. In support of this conjecture, we found a statistically significant inverse relationship between "satisfaction with how democracy works in Hong Kong" and the level of commitment to democracy (Pearson's r = -0.096, significant at the 0.05 level). We also found that democratic supporters judged the government's

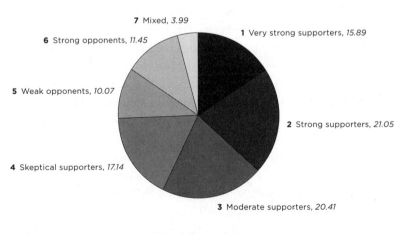

7 Mixed, *3.99*

6 Strong opponents, *11.45*

1 Very strong supporters, *15.89*

5 Weak opponents, *10.07*

2 Strong supporters, *21.05*

4 Skeptical supporters, *17.14*

3 Moderate supporters, *20.41*

Percent of respondents

FIGURE 8.5 **Patterns of Commitment to Democracy: Hong Kong**

performance during the past five years more negatively than democratic opponents. For example, while most strong supporters of democracy perceived no change in judicial independence, strong opponents of democracy were more likely to perceive improvements under the Tung regime. Likewise, strong supporters were more likely to believe that the freedom of expression in Hong Kong was decreasing, while strong opponents were more likely to see it as getting better. Similar patterns were found between the level of democratic support and other aspects of regime performance.

6. EXPECTATIONS FOR EXPANDING DEMOCRATIC GOVERNANCE

Hong Kong people know that the pace of the Special Administrative Region's democratization will be determined in Beijing, where the authorities have signaled that they want the pace to be slow. Accordingly, when we asked respondents to indicate where they expected the territory's political system to stand on a 10-point scale from dictatorship to democracy five years into the future, most were pessimistic (see table 8.4). On the 10-point scale, they expected their system to progress from 5.2 to 5.9 on the scale of democracy, an increment of only 0.7. Their expected rate of progress was the lowest of all the countries surveyed. Only about 34% believed that five years from now their government would be at least somewhat democratic, which is only slightly higher than the 32% that felt the same about the current regime, and far lower than any other political system in the survey. Although respondents who expected the regime to be dictatorial five years from now are fewer than those who considered the regime dictatorial today (29% versus 52%), most of the decrease seems to be accounted for by the "don't know" category, which amount to over 30% for the future regime. While this high level of uncertainty is not unique to Hong Kong, the other countries in the study all exhibited greater optimism about democratic progress.

We identified seven patterns of expected regime transformation based on the respondents' current and expected future regime ratings (see chapter 1, table 1.12). Among respondents who considered the current regime to be authoritarian, the majority expected little progress. Over 39% of those who indicated their expectations expected authoritarian persistence, while only slightly over half that number (22%) expected either limited or advanced democratic transition, most of them the former. Even among those who

TABLE 8.4 **CURRENT AND EXPECTED FUTURE REGIME TYPE: HONG KONG**

(Percent of respondents)

RATING	CURRENT REGIME	FUTURE REGIME	CHANGE[a]
Very dictatorial (1–2)	5.4	4.6	–0.7
Somewhat dictatorial (3–5)	46.3	24.1	–22.2
Somewhat democratic (6–8)	32.4	34.2	1.8
Very democratic (9–10)	2.6	6.7	4.1
DK/NA	13.3	30.4	17.0
Total	100.0	100.0	
Mean on a 10-point scale	5.2	5.9	0.7

Notes: N = 811.

Scale runs from 1, "complete dictatorship," to 10, "complete democracy."

Future regime is five years from time of survey.

[a] Change in percent of respondents rating the regime at the given level when the object of evaluation shifts from the current to the future regime.

considered the current regime to be somewhat democratic, the majority expected only stagnation. Nearly 30% expected Hong Kong to remain a struggling democracy, while only 7% expected the territory to be fully democratic in five years. Overall, these findings reveal a lack of optimism consistent with the perception of Beijing's timetable, and consistent as well with respondents' low sense of political efficacy and their poor evaluation of the government's performance over the past five years.

7. CONCLUSION

Our study has uncovered political frustration among the people of Hong Kong. They aspire to democracy because it embodies certain values that they treasure. The people's attachment to liberal values and their strong substantive demands on the government follow the precepts of *minben* (people-as-the-basis). These values are especially strong among residents who were born in Hong Kong and among those who are better educated, younger, and have relatively high incomes, supporting the conventional wisdom that the sources of democratic support are drawn mostly from the middle class, the younger generations, and those with a strong Hong Kong identity.

The people of Hong Kong conceivably might have done more to encourage Beijing to increase the pace of democratic change. The population's ambivalence about democracy and its sense of political powerlessness are part of the reason why this did not happen. If Hong Kong people suffer from a low sense of political efficacy, this is aggravated by the perceived nonresponsiveness of the government and by setbacks in democratic governance and the rule of law during the posthandover era. Decisions made in Beijing have helped to create a sense of powerlessness, and this sense of powerlessness has helped to create the conditions for Beijing to have its way with Hong Kong.

NOTES

1. The Urban Council and the Regional Council were the same in structure and function but responsible for the administration of different geographical districts. They were abolished in 1999.
2. We asked only one of the four policy performance questions asked elsewhere in Asia.
3. Previous studies support our argument. In a 1995 study, 63.5% of respondents agreed with the statement, "Although the current political system is imperfect, it is still the best under the circumstances." In studies conducted in 1985 and 1990, 74% and 59% respectively agreed with this statement.
4. The Political Rights rating was 4 for the years 1980 through 1992, 5 for 1993 and 1994, 4 for 1995 and 1996, 6 for 1997, and 5 for 1998 through 2006. The Civil Liberties rating was 2 for the years 1980 through 1987, 3 for 1988 through 1992, 2 for 1993 through 1996, 3 for 1997 through 2003, and 2 for 2004 through 2005.
5. The four items were grouped into two summary measures, one for perceived personal political efficacy and one for perceived system responsiveness. Each summary measure yields on an ordinal scale ranging from -4 to +4. A great majority of respondents are rated in the 0 to -2 range in both the citizen empowerment measure (84.8%) and the system responsiveness measure (85.4%). As noted in the text, the two measures are strongly correlated.
6. The difference between the desired level of democracy and the current perceived level of democracy ranged from one to nine points.

9

CHINA

Democratic Values Supporting an Authoritarian System

Tianjian Shi

AS THE SOLE NONDEMOCRACY among our eight East Asian political systems, China provides a comparative benchmark for assessing the role of values in democratic transition and consolidation. In an age when democratic values enjoy high prestige, how does an authoritarian regime make itself legitimate in the eyes of its citizens? Or, on the contrary, does the spread of democratic values present a threat to an authoritarian regime's stability? How tight, in other words, is the link between political culture and regime type?

This chapter will show that many of the same democratic values that undergird the old and new democracies of Asia are also widespread in China. Yet in China, these values functioned—at least at the time of our survey—to engender citizen support for the nondemocratic regime. The key to this paradox is the elasticity of the idea of democracy itself. For most Chinese, the current Chinese regime is already democratic in many ways that matter to them. In what sense this is so is a major theme of the analysis that follows.

Our findings suggest that citizens do not always draw the same stark contrast between democratic and authoritarian regimes that political scientists normally do. Many Chinese rate their political system more highly on the scale of democracy than citizens do in countries whose political systems are democratic in fact. Likewise, Chinese citizens trust their political institutions more than citizens in any of the other societies included in the surveys; people in China enjoy a sense of political efficacy equal to that of citizens in Japan and Taiwan; and people in China are more optimistic about their society's future democratic development than in any other society in the EAB survey except Thailand. These attitudes may be surprising. The analysis that follows explores their sources.

1. HISTORICAL AND INSTITUTIONAL BACKGROUND

At the time of our survey, the Chinese political system was what Linz and Stepan call a "mature posttotalitarian regime" (Linz and Stepan 1996b). Under the founding ruler of the People's Republic of China (PRC), Mao Zedong (1893–1976), the country had been a totalitarian system in the classic sense. Its features included a single ruling party, a dominant state, a charismatic ruler, a suppressed and atomized civil society, an enforced ideological orthodoxy, and rule by terror. After Mao's death, the Chinese Communist Party (CCP) under Deng Xiaoping (the most influential leader from 1978 to 1992) initiated a policy of "reform and opening," which involved partial marketization of the economy, limited social and institutional pluralism, liberalization of control over people's private lives, and the embrace of globalization in order to spur economic growth.

Deng's regime replaced the command economy with a "socialist market economy." Economic reform started in the villages, where the government introduced a "responsibility system" that contracted state-owned land to individual peasant households and allowed peasants to determine the way they used the land. The new policy also encouraged citizens to operate privately owned businesses in both urban and rural areas. Special Economic Zones were established in the early 1980s to attract foreign investment.

Under reform and opening, the economy grew rapidly. From 1978 to 2002, annual per capita GDP growth averaged 9.68%. GDP per capita rose from $165 in 1978 to $1,106 in 2002 (in 2000 constant U.S. dollars).[1] Rural residents moved around the country looking for work, cities grew, and a large middle class emerged. Along with these trends grew aspirations to democracy, expressed in intermittent prodemocracy movements and student demonstrations starting in 1978 and peaking in the 1989 Tiananmen student demonstrations, which were supported by weeks of citizen demonstrations in nearly four hundred cities around the country (Nathan 1985; Goldman

1994; Goldman 2005; Goldman and Perry 2002; Zhang 2002). After a period of indecision and internal power struggle, the party violently repressed the 1989 prodemocracy movement and reimposed political control.

The party did not, however, permanently roll back either economic reform or social liberalization. These continued after Deng's death in 1997 under the leadership of Jiang Zemin (CCP General Secretary 1989–2002). At the time of our survey (March through June 2002), the party was preparing to transfer leadership to Hu Jintao (born in 1942). Based on Hu's image and the signals surrounding the transition, our respondents would not have expected marked changes in the ruling party's policies toward political pluralism, individual freedom, the economy, or in other domains; indeed, in the event, no radical policy changes occurred after the transition (Nathan and Gilley 2003).

From the point of view of a citizen, the Chinese political system in 2002 displayed a combination of old and new features. On the side of continuity with the past, the CCP was still a selective political elite consisting of about 8% of the population. Party members answered to tight political discipline from the party leadership in Beijing, which controlled their careers and issued bulletins instructing them what to think and say. Through its members serving as officials in state organs, the party controlled government agencies, the national, provincial, and local legislatures, and the courts. Party members dominated life in the villages and kept an eye on the daily activities of urban residents. The party exercised dominant influence in the military, finance, heavy industry, education, and journalism. In some spheres of the economy and culture the party shared influence with nonparty elites so long as they presented no challenge to the monopoly of political power.

Political life also showed some new features. Thanks to the growth of private and foreign-invested enterprises under Deng's economic reforms, the state was no longer the sole employer. The party gave up trying to make citizens believe in its ideology (as long as they did not publicly challenge it) and abandoned the classic Maoist control mechanisms of self- and mutual monitoring by citizens and mass campaigns against class enemies. While the media remained party controlled, they competed for market share by carrying sensational news and a variety of opinions on nonsensitive matters. The widespread use of the Internet, email, and instant messaging increased the government's difficulties in controlling the flow of information.

Modest institutional changes were introduced, but fell short of democratization. The National People's Congress (NPC) in 1979 passed a law that allowed for the direct election of delegates to township and county-level people's congresses under controlled circumstances (Shi 1999b). Elected deputies to various levels of people's congress occasionally asserted some independence. For example, three provincial congresses elected candidates not endorsed by the CCP as deputy governors in 1987 and 1988. There were five such cases in the 1992 and again in the 1996 elections.[2] Some seven hundred party nominees to county-level offices were rejected by local people's congresses in each election.[3] The NPC itself started to play a more assertive role (O'Brien 1994b; O'Brien 1990).

The change that affected the largest number of citizens was the introduction in 1987 of semicompetitive elections for members and officers of village committees. The village in China is considered a self-governing grassroots unit of society rather than part of the hierarchy of government. Still, village officials are responsible for allocation of land (for agricultural use and housing), tax collection, family planning, and economic development. The village elections were introduced by the chairman of NPC, Peng Zhen, who thought the party's control over the villages depended on finding local leaders whom rural residents could accept. Over the course of a protracted struggle between central-level reformers and entrenched local officials, the village committee election process became increasingly competitive. By the third or fourth round of elections, which took place at different times in different villages, peasants learned that they could use the process to get rid of unpopular local leaders, although they could not affect the central government policies that all local leaders were obligated to enforce (Li and O'Brien 1999; O'Brien and Li 2000; Shi 1999c). At the time of our survey, 81.6% of the villages we surveyed had held elections, 70% of which involved multiple candidates.

The Chinese political system in 2002 was thus authoritarian, but had undergone significant liberalization affecting citizens' economic activities and private lives, while promoting a rhetoric and some minor practices of democracy.

2. THE MEANING OF DEMOCRACY

Given this rapidly changing environment, Chinese citizens could be expected to have a complex and perhaps internally contradictory set of ideas about democracy. Discussion of democracy had been pervasive in Chinese political life for over a century. Since the fall of the last imperial dynasty in 1911, every Chinese regime, no matter how authoritarian in practice, has claimed to pursue democracy for its citizens.[4]

But democracy can mean many things. After 1949, the Chinese communist regime indoctrinated its citizens in the idea of "socialist democracy." Based on a Marxist analysis of social classes, socialist democracy is described as more advanced than "bourgeois democracy" because it serves the majority of the population ("the people") while depriving of rights those who would exploit others or destabilize the state ("enemies of the people"). Under socialist democracy the ruling party listens to the people (the "mass line") and may consult with experts, but it does not adopt Western-style political competition or separation of powers, which the theory claims are tools used by the bourgeoisie to hoodwink the majority (Mao 1949).

To what extent are the Chinese public's ideas of democracy marked by these concepts, and to what extent are they instead influenced by global trends that identify democracy with civil liberties and political pluralism? The EAB survey posed an open-ended question, "What does democracy mean to you?" Each person was encouraged to give up to three answers. The responses were coded under a common scheme applied to all eight societies. The results are presented in chapter 1, table 1.3.

The table shows that China has a high level of "don't know/no answer" responses to this question, second only to Japan in the EAB surveys. Before proceeding with the rest of the analysis, it is important to find out whether the high level of item nonresponses in China was attributable to the fact that the meaning of democracy was really beyond the comprehension of many respondents (as the answer "don't know" implies), or was instead a response to the fear of answering such a controversial question when living under an authoritarian regime (Shi 1996). This issue—cognitive deficiency versus political fear—will affect our interpretation of both this table and the answers to other sensitive questions throughout the China questionnaire.[5]

Three statistical tests help to answer this question. First, if DKs and refusals were used by respondents to hide their true opinions, educated people would be more likely to give DKs and refusals than people with less education, since educated people are more likely to have opinions independent of official ideology that they are afraid to express. If, however, "don't know" really means "don't know," education should be inversely correlated to nonresponse. Second, we can assume that those who describe themselves as interested in politics are more likely both to provide a meaning for the word *democracy* and to be aware of any risks involved in sharing their views. Thus, under the political fear hypothesis those who say they are interested in politics should be more likely than other respondents to give nonresponses to the question, while under the cognitive deficiency hypothesis nonresponses should be more likely to come from those who say they are not interested in politics.

Third, if the political fear hypothesis is correct, we should find item nonresponse to be positively correlated with a measure of political fear, while we expect to find no such correlation if cognitive deficiency is at work. The China version of the EAB questionnaire included two items designed to assess political fear, asking whether respondents were afraid of being reported if they criticized government policies or national leaders. Substantial numbers of people answered in the affirmative: 27.6% said yes to the first question and 22.5% to the second.[6]

The results of the three tests are displayed in table 9.1. The analysis separates "don't know" from "no answer" in order to see whether there is any difference in the correlates of the two forms of nonresponse. One might theorize, for example, that those who refuse to respond out of political fear are more likely to say "no answer" than "don't know." But there is no difference. The results in all six cells support the conclusion that both forms of nonresponse are the result of cognitive deficiency and that neither is the result of political fear. Less-educated persons and those who say they are not interested in politics are more likely to decline to answer the question with either "don't know" or "no answer." Although political fear exists in China, it does not affect respondents' decision whether or not to give substantive answers to this question.

Among those who gave substantive answers to the question, democracy was perceived in positive terms by every respondent, a remarkable degree of unanimity in a survey research setting. While democracy's image is overwhelmingly positive throughout Asia (the highest percentage of negative

TABLE 9.1 **CORRELATION OF POLITICAL FEAR WITH NA AND DK**

(Pearson's *r*)

	NO ANSWER	DON'T KNOW
Education	-.078**	-.341**
Interest in politics	-.122**	-.245**
Fear of criticizing government	-.017	-.035

Notes: N = 3183.

** Correlation significant at 0.01 level (two-tailed).

responses was around 5%, found in Hong Kong and Taiwan), China was the only one of our eight political systems where the substantive responses were entirely positive.

Chinese were more likely than other respondents in Asia to associate democracy with populism ("by and for the people"). More than one-quarter of Chinese respondents gave answers in this category, compared to numbers under 10% in other parts of Asia, with the exception of Taiwan. The two most frequent responses that we coded under this heading were "the people are masters of the country" and "the authorities listen to people's opinions." Both of these responses are compatible not only with the doctrine of socialist democracy but also with classic Confucian ideas of benevolent dictatorship, since they do not require competitive political pluralism to be put into effect. We also coded in this category the more than 3.9% of respondents who defined democracy by reference to the official CCP concept of "democratic centralism."

The next-largest clusters of ideas about democracy were those associated with universal liberal-democratic values, which we coded as "political rights, institutions, and processes" and "freedom and liberty." Over one-fifth of the sample said that democracy involves political participation in ways such as voting in elections, exercising influence over decision making, and exercising majority rule. Here the Chinese sample stood around the middle of the Asian samples, mentioning participation less often than respondents in Thailand and Mongolia and more often than respondents in Taiwan, Hong Kong, Korea, Japan, and the Philippines.

More than one-quarter of our respondents equated democracy with ideas like freedom of the press, freedom of belief, freedom of religion, and general political freedom. Some specifically mentioned freedom of association, even though it remains officially prohibited. Although this percentage is not low, all the other Asian samples gave higher percentages of responses in this category.

The analysis so far shows the mixed effects of decades of indoctrination in the official concept of socialist democracy plus a quarter-century's exposure to Western liberal ideas of democracy. To explore more precisely the relative influence of these two sets of ideas, we compared the percentage of respondents who gave answers in *only* the categories of "social equality and justice," "good governance," and "by and for the people" (who may be seen as thinking exclusively in terms of the ideas promoted by the party) with the percentage of respondents who gave answers in *both* the categories of "freedom and liberty" and "political rights, institutions, and processes" (who may be seen as incorporating both prongs of the Western idea of democracy as rights plus participation).[7] The result of this exercise is that 18.3% of respondents defined democracy exclusively in populist and/or socialist terms, and 15.4% defined democracy in terms of both liberty and participation. This suggests that the official view of democracy remains dominant among the Chinese public but that views from the West have made considerable headway. Indeed, an additional 19.9% of respondents mentioned liberty or participation once, and 6.2% mentioned values in these categories more than once, implying that liberal notions of democracy have established a strong beachhead in Chinese popular thinking.

To probe further how popular liberal-democratic ideas are in China, the China questionnaire included six additional questions. The responses, which are reported in table 9.2, reinforce the conclusion that the concept of democracy among people in China is a mixed one. In the first two items, we asked respondents whether they would support selecting national-level leaders through competitive elections and a system of competition among multiple political parties. Both of these practices are central to liberal democracy and are ruled out in the official concept of socialist democracy. Seen from a liberal-democratic perspective, the responses were contradictory. While 84% of respondents agreed or strongly agreed with having elections for national leaders, only 16.3% agreed or strongly agreed with multiparty competition. A liberal democrat would argue that elections for national leaders cannot be meaningful without political party competition to organize the election around competing interests. Most Chinese respondents, however, did not appear to make this connection.

Another standard component of liberal democracy is rule of law. We asked respondents whether it would be acceptable for the government to disregard the law when the country faces a difficult situation, and whether they think a judge should accept the views of the executive branch when deciding important cases. Nearly 86% of respondents believed the government should obey the law even in times of emergency. Yet nearly half were willing to see judges guided by the executive branch in important cases, while another fifth said they did not know the answer to this question; only about one-third dissented from this stance. These views show the influence of the ruling party's position. The party claims that the extraordinary measures it has sometimes taken in times of crisis are lawful. It also states that law is political and that judges should therefore accept the guidance of the party in important cases.

TABLE 9.2 LIBERAL CONCEPTS OF DEMOCRACY: CHINA

(Percent of respondents)

	STRONGLY LIBERAL	LIBERAL	NONLIBERAL	STRONGLY NONLIBERAL	DK
National leaders should be elected (agree)	16.7	67.3	6.0	0.2	9.9
Multiparty competition should be allowed (agree)	1.4	15.9	54.9	7.0	20.8
The government should obey laws even in a time of emergency (agree)[a]		85.6	3.4		11.0
On important cases, judges should seek the opinion of the local government (disagree)	2.2	33.5	42.5	2.1	19.8
The NPC should not constantly check the administration (disagree)	1.3	36.4	27.1	0.4	34.8
Political leaders should concentrate on their goals and ignore established procedures if necessary (disagree)	2.4	46.8	20.6	0.5	29.7

Notes: N = 3183.

Strongly liberal = strongly agree or strongly disagree, depending on the question. Liberal = agree or disagree. Nonliberal and Strongly nonliberal = the reverse.

[a] Original response categories are binary.

The last two questions were directed at the idea of constraints on political power. One asked whether respondents agreed that if the administration is constantly checked by the legislature (the National People's Congress), it cannot accomplish anything. The other asked whether respondents agreed that the most important thing for a political leader is to accomplish his goals even if he has to ignore established procedure. Respondents were again divided, with a plurality taking the liberal position on the question of legislative interference and a strong plurality taking the liberal position on the question of established procedures.

This exploration of what democracy means to Chinese respondents begins to explain the paradox noted at the outset of this chapter: that Chinese citizens support both the general idea of democracy and many of its specific components, while also supporting many attributes of what Westerners call authoritarian regimes—and they hold these views without an apparent sense of contradiction.

3. EVALUATIONS OF THE CURRENT REGIME

The Chinese regime also derives support from citizens' favorable perceptions of its performance. The EAB surveys invited respondents to evaluate their current regimes in several ways. One was to ask citizens to compare the degree to which the current and past regimes were democratic. The other was to ask citizens to evaluate the current regime's performance in providing both democratic liberties and effective public policies.

3.1. PERCEPTIONS OF CHANGE

We asked respondents to rate their current and past regimes on a 10-point scale. Since the other regimes included in this study are democratic (or in the case of Hong Kong, partially democratic), people in those societies were asked to rate, in addition to their current regimes, the regimes in place at the time of the "most recent authoritarian rule." In China, even though democratic transition has not occurred, we still wanted to get a sense of how people perceived the changes in political life that had taken place in the quarter century since Deng Xiaoping's rise to power. So we asked people to rate the system's level of dictatorship or democracy at two earlier points before the current period:

TABLE 9.3   **PERCEPTIONS OF PAST AND CURRENT REGIMES: CHINA**

(Percent of respondents)

REGIME TYPES	1970S REGIME	MID-1990S REGIME	CURRENT REGIME
Very dictatorial (1–2)	9.6	1.2	1.2
Somewhat dictatorial (3–5)	37.1	25.6	10.9
Somewhat democratic (6–8)	17.4	38.9	44.5
Very democratic (9–10)	4.3	6.4	18.4
DK/NA	31.6	28	25.1
Total	100.0	100.0	100.0
Mean on a 10-point scale	4.7	6.1	7.2

Notes: N = 3184.

DK/NA = Don't know/no answer.

before 1979 (Deng came to power at the end of 1978), and in the mid-1990s (when Deng's reforms were well advanced and appeared irreversible).

Table 9.3 reports the scores and mean ratings for the three time periods. The figures show that Chinese respondents perceived a marked level of political change in the democratic direction. DK/NA levels were the highest in Asia, ranging from one-quarter to nearly one-third of respondents, with the largest percentage of people feeling unable to rate the regime most distant in time. Over sixty percent of respondents described the current system as democratic in some degree. Only 12.1% rated it as somewhat or very dictatorial. As shown in figure 9.1, over 80% of respondents who answered the questions on the two regimes perceived a change in the democratic direction of 1 to 9 points in magnitude.

These figures are comparable to the other political systems in our study. In Japan, for example, 77% of respondents described the current system as democratic and 14% as dictatorial. In China, the mean evaluation of the old regime before Deng was 4.7, comparable to the means given to the authoritarian regimes in Korea, Taiwan, and the Philippines. The mean evaluation of the current regime was 7.2, higher than the levels in Korea, Mongolia, the Philippines, and even Japan.

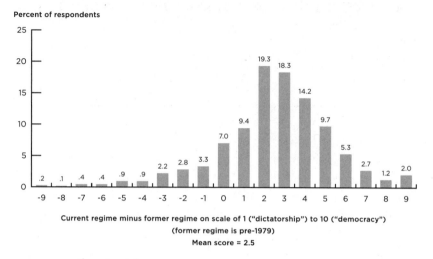

Percent of respondents

Current regime minus former regime on scale of 1 ("dictatorship") to 10 ("democracy")
(former regime is pre-1979)
Mean score = 2.5

FIGURE 9.1   Perceived Regime Change: China

Indeed, the evaluation of the direction of change among citizens in China is equally or more positive than among the citizens of any other political system we surveyed except Thailand and Japan. This emerges in the comparison of the eight systems in table 1.7, chapter 1. Nearly 59% of Chinese who compared the current system with that before 1979 perceived a change in the direction of democracy. Excluding "don't knows," 63.9% of the population in China believed the nature of the regime had changed in a positive direction. If we add those who believe that democracy was continuing, then 89.8% perceived the regime in a positive way. Only 10.1% saw the regime as remaining authoritarian or as having retreated from a more democratic to a more authoritarian condition over the twenty years since the reform started in China in 1979. Respondents were more negative about the direction of change in four of the other seven societies in the EAB survey (Hong Kong, Taiwan, Mongolia, and the Philippines).

It may seem paradoxical that people living in an authoritarian political system evaluate their regime's level of democratic change more generously than respondents living in some real democracies. But the puzzle is resolved if we remember that the regime ratings we asked for are not objective measures against a universal standard, but are generated by respondents as a function, first, of their own conceptions of democracy, and second, of the baseline against which they measure change. As we saw above, for many Chinese a paternalistic government that denies political competition is consistent with their conception of democracy. And for many, the limited increase in freedom they have enjoyed since Mao's death marks a real improvement from the past.

In a third-wave democracy like the Philippines, by contrast, respondents may measure the regime against a demanding set of ideals that came to the fore during the transition or which they idealize as having characterized the country's first experiment with democracy before World War II. In a mature democracy like Japan, citizens' current dissatisfactions may loom larger than positive changes that took place before many of our respondents were alive. The information on perceived regime change, then, does not measure the actual level of democratic development, but shows how change is perceived by ordinary citizens—a perception that may influence their level of support for the current regime.

3.2. COMPARING THE PERFORMANCE OF FORMER AND CURRENT REGIMES

To go more deeply into respondents' comparisons of the current regime with the past regime, we asked them to rate each of nine major government performance domains. The results for China are presented in table 9.4. Again respondents in China offered a relatively high proportion of "don't knows" (reflected in lower valid percentages in this table than in the versions of this table in the other country chapters). Nonetheless, the results are striking, and consistent with the discussion in the preceding section. There is a substantial consensus among people in China that there has been improvement since 1979 in the domain we call "democratic performance." Of the five areas we asked about, respondents found the greatest improvement in freedom of expression, followed by freedom of association (despite the fact that China outlaws the kinds of activities that are considered free association in the West, such as the organization of trade unions and political parties and participation in autonomous religious organizations). Citizens also saw improvement in judicial independence. By contrast, with regard to the ability of citizens to influence government, nearly half saw no change and only 39% saw positive change, reflecting the reality that significant steps in political democratization have yet to occur. Fewer

TABLE 9.4 PERCEIVED PERFORMANCE OF CURRENT AND PAST REGIMES: CHINA

	MEAN[a]	SD[a]	NEGATIVE CHANGE[b]	POSITIVE CHANGE[b]	NO CHANGE[b]	PDI[c]	VALID %[d]
Democratic performance							
Freedom of speech	1.00	0.67	2.9	85.0	12.2	82.1	80.4
Freedom of association	0.79	0.69	4.8	74.2	21.0	69.4	60.8
Equal treatment	0.50	0.93	16.2	60.4	23.4	44.2	77.3
Popular influence	0.26	0.82	13.8	39.0	47.1	25.2	61.7
Independent judiciary	0.49	0.91	17.1	61.8	21.1	44.7	50.2
Average	0.61	0.81	11.0	64.1	25.0	53.1	66.1
Policy performance							
Anticorruption	-1.21	1.05	83.2	12.4	4.4	-70.8	80.7
Law and order	-0.19	1.33	48.5	45.3	6.1	-3.2	89.6
Economic development	1.53	0.64	1.8	96.6	1.6	94.7	91.2
Economic equality	-1.01	1.28	74.7	21.3	4.1	-53.4	88.7
Average	-0.22	1.07	52.1	43.9	4.0	-8.2	87.6

Notes: N = 3183.

Past regime is defined as pre-1979.

[a] Scale ranges from -2 (much worse) to +2 (much better).

[b] Percent of valid sample.

[c] PDI (percentage difference index) = percent seeing positive change minus percent seeing negative change.

[d] Percent of sample giving a valid answer to this question.

than one-fifth saw negative change in any of the five areas of democratic performance. Clearly, the political liberalization that has occurred in China is acknowledged by the majority of respondents.

These findings contrast with outside evaluations such as the Freedom House scores on China's civil liberty and political rights (Freedom House, 1999–2003). From 1998 to 2002, China got the worst-possible Freedom House score, 7, for civil liberties and the next-to-lowest score, 6, for political rights. While the Freedom House ratings compare China to the standards of advanced liberal democracies, our respondents' point of comparison is 1979, and as argued earlier, the frame of reference used by many of them is the concept of socialist democracy.

We also asked about four areas of policy performance relating to the administration of society and the economy. On the overall economic situation, 96.6% said the situation today is better than in 1979. At the same time, however, nearly three-quarters said that the economy has become less equal. Opinions were also negative regarding the government's effort to control corruption, and were divided on the issue of law and order, with close to half the respondents saying the situation has gotten better and half saying it has gotten worse. Unlike the findings on democratic performance, these perceptions are in line with the views of outside experts, who believe the Chinese economy has grown rapidly while inequality and corruption have worsened. The views of the Chinese were also consistent with those elsewhere in Asia: most of our respondents in other societies also believed that the greatest improvements since the transition from the previous regime had taken place in the domain of democratic performance, while the new regime's performance in the policy areas we asked about had been less impressive.

4. THE STATE AND THE CITIZEN

In each of our eight political systems, the EAB survey tried to discover some of the key attitudes citizens hold toward the institutions of the state and toward themselves as political beings. The guiding theory is that democracies are healthy when citizens trust state institutions and see themselves as competent to perform the role of citizen. The China survey enables us to compare the levels of perceived corruption, institutional trust, and citizen efficacy in an authoritarian society to the levels of these variables in neighboring democratic societies.

4.1. CITIZEN EFFICACY AND SYSTEM RESPONSIVENESS

Even though the Chinese system does not fulfill the minimal attributes of what we define as democracy—freedom to organize and competitive elections—the regime nonetheless claims to provide responsive government under its concept of socialist democracy. Do Chinese citizens agree? We asked them about both sides of the citizen-government relationship: citizen's "internal efficacy" (that is, self-perceived empowerment) and government's responsiveness (sometimes referred to as "external efficacy") (Craig et al. 1990:289–314; Easton and Dennis 1967:25–38; Madsen 1987:571–581).

To probe the self-perceived empowerment of respondents, we asked them to tell us how they evaluated their own ability to understand the complexities of politics and their capacity to participate in politics. Chinese responses to this question are displayed along with those from Asian democracies in chapter 1, table 1.4. We found the Chinese somewhere in the disempowered side of our sample of Asian systems, ranged perhaps incongruously with the Taiwan respondents. In both systems around 60% of the public felt that they could neither understand nor participate in politics. In China, only 7.4% expressed confidence in their ability to do both. Only the citizens of Hong Kong felt more disempowered. The low sense of political efficacy in China is no doubt related to the fact that citizens really do lack channels either for knowing much about politics or for participating effectively. In the post-Mao period, Chinese citizens participated most actively in the local-level work unit, or *danwei* (Shi 1997). As economic reform destroyed the effectiveness of the *danwei*, effective new channels of participation were not created to replace it.

To assess respondents' views of government responsiveness, we asked how strongly they agreed or disagreed with the following two statements: "The nation is run by a powerful few and ordinary citizens cannot do much about it," and "People like me don't have any influence over what the government does." Citizens were split in their responses. On the negative side, 36% believed that the government is run by powerful interests, and over 70% said that the government is not subject to their influence. Taking a more positive view were the nearly 42% of respondents who disagreed with the statement that the nation is run by a powerful few, and the 14.1% who said that people like themselves could have influence over government. (The rest of the respondents to each question gave "don't know" or "no answer" responses.) In short, views were mixed. Although most people did not think that the government responds to popular influence, neither did most believe that the government is run by big interests.

These questions, however, implicitly refer to the central government. In China's system much resource allocation relevant to citizens' daily lives takes place in local governments and work units (for further discussion, see Shi 1997, chapter 1). To assess the perceived responsiveness of these levels of the system we asked three additional questions (in China and Taiwan only). First, "If you needed the help of government officials for something, would you ask for it?" Nearly 79% of respondents in China told us that they would. Second, did the respondent think that such a request would get a helpful response? Nearly 40% said yes, while slightly fewer than 40% were not sure. Third, we asked respondents to agree or disagree with the statement, "There are many ways for people in our country effectively to influence government decisions." Some 34% agreed while 33.6% disagreed.

These responses suggest that Chinese citizens see their system as fairly responsive at the local level and less so at the central level. This reflects the reality that the Chinese system provides citizens with the possibility to exert influence over the output side of the policy process but not over the input side. In Almond and Verba's terms, the Chinese are politically competent as subjects, less so as citizens (Almond and Verba 1963). In this sense, the official notion of socialist democracy is more than a myth: it has some correspondence in citizens' perceptions of their own relationships with the state. At the same time, it falls short of—indeed, it does not aspire to—the same forms of citizen competence that liberal-democratic systems value most highly.

4.2. PERCEPTIONS OF CORRUPTION

Corruption is a threat to the legitimacy of any regime, democratic or authoritarian. In China, charges of corruption were a leading issue in the 1989 prodemocracy movement, and the party has continued to treat corruption as a mortal threat to its stability (Shi 1990:1186–1205; Lu 2000; Nathan 2003:6–17). As table 9.4 showed, despite the government's efforts, in 2002 most respondents still believed that corruption had increased since 1979. To find out more about where they thought corruption existed, we asked respondents to specify their perception of the scope of corruption at two levels: in the local government and in the central government. The distribution of the answers to these questions is presented in table 9.5.

TABLE 9.5 PERCEPTION OF POLITICAL CORRUPTION AT NATIONAL AND LOCAL LEVELS: CHINA

(Percent of total sample)

		NATIONAL GOVERNMENT				
LOCAL GOVERNMENT	Hardly anyone is involved	Not a lot of officials are involved	Most officials are corrupt	Almost everyone is corrupt	DK/NA	Total
Hardly anyone is involved	3.6	1.9	0.2	—	2.5	8.3
Not a lot of officials are involved	4.5	**13.7**	0.7	—	**13.1**	**32.1**
Most officials are corrupt	2.1	9.7	4.9	0.2	**17.0**	**33.7**
Almost everyone is corrupt	0.3	0.8	0.6	0.2	2.0	4.0
DK/NA	0.3	1.6	0.4	-	**19.6**	**21.9**
Total	**10.9**	**27.7**	6.8	0.3	**54.2**	**100.0**

Notes: N = 3183.

Blank cell means no cases.

Percentages above 10 are in boldface.

As with a number of questions in China, we encountered a high proportion of DK/NA responses to this question. Just as 19.3% of respondents had been unable to evaluate the government's performance in fighting corruption (as seen in the "Valid %" column in table 9.4), so 19.6% of respondents were unable to say what degree of corruption existed at either of the two levels of government. But this uncertainty was not equally distributed. More than twice as many people did not know how to characterize corruption in Beijing as the percentage who did not know how to characterize it at the local level. This reflects the facts that the central government is far away from the lives of ordinary people, and that the regime-controlled media seldom carry news of central-level corruption.

Instead, the media portray corruption as a local phenomenon that the center is battling against. It makes sense, then, that among those who had a view, corruption was perceived as chiefly a local problem. Answering our question about the local level, 37.7% of respondents said that most or all officials were corrupt, compared to only 7.1% who said the same for the central government. This central-local contrast was the sharpest we observed in any of the eight political systems in the study. Moreover, those who saw corruption as systemic—that is, who said that most or all officials were corrupt at both local and central levels—constituted only 5.9% of the sample. This again was the lowest number in Asia, compared, for example, to 32.3% for Japan, and 42.1% for Taiwan.

When asked further whether they or their families had personally witnessed corruption or bribe-taking by politicians or government officials in the past year, only 20% of respondents in China said yes, the fourth-lowest percentage among our eight political systems after Japan, Hong Kong, and the Philippines. Thus, more people suspected that corruption was prevalent than had direct knowledge of it. This is probably the result of the official media's energetic publicity for official anticorruption efforts. During pretest for the questionnaire, we asked those who said corruption was a serious problem, but had no direct or indirect evidence, to tell us how they knew about it. Most referred to the official newspaper, *People's Daily*, and named as examples the then famous cases of Hu Chengqing, former deputy governor of Anhui Province, and Cheng Kejie, former vice-chairman of the NPC, both of whom had recently been executed for corruption.

Corruption in China may be worse than our respondents think, but at the level of public perception, our findings suggest that as of 2002 the problem was less intense in China than in Asia's democracies.

4.3. TRUST IN INSTITUTIONS

Institutional trust gives room for maneuver at times when a regime encounters difficulties, and is therefore an important determinant of the political stability of any kind of regime, democratic or otherwise. With this in mind, we asked respondents to report how much they trusted sixteen institutions plus the country itself.[8] The results are reported in figure 9.2.

We found high levels of trust in four central-level political institutions: the national government, the NPC (national legislature), the CCP, and the People's Liberation Army (PLA). The percentage of respondents claiming that they did not trust these institutions ranged from one to two percent, by far the lowest levels of distrust for any institutions across Asia.

The level of trust in local institutions was lower than that in central institutions, but still high compared to elsewhere in Asia. Seventeen percent of respondents reported that they did not trust the courts, 21% did not trust local government, and 23% did not trust civil servants. (Since there is no distinction in China between political appointees and career officials and little clarity about the difference between party and government officials, distrust of civil servants can be understood as distrust of power holders in general.) The most distrusted government institution was the local police station (*paichusuo*), distrusted by one-quarter of respondents. The finding is in contrast to the higher level of trust in the public security apparatus as an institution: only 18% of respondents claimed that they did not trust the public security bureau (PSB), which is the same level of distrust as the court system. These findings suggest that people in China trust political institutions that are removed from their daily lives more than they trust institutions with which they have regular contact. This is consistent with the traditional mentality that believes that the emperor is good even if local officials are bad.

Media in China play a different role from the one they play in democracies. Rather than independently providing information, the media serve the party and government to mobilize popular support. We asked respondents first whether the media in general can be trusted and then whether they trusted newspapers in particular. The analysis shows that the media enjoyed a high level of trust. Eight percent of respondents told our interviewers that they did not trust the media in general, and 15% said that they did not trust newspapers.

NGOs proved to be the least trusted institutions we asked about. This may reflect the tradition in both precommunist and communist China of citizen dependency on government. As nongovernmental bodies, NGOs

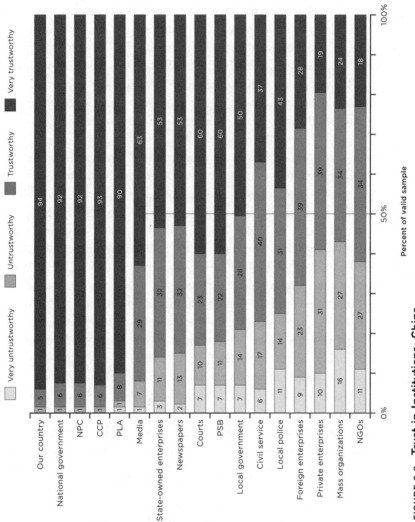

FIGURE 9.2 Trust in Institutions: China

Legend: Very untrustworthy | Untrustworthy | Trustworthy | Very trustworthy

Percent of valid sample

Institution	Very untrustworthy	Untrustworthy	Trustworthy	Very trustworthy
Our country	1	5		94
National government	1	6		92
NPC	1	6		92
CCP	1	6		93
PLA	11	8		90
Media	1	7	29	63
State-owned enterprises	3	11	32	53
Newspapers	2	13	32	53
Courts	7	10	23	60
PSB	7	11	22	60
Local government	7	14	28	50
Civil service	6	17	40	37
Local police	11	14	31	43
Foreign enterprises	9	23	39	28
Private enterprises	10	31	39	19
Mass organizations	16	27	34	24
NGOs	11	27	34	18

are perceived to lack prestige and effectiveness; by contrast, citizens believe they can appeal to higher levels of government for help when they run into problems with local authorities. Additionally, NGOs say that they represent special interests, an idea that strikes many Chinese as selfish rather than public spirited. By contrast, government institutions say they represent the interests of whole population.

Why do political institutions in China's authoritarian system enjoy higher trust than similar institutions in Asian democracies? No doubt the regime's control over information contributes to this result. The fall-off in trust from national to local institutions reflects the fact that official media are allowed to criticize local officials, within certain limitations, but can only praise national institutions. In addition, people have closer contact with local government, and local governments' decisions have more obvious impacts on people's lives.

Another contributing factor is the widespread belief in norms of hierarchy and collectivism. In previous research I demonstrated that trust in both incumbents and institutions is correlated in China with these two cultural attributes (Shi 2001:401–419). This finding is supported by the regression analysis in table 9.6. The dependent variable is an index of respondents' reported levels of trust in five institutions: the central government, CCP, the NPC, local government, and the courts. The analysis shows that age and education have little impact on the dependent variable. Nor does media access affect institutional trust, a finding that suggests that the regime's propaganda is ineffective in shaping citizens' perceptions of the government. Income is negatively associated with institutional trust. This may be because those with higher incomes are more likely to be in business and to have direct contact with government agencies, generating feelings of distrust as a result of encounters with official corruption or other unpleasant interactions. Likewise, the perception that government actions have an influence over one's life is negatively correlated with trust, perhaps because those who perceive this influence are more likely to blame the authorities for whatever problems they have.

Three variables do exert a significant positive impact on institutional trust. Two of these are cultural variables that work as hypothesized. Both reciprocal orientation, which is the opposite of hierarchical orientation, and individualistic orientation, which is the opposite of collectivism, have statistically significant negative impacts on trust in political institutions.

The third variable that positively affects institutional trust is satisfaction with local government performance. The connection seems obvious: those who are more satisfied with what government institutions have done are more likely to trust them.[9]

Our findings in this section call into question the claim made by some theorists of democratic transitions: that authoritarian regimes lack the safety cushion of public support enjoyed by democratic regimes because authori-

TABLE 9.6 **REGRESSION ANALYSIS OF TRUST IN POLITICAL INSTITUTIONS: CHINA**

	B	BETA
Constant	25.45***	
Age	.007	.033
Education (years of formal schooling)	-.002	-.002
Media access[a]	.007	.005
Annual family income	-.000*	-.049
Perceived impact of local government[b]	-.076***	-.083
Reciprocal orientation[c]	-.963***	-.098
Individualistic orientation[c]	-.688*	-.042
Satisfaction with local government performance[d]	1.725***	.382
Adjusted R^2=.193		

Notes: * $p < .05$ ** $p < .01$ *** $p < .001$

The dependent variable is an index composed of five variables: trust in the courts, the central government, the CCP, the NPC, and the local government. It ranges from 0 (the respondent finds all five institutions completely untrustworthy) to 30 (the respondent finds all five institutions completely trustworthy).

[a] Media access is the number of times respondent listened to radio broadcasts and watched TV news in the past week.

[b] Perceived impact of government is measured by asking respondents if they think township and local governments and their polices have any impact on their daily life.

[c] Reciprocal orientation is measured by disagreement with the following statements: "If a conflict occurs, we should ask senior people to uphold justice"; "Even if parents' demands are unreasonable, children should still do what is asked of them"; and "When a mother-in-law and a daughter-in-law come into conflict, even if the mother-in-law is in the wrong, the husband should still persuade his wife to obey his mother." Individualistic orientation is measured by disagreement with the following statements: "A person should not insist on his own opinion if people around him disagree"; "If various interest groups compete in a locale it would damage interests of everyone"; and "The state is like a big machine and the individual, a small cog, should have no independent status."

[d] Satisfaction with government performance is measured by a question asking whether the respondent is satisfied with the performance of local government.

tarian governments enjoy support only insofar as their leaders maintain attractive personal images (charismatic legitimacy) or their policies deliver economic benefits (performance-based legitimacy). In China at the time of our survey, performance-based legitimacy certainly existed, as shown above, but it had to some extent also been converted into what David Easton calls diffuse support (1975). The analysis in this section further shows that traditional values of hierarchy and collectivism contributed to generating diffuse support in China.

The existence of diffuse support might provide a degree of resilience for the Chinese regime if it encountered a downturn in some of its performance indicators, although there is no way of estimating the depth of this reservoir of support (Nathan 2003). Certainly, the data on institutional trust reinforce the sense developed in earlier sections of this chapter that the regime in 2002 faced no mass defection that might push it toward democratization.

5. COMMITMENT TO DEMOCRACY

How committed are people in China to democracy? Some argue that the Chinese do not want democracy and prefer authoritarianism. Indeed, this is one of the arguments given by the regime for not introducing democratic reform. Others argue that there is no difference between people in China and elsewhere: the desire for democracy is built into human nature.

5.1. DEMOCRATIC ATTACHMENT AND AUTHORITARIAN DETACHMENT

We asked five questions in each of our eight Asian systems to explore people's attachment to democracy. The results are reported in chapter 1, table 1.8.

Like other people in Asia, the Chinese are overwhelmingly supportive of democracy. Strong majorities consider democracy desirable, suitable, effective, and preferable. China ranked in the middle of the group of political systems surveyed for four of the five democratic attachment variables. Only in the percentage of people who considered democracy "desirable now " was China was tied for last place, with Taiwan. But it ranked above both Hong Kong and Taiwan in the percentage of people who gave prodemocratic answers to the other four questions.

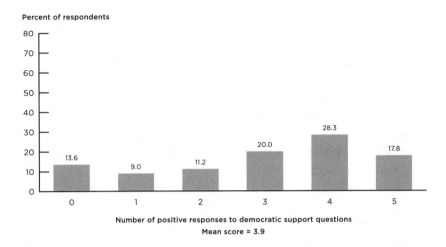

Percent of respondents

Number of positive responses to democratic support questions
Mean score = 3.9

FIGURE 9.3 **Democratic Support: China**

Only in regard to democracy's priority over economic development did Chinese respondents give less than majority support, and again in this respect, the Chinese were not markedly different from respondents elsewhere in the region. Indeed, the size of the prodemocracy minority on this question was larger in China than in five of our other survey sites.

In short, the Chinese were generally as supportive of democracy as respondents in Asia's old and new democracies, and in some respects more so. This is further illustrated in figure 9.3, which shows that two-thirds of Chinese respondents gave two or more prodemocracy answers to our five democratic attachment questionnaire items.

The EAB survey also probed citizens' levels of authoritarian detachment, defined in this volume as the rejection of four types of authoritarian regime. Because it is illegal in China to call into question two of these authoritarian institutions (a strong leader and rule by a single party), we could only ask respondents how they felt about the other two: rule by the military and rule by technocratic experts. The China data are included in chapter 1, table 1.9. Here again, the Chinese did not stand out from other Asians. A majority rejected both authoritarian projects. A higher percentage was willing to accept military rule than in other countries, but the percentage was close to that in the Philippines.[10] Chinese rejected rule by technocratic experts at about the same rate as citizens in Asian democracies.

5.2. OVERALL COMMITMENT TO DEMOCRACY

Figure 9.4 summarizes the patterns of democratic attachment and authoritarian detachment in terms of five patterns of regime orientation (definitions are given in the notes to table 1.11, chapter 1; however, the China figure differs slightly from those in other chapters because we were only able to ask two of the four authoritarian detachment questions). The figure classifies those with the most consistent prodemocratic and antiauthoritarian views as moderate supporters of democracy, those with consistent antidemocratic and proauthoritarian views as strong opponents, and so on.

By these standards, the majority of people in China were committed to democracy. Over one-third of the population were moderate supporters and another 13% were skeptical supporters. These two groups represent close to half the population. Elsewhere in Asia, there was a greater prevalence of mixed views and of weak and strong opposition to democracy. However, China also had the highest percentage of opponents to democracy of all the nations studied. In this sense, opinion on democracy can be said to be more polarized in all three Chinese societies than it is elsewhere in East Asia.

The data show that modernizing social change has worked in China much as theory would predict, moving popular attitudes away from support for authoritarianism and toward support for democracy. For strong opponents of democracy, the mean number of years of education was 3.81, for weak opponents 6.57, for mixed group 6.34, for skeptical supporters 7.7, and

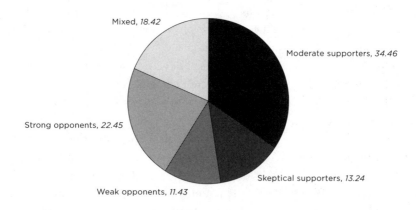

Percent of respondents

FIGURE 9.4 Patterns of Commitment to Democracy: China

for moderate supporters 8.9. In other words, the average strong opponent had not completed primary school while the average moderate supporter had nearly nine years of education. The mean yearly family incomes for strong opponents, weak opponents, mixed, skeptical supporters, and moderate supporters of democracy respectively were RMB 7,047 (approximately $859), RMB 9,106 ($1,110), RMB 9,240 ($1,126), RMB 14,075 ($1,716) and RMB 14,289 ($1,742).[11] That is, skeptical and moderate supporters of democracy earned on the average twice as much as strong opponents. Urban residents are more likely to support democracy than rural residents. Age also had an effect: strong opponents of democracy were on average nearly five years older than those in any of the three other categories.

6. EXPECTATIONS FOR CHINESE DEMOCRACY

The EAB survey tried to gauge citizens' optimism for the future of Chinese politics by asking them to predict the level of democracy of the regime five years into the future. The results are presented in chapter 1, table 1.12.

The findings for China reveal a pervasive optimism. Only 3.3% of valid respondents expected the future regime to have a score of 5 or below, the range we classify as authoritarian. All other valid respondents placed the future regime somewhere in the democratic range of 6 or above. These optimists in turn consisted of two categories: a minority of 13%, who considered the current regime authoritarian but expected it to democratize (the third and fourth rows in the table), and a large majority of 83.6% who considered the current regime already democratic and expected it to remain so or to become even more so. In short, respondents saw the country on a trajectory toward democracy, although from a variety of starting points.

This does not, however, reflect an expectation of regime change. As we saw in table 9.3, nearly two-thirds of respondents answering the question rated the current regime as already democratic.[12] For them, further movement toward democracy would mean the intensification of trends already visible in the current regime rather than a change in the type of regime.

7. CONCLUSION

Earlier chapters suggested that disillusionment with democracy in places like Taiwan and Japan does not portend inevitable retrogression to authoritarianism, because citizens reject authoritarian alternatives as strongly as they express dissatisfaction with democratic realities. Conversely, in China we cannot assume that widespread support for democracy portends a likely transition in the regime. On the contrary, the China case shows that a high level of popular support can be sustained for an authoritarian regime even as the forces of socioeconomic modernization and cultural globalization bring increasing public support for the abstract idea of democracy.

We have identified three factors that make this possible in the case of China (we do not have evidence for whether the same factors operate in these ways in other authoritarian systems). First, the regime has been able to define democracy in its own terms, drawing on ideas of good government with deep roots in the nation's historical culture and more recent roots in its ideology of socialism. Second, the regime draws support from the public's perception that it is performing better than the previous regime, in both the political realm (greater freedom and accountability) and some aspects of the policy realm (economic growth). Third, persisting norms of hierarchy and collectivism support trust in political institutions, especially those at the national level with which citizens have less direct personal contact.

While performance legitimacy—the second factor just listed—is vulnerable to changes in economic or political performance, the other two factors point to cultural roots of diffuse political support that are likely to change more slowly, if at all. This is why the spread of prodemocracy attitudes—which our analysis shows is certainly happening—does not necessarily point toward regime change in any foreseeable time frame. Such change could happen. But it is also possible that the spread of prodemocracy attitudes will generate even stronger support for the regime in power if it is able to continue to align its own image and performance with citizen values as these evolve.

NOTES

1. The per capita GDP with PPP adjustment in 2000 international dollars grew from $673 in 1978 to $4,568 in 2002; see http://devdata.worldbank.org/dataonline.
2. Interview with officials of the National People's Congress (NPC), conducted in Beijing in October 1993.
3. Interview with officials of the research department of the NPC, conducted in Beijing in 1999.
4. The trivial exceptions were Yuan Shikai's and Zhang Xun's attempted imperial restorations in 1915 and 1917 respectively.

5. Since China is the only nondemocracy in our study, we do not think the same question arises for the other seven surveys.

6. The fact that such high percentages of respondents said yes to these questions is itself a sign that they felt safe expressing controversial views to our interviewers. The interviewers were retired middle-school teachers who were instructed, of course, to give respondents an assurance of confidentiality. Apparently many respondents accepted this assurance.

7. Because of the different way they are calculated, these figures cannot be derived from the table. For the purpose of this analysis, respondents giving substantive answers to the question that do not fit into the two special categories we have just defined would be considered as responding in mixed ways to the influences of both the CCP and the West.

8. In the China questionnaire respondents were allowed to chose among three levels of trust and three levels of distrust for a 6-point scale. In figure 9.2 this scale has been collapsed into four categories for comparability with the figures in other chapters.

9. The relationship between political trust and government performance, incidentally, confirms again the validity of survey results gathered in an authoritarian society. If political fear explained the high reported levels of trust in Chinese government institutions, we would expect reported trust to correlate weakly or not at all with a respondent's satisfaction in the performance of government. Since it does correlate, we have reason to think that respondents' self-reports of their trust in government institutions are valid. This is an instance of the "external consistency" test for the validity of an indicator, and also applies to the other regression coefficients reported in table 9.6. The validity of an indicator gains credibility when the indicator is correlated with other variables in a theoretically predicted way. For discussion of the external validity test, see, among others, Balch 1974:1–43; Hill 1982:33–46; Citrin 1974:973–988.

10. The relatively low rate of rejection of the idea of military rule may have something to do with the episode during the Cultural Revolution when Mao ordered the military to intervene to stop warring civilian factions from killing each other. In 1989, the party also declared martial law in parts of Beijing to put an end to the hunger strike and prodemocracy demonstrations there, which many Chinese citizens view in retrospect as having posed a dangerous challenge to social order. Such experiences may have persuaded some Chinese that military rule is sometimes necessary in times of emergency.

11. The conversions use the 2002 exchange rate of U.S.$1 = RMB 8.20.

12. Tables 1.12 and 9.3 report different percentages of people who consider China a democracy and a nondemocracy because the former table reports percentages of the valid sample and the latter table reports percentages of the total sample.

10

CONCLUSION

Values, Regime Performance, and Democratic Consolidation

Yun-han Chu, Larry Diamond, and Andrew J. Nathan

IF ASIA'S DEMOCRACIES ARE in trouble today, the lesson is not that this form of government cannot find cultural roots in the region, but that democratic governments must win citizens' support through better performance. The Asian cultures that we studied are open to democracy, but not committed to it. This shows that consolidation is a longer process than many third-wave optimists foresaw, and its success is not a foregone conclusion.

Our surveys took place against the background of political strife, bureaucratic paralysis, and economic distress in the region's five new democracies. In Taiwan and the Philippines, the results of presidential elections had been challenged by the losers. In the Philippines the president had recently been forced out of office. In South Korea (hereafter Korea) the incumbent president was crippled by domestic challenges. Mongolia was mired in party stalemate. Even the region's oldest democracy, Japan, found itself rudderless, with a stream of prime ministers resigning amid economic and political turmoil. Throughout the region economic growth had slowed as a result of the financial crisis of 1997 and 1998—except in authoritarian China.

Distrust of democratic institutions was widespread. As we have seen in the chapters in this volume, majorities of respondents in every country except Thailand and China expressed distrust for political parties. Majorities distrusted parliament in Taiwan, the Philippines, Korea, and Japan. Corruption was described as pervasive at either the local or the national level, or at both levels, by majorities in Japan, the Philippines, Taiwan, and Mongolia. Table 10.1 reminds us that seven of the eight publics (excluding Hong Kong) acknowledged that their new regimes were doing better than the old regimes in measures of democratic performance, that is, in providing political freedoms and opportunities for public influence. But only four of the publics gave positive evaluations of their new regimes' performance in dealing with the policy issues we asked about—corruption, law and order, economic development, and equity—and of these, only the Thai public saw more than modest improvement.

Authoritarianism remained a strong competitor to democracy in the region. Non- and semidemocratic regimes govern much of East Asia and have displayed greater resilience than their newly democratized neighbors. Over recent decades, China in particular has made a smooth transition from a rigid older form of authoritarianism to a new, adaptive form that by comparative Asian standards scored high levels of public support in the EAB survey. China's model—labeled "resilient authoritarianism" by one of us (Nathan 2003)—has been studied by socialist and authoritarian siblings like Vietnam, Laos, Myanmar (Burma), and to some extent, North Korea. Unless China embarks on a path of democratization, the

TABLE 10.1 **AVERAGE PDI OF PERCEIVED PERFORMANCE OF CURRENT AND PAST REGIMES**

	DEMOCRATIC PERFORMANCE	POLICY PERFORMANCE
Japan	60.8	15.2
Hong Kong	-24.1	1.3
Korea	31.5	-23.1
China	53.1	-8.2
Mongolia	51.8	-16.8
Philippines	26.8	8.9
Taiwan	50.0	-11.1
Thailand	69.7	57.3

Note: Based on "Perceived Performance of Current and Past Regimes" tables in each chapter.

prospects for democratic breakthroughs in the recalcitrant states in its orbit appear to be dim.

The East Asia Barometer surveys underscore that the new democracies in Asia experienced slow and uneven growth in democratic legitimacy. While an average of 88% of respondents across the five new democracies surveyed (Taiwan, Korea, Mongolia, Thailand, and the Philippines) deemed democracy to be "desirable for our country now," only an average of 59% considered it "preferable to all other kinds of government" and an average of 35% said it was "equally or more important than economic development" (cf. chapter 1, table 1.8).

Democracy is a good word across the region—a label claimed by even authoritarian regimes—but fundamental democratic values have fragile support. The theory of Asian values promoted by authoritarian leaders in the region, privileging economic development and social harmony over Western-style civil and political freedoms, showed broad appeal to scholars, activists, and social movement leaders (Bauer and Bell 1999). Our surveys revealed that it also appeals to ordinary citizens, although to differing degrees in different countries. An average of 35% of respondents across seven of the eight publics (excluding China) disagreed with view that the government should not disregard the law. In all eight surveys, an average of 40% did not agree that government leaders should follow procedure. In addition, an average of 49% agreed with the proposition that judges should accept the view of the executive in deciding important cases, and an average of 57% agreed with a similar proposition opposing a legislature that checks the executive (based on chapter 1, table 1.13).

EAST ASIAN VIEWS IN COMPARATIVE PERSPECTIVE

East Asia, however, is not alone in its publics' ambivalent support for democracy. We are able to compare East Asian attitudes toward democracy with those in several other regions thanks to the recent emergence of parallel efforts to assess attitudes and values toward democracy in Latin America (the Latinobarómetro), Africa (the Afrobarometer), and the postcommunist states of Central and Eastern Europe and the former Soviet Union (the New Europe Barometer). For this comparison we narrow the focus to the six democracies in East Asia—the five new democracies plus Japan—leaving out China and Hong Kong as less relevant for this purpose. This renders our analysis comparable with the regional barometers in the other regions, which have surveyed countries that are electoral democracies or at least have regular, multiparty elections.

Before proceeding, it is important to stress a methodological caveat. As we have seen throughout this study, measured levels of public support for democracy and evaluations of how well it works depend on how a question is worded and the response options that people are given. It is hard enough to compare national responses to questions that are identically worded but then must be translated into a number of different languages—and, underlying them, into quite different cultural contexts as well. Throughout this project, we struggled with the challenge of achieving a sufficiently high degree of standardization in questionnaire design and administration so that the answers would be comparable across our eight East Asian societies. But if this is difficult across countries within one regional survey, it is even more challenging across the different regional barometers, despite growing efforts to standardize questions and methods. Understanding how sensitive public responses can be to differences in question wording and design, we try as much as possible to confine our comparative treatment to more or less identical items.

Support for democracy. Compared to levels of democratic support in other regions, our six East Asian democracies appear about average. When asked whether democracy is always preferable to any other type of regime, the mean support across the EAB's six democratic regimes was 60%.[1] This is only slightly lower than the 62% recorded in Africa in 2002 and 2005,[2] the same proportion as in the five South Asian countries surveyed in 2004,[3] and higher than the mean level in Latin America (53%; Latinobarómetro 2005:56) and Eastern Europe (also 53%; Rose 2005:68).[4]

Other measures, however, indicate a more positive East Asian view of democracy. More than three-quarters of the respondents in every democracy in the EAB study thought democracy was "suitable" for their society, except for Taiwan; even there the suitability assessment rose from 59% in 2001 to 67% in 2005. (In the Philippines, however, reflecting the country's woes in the years after our first-round survey, the suitability figure dropped from the 80% revealed in the EAB survey to 57% in a survey conducted in 2005.) Likewise, most East Asians thought democracy could be "effective" in solving the problems of their society: nine of ten Thais, seven of ten Koreans and Mongolians, six of ten Japanese and Filipinos—but again, only slightly less than half the public in Taiwan. On average, over two-thirds of people in our six East Asian democracies (68%) thought that democracy could be effective in solving the problems of society, compared to an average of only about half of Latin Americans[5] (see table 10.2).[6]

TABLE 10.2 REGIONAL DIFFERENCES IN DEMOCRATIC ORIENTATIONS

Percent of respondents

QUESTION	AFRICA 2000	AFRICA 2002	AFRICA 2005	EAST ASIA 2002[a]	SOUTH ASIA 2004–2005	LATIN AMERICA 2000	LATIN AMERICA 2005	EASTERN EUROPE 1995	EASTERN EUROPE 2004	EU 15 2006
Democracy always preferable	69	62	62	60	64	57	53	—	53	—
Reject all 4 auth. options	48	—	—	48	—	—	—	—	59	—
Reject all 3 auth. options	—	—	—	53	—	—	—	67	67	—
Reject military rule	82	78	73	83	60	—	—	—	—	—
Reject 1-party rule	—	71	71	71	—	—	—	—	—	—
Reject strongman	—	78	73	73	33	—	—	—	—	—
System efficacy: democracy can solve problems	—	—	—	68	—	48[b]	53	—	—	—
Satisfaction with democracy	58	52	45	61	48	36	31	—	38[c]	66[d]
Trust in:										
National govt.	—	—	—	46	69	—	36	—	—	—
Courts	—	—	62	57	72	—	31	—	26	—
Parliament	—	—	56	36	59	—	28	—	16	—
Parties	—	—	46[e]	29	48	—	19	—	10	—
Military	—	—	65	64	81	—	42	—	42	—
President	—	—	64	—	—	—	43	—	51	—

[a] East Asia percentages are for the six democratic countries, excluding China and Hong Kong.

[b] This figure is from the 2002 Latinobarómetro.

[c] 2006 Eurobarometer average for eight new East European members of EU, plus Romania and Bulgaria.

[d] Figure for the original fifteen EU members.

[e] This is an average of 56% approval of the ruling party and 36% approval of the opposition parties.

Regime evaluations. Another important dimension of public opinion of democracy is how citizens evaluate the performance of their democratic system. A question in many regional barometers asks, "How satisfied are you with the way democracy works in our country?" By this measure, on average six in ten citizens in East Asian democracies were satisfied. Only in Japan and Taiwan was the proportion satisfied below half (about 45%), although in Taiwan it rose to 56% by 2005.

This is slightly better than in Europe, where the Eurobarometer finds that satisfaction has oscillated in recent years in the neighborhood of 56% (the average level among the European Union member states in 2006). In South Asia, democratic satisfaction averaged 51% across the three democracies in the region (India, Sri Lanka, and Bangladesh). In Africa, across the twelve countries surveyed in all three iterations of the Afrobarometer, the overall percentage satisfied with the way democracy works dropped from 58% in 2000 to 45% in 2005. The Latinobarómetro finds Latin Americans persistently dissatisfied with the performance of their democracies, with mean levels of satisfaction among countries in the region oscillating between 25% and 40% over the last decade. In 2005, the average among regional countries was less than a third (31%), with majorities satisfied only in Uruguay and Venezuela. In Peru, Ecuador, Nicaragua, and Paraguay, fewer than a fifth of citizens were satisfied; in Mexico and Brazil, fewer than a quarter.[7]

Authoritarian detachment. An even more encouraging indicator of democratic legitimacy in East Asia in comparative perspective is the degree to which democracy is preferred to authoritarian alternatives. As we saw in chapter 1, large majorities of East Asians rejected the authoritarian options they were asked about. In each of the six EAB democracies, over 80% opposed military rule, save for the Philippines, where the proportion was 63%. Over three-quarters of Thais, Koreans, and Japanese, seven of ten respondents in the Philippines and Taiwan, and six out of ten Mongolians rejected a surrender of government to a "strong leader." The pattern was roughly similar for the option of a one-party system. In each of the six democracies, at least seven out of ten citizens (and over eight of ten in Korea and Japan) opposed letting "experts decide everything," save in Mongolia, where the proportion was two-thirds.

Again in this respect, East Asians appear similar to Africans. On average in the eighteen African countries in 2005, 73% opposed military rule, compared to 83% in the six East Asian democracies. In both East Asia and Africa, averages of about seven in ten opposed the option of one-party rule, and about three-quarters (slightly more in Africa) rejected the option of rule

by an authoritarian strongman. By the most demanding standard of rejecting all four authoritarian options (including traditional rule in Africa and
technocratic rule in Asia), the average proportion drops to just below half
(48%) in both Africa and East Asia.

Across the ten democracies of postcommunist Europe (surveyed in late
2004 and early 2005), on average 59% of the public rejected all four proffered
authoritarian options (army rule, communist rule, a dictator, or suspending
parliament and elections in favor of a strong leader), a figure higher than in
Africa or East Asia (Rose 2005:19). But a pattern of intraregional divergence
is apparent. In the eight states which acceded to EU membership on May
1, 2004 (the Czech Republic, Slovakia, Hungary, Poland, Slovenia, Estonia,
Latvia, and Lithuania), an average of 61% of the public rejected all four authoritarian alternatives. Likewise, in Romania, which (with Bulgaria) joined
the EU in January 2007, 64% rejected all authoritarian alternatives. By contrast, publics in the former Soviet republics of Ukraine, Russia, and Belarus
were relatively welcoming of authoritarian options. Only 45% in Ukraine,
27% in Russia, and 23% in Belarus rejected all four. Nearly half of Russians
said they could support suspension of parliament and elections, and over
40% endorsed a return to communist rule, while nearly two-thirds in Belarus endorsed the option of a dictator. Also in Bulgaria only 46% rejected
a return to autocracy in some form.

On the only partially comparable item we have for Latin America, respondents were asked in 2005 if they would "support a military government
to replace the democratic government if the situation got very bad"; on
average 62% in the region said no (Latinobarómetro 2005:51).[8]

Of all the regions, South Asia displayed the weakest resistance to authoritarian rule. Only about a quarter of South Asians rejected the option of a
strong leader (and even if the large number of nonresponses to the question
is discarded, the proportion rises only to a third). Even in long-democratic
India, which voted overwhelmingly in 1977 to bring down the authoritarian emergency rule of Indira Gandhi, only about half (52%) of those with
an opinion opposed the option of a "strong leader who does not have to
bother about elections."[9] About half of South Asians overall (and 62% who
answered the question) rejected military rule, but only small percentages
rejected rule by a king.

Assessing Past, Present, and Future Regimes. A final way to compare how
citizens feel about their democracy is to assess how far they feel their regime has come as a democracy, and how far they expect it may go. On our
survey's 10-point scale of degree of democracy, citizens of the six East Asian

democracies rated their past regimes on average at 3.8, their present regimes at 7.1, and their expectations for the regimes of the future at 7.9. In other words, each East Asian public saw its old regime as clearly authoritarian, the new regime as well past the midpoint of 5 on the democracy scale, and the future regime as expected to demonstrate some degree of progress. Only the Japanese expressed little expectation of future progress, not surprisingly since their regime has already been democratic for half a century.

There are no directly comparable data from the other regional barometers, but we can place East Asian attitudes in perspective by examining the New Europe Barometer's "heaven-hell" scale of approval and disapproval of past, present, and future regimes, which ranges from +100 to –100. Among the eight postcommunist states that entered the EU in 2004, publics saw not much difference between the old regime (which had an average approval of +12 points) and the current one (+11 points), but expressed a clear sense of optimism about the future, with a mean expected approval level of +29 points (Rose 2005:47–51). Put otherwise, Asians saw the trajectory from the past to the future regime as traversing, on average, 41% of the 10-point scale from authoritarian to democratic, while postcommunist publics saw the distance traveled as 8.5% of a 200-point disapproval-approval scale. While the two scales are too different to permit strict comparison, the contrast seems striking enough to justify the conclusion that the political mood in East Asia was relatively optimistic, despite the region's travails.

The cross-regional comparisons suggest that if democracy is in trouble in Asia, it also suffers serious, and in some respects more acute, vulnerabilities in other regions. But an alternative reading is possible: perhaps we should not be too quick to take alarm at public discontent and value ambivalence in Asia or elsewhere. After all, democracy has survived for over half a century with modest levels of support in Japan. To clarify our data's meaning for democratic consolidation, we will have to situate them in a broader framework of analysis.

CONSOLIDATION IN MULTIDIMENSIONAL AND DYNAMIC PERSPECTIVE

We argued in chapter 1 that public attitudes work in combination with other normative and behavioral factors to determine the fragility or robustness of democratic regimes (see table 1.1). The EAB surveys examined what ordinary people believe and value without investigating the attitudes and behaviors of other key actors such as political elites and organizations. Thus it should not be completely surprising that a coup occurred in Thailand, even though our survey showed that the broad public supported democratic norms and values. Thai democracy fell short of consolidation at the elite not the mass level: significant leaders neither believed in democracy nor constrained their behavior by its principles.

Yet the domain of mass norms and beliefs is crucial to consolidation. Absent deep and resilient public commitment, a democratic regime is vulnerable to decay in the other five consolidation domains. Thus, although survey data cannot tell us whether a given democracy will certainly survive, they can alert us to whether the mass base provides the support necessary for consolidation across the other five domains or instead is dangerously fragile. Specifically, as one of us has argued elsewhere, democracy can be considered normatively consolidated at the mass level if at least 70% of the public believe that democracy is preferable to any other form of government *and* is suitable for the country, and if no more than 15% prefer an authoritarian alternative (Diamond 1999:68).

By this standard, at the time of the EAB survey democracy fell short of consolidation by considerable distances in all five new democracies, and even in the old democracy of Japan. Five of the six cases exceeded the 70% threshold for democracy's suitability; the exception was Taiwan where only 59% of the population considered democracy suitable now. However, the percentage preferring democracy to all other kinds of government topped the benchmark 70% only in Thailand (see chapter 1, table 1.8). On the authoritarian alternatives measure, each of the EAB democracies had significant proportions above 15% supporting at least two of the authoritarian alternatives. Indeed, each of the first three authoritarian options (leaving aside "experts decide everything") attracted more than 30% support in the Philippines, while 36% of Thais endorsed a one-party system and 40% of Mongolians embraced rule by a strong ruler (see chapter 1, table 1.9).

In these respects, once again, East Asia is not alone. The same exercise conducted across the Latino-, Afro-, and New Europe barometers produces similar results. With respect to authoritarian options, for example, an average of 30% of Latin Americans in 2005 said they "would support a military government if things get bad" (Latinobarómetro 2005:50). Among the eight postcommunist countries admitted to the EU in 2004, an average of 27% support getting rid of parliament and elections and having "a strong leader who can quickly decide everything," while 26% support suspending parliament and elections, and 15% favor a return to communist rule (Rose 2005:19). In the 2005 Afrobarometer, 15% or more of the population favored abolishing elections and parliament in four of eighteen countries surveyed, 15% or more favored army rule in seven of the countries, and 15% or more favored single party rule in ten of the countries (Afrobarometer 2006:table 1). At least one authoritarian option received support from at least 15% of the population in thirteen of the eighteen countries surveyed. Thus, by the standards of table 10.3, democracy remains attitudinally unconsolidated throughout all the regions where it was established since the 1970s except Western Europe.

But there is more. The definition proposed in table 10.3 stipulates that democracy is not attitudinally consolidated until the benchmark levels of support have been maintained "over some period of time" (Diamond 1999:68). To be sure that democracy is consolidated, one would want to see evidence of broad support for democracy and low levels of endorsement of authoritarian alternatives, sustained consistently in public opinion surveys for at least a decade. Although the data reported in this book are of course single-time snapshots of attitudes in each political system, the EAB country teams have accumulated some longitudinal data as well, partly from surveys conducted before the EAB joint project, and partly from surveys conducted after the EAB survey under the umbrella of the Asian Barometer (described in chapter 1). This body of data reveals that public attitudes toward democracy in Asia are labile, fluctuating dramatically over relatively short periods of time. There is evidence of this phenomenon in the other Global Barometer Surveys as well, as suggested by information provided in the preceding section of this chapter.

Support for democracy can rise dramatically in a short time. For example, as shown in the preceding section, the assessment of democracy's suitability rose from 59% in 2001 in Taiwan to 67% in 2005. But democratic support does not benefit from a ratchet effect. It declines readily and sometimes dramatically in response to unfavorable events. For example, in Korea, the preference for democracy fell from 69%, just before the East Asian financial crisis, to 54% in 1998 and 45% in 2001, before recovering to 49% in 2003, and then to 58% in 2004 (Shin and Lee 2006). In the Philippines, as a result of protracted political polarization and crisis, the assessment of democracy's suitability declined from 80% in 2002 to 57% in 2005, while preference for democracy fell from 64% in 2001 to 51% in 2006. Democratic preference fell more modestly in Thailand, from an exceptionally high level of 83% in 2002, to 71% in 2006.

These data come from too short a time frame to allow full understanding of the dynamics of democratic support. We cannot yet judge whether there are unseen barriers beyond which measures of democratic support do not normally move. Nor do we know where the thresholds lie at which changes in mass public support have effects in the other five consolidation domains. We need to sustain comparative research over a period of time to discover answers to these questions.

It is not too early, however, to ask what forces generate the observed ups and downs in public support. The chapters in this book focused on the factors that affect democratic support in the short term; the EAB data, however, will also make possible further investigation of the factors that affect the growth (or decline) of deeper democratic values in the long term. What we have shown in this volume is that regime performance produces rapid ups and downs in attitudinal support for democracy. What remains to be more fully examined is how at the same time, but on a longer timeline, socioeconomic modernization affects the prevalence of fundamental democratic values.

In every political system that we surveyed, East Asian publics told us that they recognized democratic progress. They assessed their current regimes as markedly more democratic than the previous ones (chapter 1, table 1.6). As seen earlier in table 10.1, they acknowledged the current regimes' performance in providing rights and freedoms. Yet when it came to the new regimes' policy performance, our respondents' evaluations in the six democracies were weak or negative (again table 10.1). In addition, publics withheld trust from core democratic institutions like parties and parliaments, and told us that they perceived high levels of corruption in their central and/or local governments.

How do the two kinds of perceived performance affect support for new democratic regimes? Earlier studies suggested that both kinds of performance matter, but that democratic performance matters more than policy performance in building support for democracy (Diamond 1999:192–196). Table 10.3 supports this conclusion. The table describes the impact in six of our survey sites of perceived democratic performance and perceived policy performance on the key measures of democratic support and authoritarian detachment we have been discussing in this chapter, when several other relevant variables are controlled in a regression equation. In general, both kinds of performance affect democratic support, although in different ways in different countries. Overall, democratic performance matters more; it has statistically significant effects in fourteen of the possible eighteen cells compared to eleven of eighteen cells for policy performance, and its effects are more often statistically significant at the demanding .ooo level.

The greater effect of democratic performance is particularly marked for the variable we call authoritarian detachment. If respondents think a regime performs well in providing democratic rights and freedoms, then in every location except the Philippines they reduce their support for authoritarian alternatives. But the impact of policy performance on democratic support is less distinct. Respondents reward the regime for improved policy performance with increased authoritarian detachment in only one of the six political systems, Thailand. In two countries perceived policy performance has no statistically significant effect on authoritarian detachment. In three countries (Korea, Mongolia, and the Philippines) it even has a negative effect. Our provisional interpretation of this finding, yet to be fully tested, is that the citizens who most firmly reject authoritarian alternatives are also likely to be most critical of a regime's policy performance, regardless of the type of regime, while those who are more open to authoritarian options are also likely to be more deferential to the regime's policy actions, regardless of the type of regime.[10] In any case, the big picture is that regime performance increases support for democracy. Citizens have an opinion about whether their democratic regime is doing a good job, and if they think it is they give it more support.

The cross-regional perspective reveals that these patterns are again not unique to Asia. In Africa, appreciation of progress in providing democratic freedoms generates public attitudes in support of democracy. Support for democracy rises after free, competitive elections and declines linearly, according to Michael Bratton, "the farther back in the past an electoral alternation (or failing that, a transition to competitive elections) had occurred" (2004:155). Corruption, on the other hand, "is corrosive ... to citizen acceptance of democracy."[11] And on average, Africans think that the majority of their elected representatives are corrupt.

Likewise, in Latin America, large proportions of the public (between 75% and 90%) say each year that corruption has increased in the past five years. More than nine in ten Latin Americans (most recently 97% in 2001) say the problem of corruption is serious or very serious. Less than one out of three of Latin Americans (30% in 2005) perceive at least "some" progress in reducing corruption in their country. The four countries in which the proportions are 40% or higher—Chile, Venezuela, Uruguay, and Colombia—are the places where support for democracy has been strong or increasing in recent years. Trust in politicians is a casualty of these perceived

TABLE 10.3 IMPACT OF REGIME POLICY PERFORMANCE ON SUPPORT FOR DEMOCRACY

(Standardized regression coefficient)

	TAIWAN		KOREA		MONGOLIA		THAILAND		PHILIPPINES		JAPAN	
	Democ	Policy	Democ	Policy	Democ	Policy	Democ	Policy	Democ	Policy	Democ	Policy
Democracy desirable for our country now[a]	**.154**	.143	**.188**	*.068*	*.108*	*-.098*	.088			*.097*		*.158*
Democracy suitable for our country now[a]	**.177**	.173		.173	*.108*		.086			*.079*		*.162*
Authoritarian detachment[b]	**.182**		*.064*	-.176	**.217**	-.227	**.150**	**.187**		-.136		**.184**

Notes: Entries are the standardized regression coefficients (betas) in an ordinary least squares regression in which the dependent variable is the measure of democratic support indicated in the left column, and the other independent variables controlled for are age group, years of education, and urban or rural residence.

Democ = perceived democratic performance. Policy = perceived policy performance. These are operationalized as the average improvement or decline perceived by each respondent in government performance on the five measures of democratic performance and four measures of policy performance respectively.

Entries in boldface are significant at the .000 level. Those in italics are significant at the .05 level or higher. In empty cells the coefficient is not statistically significant.

[a] Six or above on a 10-point dictatorship-democracy scale of where the country should or could be now.
[b] The number of authoritarian options the respondent rejects, ranging from 0 to 4.

failures. While 71% of Latin Americans surveyed trust the church and 55% trust radio, trust for the military, the president, and television average only slightly over 40%. Barely a quarter of Latin Americans trust the congress and only a fifth trust political parties (Latinobarómetro 2005:61).

As in Africa, Asia, and Latin America, newly democratized publics in Eastern Europe also perceive that they have greater freedom while condemning their governments for poor policy performance. When asked if they felt freer than before the fall of communism to say what they think, join organizations, take an interest in politics or not, and choose in religious matters, 63% answered yes to all four questions; 79% saw greater freedom of speech, and 81% greater freedom of association. More than half (52%) thought the government had some or a lot of respect for human rights, although here there was unusually wide variation, from 76% in Hungary to 30% in Romania. At the same time, however, nearly three-quarters of citizens (72%) in these ten democracies believed that half or "almost all" officials are corrupt, and roughly the same proportion think the government treats them "definitely" or "somewhat" unfairly. And more citizens in these ten countries approved of the old economic system (69%) than the new one (57%). Moreover, nowhere are levels of trust in parties and representative institutions lower than in the postcommunist states, where citizens had their fill of "the party" by the time the Berlin Wall came down. Parties are trusted on average by just 10% in the new democracies of the region, and are actively distrusted by three-quarters of the population.[12] Parliament fares little better (16% trust, 63% distrust). The postcommunist malaise is also apparent in the comparison between the average level of satisfaction with the way democracy works in the original fifteen (West European) EU members—66% in 2006—and satisfaction in the typical postcommunist state—38% across the eight new East European members, plus Romania and Bulgaria.

Previous research has shown that these political assessments have important consequences for commitment to democracy in postcommunist states. Trust in institutions and the perceptions of increased political freedom, greater fairness, and increased citizen ability to influence government have independent and significant positive effects on support for the current system of democratic government. The perception of greater political freedom also increases the rejection of authoritarian alternatives (as does patience with the new regime). The objective reality also appears to matter independently; increased freedom (as measured by Freedom House) significantly increases levels of regime support, while higher levels of corruption (by independent expert assessments) bring about significantly higher levels of support for authoritarian alternatives (Rose, Mishler, and Haerpfer 1998:158, 193).

While perceived regime policy performance helps explain short-term ups and downs in regime support, we believe a long-term evolution is also taking place in deeper democratic values under the influence of forces of economic and social change that are at work across the Asian landscape. Since value evolution has not been a major theme of this book, we will discuss the subject only briefly here. As we saw in chapter 1, citizens in most countries in East Asia are supportive of most of the rule-of-law values we asked about (chapter 1, table 1.13).[13] Our evidence suggests that this level of value support is likely to increase so long as Asia continues to modernize. Table 10.4 dramatizes the point by displaying the impact in each of six survey sites of education and urban residence—variables whose levels in a society increase with modernization—on respondents' commitment to rule of law, controlling for age group.[14] Education has strong positive effects on commitment to rule of law everywhere except Thailand. Urbanization has positive effects in Taiwan, Korea, and Thailand. The negative correlation in Mongolia may reflect the concentration of the old communist elite and state bureaucracy in the capital city, Ulaanbaatar.

That this should be so is not surprising: the power of modernization to change values is well established in the literature (Lipset 1959; Inkeles and Smith 1974; Diamond 1992; Inglehart and Welzel 2005). Of course, modernization does not work in an invariant way across all societies. We suspect that East Asia's democracies will be slower to develop value commitments to democracy than the new democracies of Western Europe (Diamond 1999:chap. 5). Portugal, Spain, and Greece had the advantages of having experienced democracy in earlier historical periods, of being located in an overwhelmingly liberal and democratic region, and of being spurred by the (then) European Community to fulfill demanding democratic conditions as a condition for entry. The democracies of East Asia (save for Japan and the Philippines) went through transitions to democracy without much prior experience of this form of government, in a less-supportive regional environment, and with fewer material enticements for democratic consolidation. Nonetheless, as these Asian societies become more highly educated and more urbanized we expect their citizens' values to change. Much research remains to be done, however, to determine *how* modernization acts upon values in Asia. Among other questions, we need to explore whether the move toward prodemocracy attitudes under conditions of modernization is invariant in direction, how much variation can be

TABLE 10.4   **IMPACT OF MODERNIZATION ON COMMITMENT TO RULE OF LAW**

(Standardized regression coefficient)

	TAIWAN	KOREA	MONGOLIA	THAILAND	PHILIPPINES	JAPAN
Education	**.261**	*.072*	**.156**	—	**.114**	**.230**
Urban residence	*.060*	**.105**	**-.123**	*.091*	—	—

Notes: Entries are the standardized regression coefficients (betas) in an ordinary least squares regression in which the dependent variable is the number of liberal responses, from 0 to 4, given to questions testing whether the respondent believes in rule of law; the other independent variable controlled for is age group.

Entries in boldface are significant at the .000 level. Those in italics are significant at the .05 level or higher. In empty cells the coefficient is not statistically significant.

observed in the strength of the association between modernization and value change in different countries and under different types of regimes, and how long-term changes in democratic values interact with short-term changes in democratic support.[15]

We cannot, however, expect citizens' growing empathy for democratic values to translate directly into steady regime support. What we have seen instead in this volume is that independently of the public's value commitments, support for democratic regimes fluctuates widely in sensitive response to changing perceptions of these regimes' performance, levels of corruption, and the trustworthiness of their political institutions. Asian publics are open to democracy and we expect they will grow more open to it over time. But they are not captive to its charms. In politics as in daily life they are skeptical consumers. They must be shown that democracy works, and for the time being many of them doubt that it does.

CONCLUSION

In East Asia and elsewhere, we have learned a lot about the health of new democracies by listening to the people. Ultimately, if democracy is to be consolidated, it must work to improve people's material lives, advance economic development, and provide good governance. Several East Asian democracies climb a steep hill of expectations in this regard because the economic and administrative performance of the previous authoritarian regimes was relatively successful. But in the near term, what people expect at a minimum is that democracy will work to deliver fair, honest, and responsive government, with greater freedom. To the extent that democracy works to provide the political substance people expect of it—individual freedom, accountability, free and fair elections, a rule of law, and some degree of fairness to all citizens—people will come to value it, even if somewhat hesitantly, and will resist the temptation to embrace alternative forms of government.

Unfortunately, there remains too much in East Asia of what Diamond (1999:49) calls "hollow, illiberal, poorly institutionalized democracies." At the time of our surveys the Philippines had suffered serious challenges to civil liberties, good governance, and the rule of law; Thailand struggled with ongoing problems of corruption and vote buying; and in Taiwan, political polarization was manifested in deep divisions not only over policies but also over the meaning of the constitution itself and whether it should be fundamentally changed, a debate that signified a lack of institutional consolidation and of elite agreement on the rules of the democratic game. While Taiwan and Korea made remarkable progress in civil and political freedom and the rule of law in the decade prior to our surveys, they were markedly less successful in producing accountable government and finding a satisfactory balance between the extremes of imperial presidential power and opposition legislative obstruction (Chu and Shin 2005). Democracy is not merely about elections, but involves multiple and finely graded degrees of quality that, our studies suggest, are visible to the public. In East Asia's democratic regimes, a critical mass of citizens wants not just democracy as such but more and better democracy: more accountability, more responsiveness, more transparency, and less corruption.

The consolidation of democracy in East Asia will require steps to make democratic systems more effective, responsible, and democratic. Among the priorities are reforms to develop structures of horizontal accountability, including legislative capacity and oversight, judicial competence and independence, and economic scrutiny and regulation; to monitor, deter, and punish corruption; and to improve party and campaign finance so as "to arrest the encroachment of money into politics" (Chu and Shin 2005:209). In some countries constitutional reforms may be necessary to repair the recurrent tendency of presidential systems toward polarization and deadlock. While citizens in the region are unlikely to see again the phenomenal rates of economic growth of the previous generation, consolidation will be aided if economies continue to produce at least moderately good records of economic growth and distribution while adapting to changing international market conditions.

East Asian democratic regimes face these challenges in a difficult global context. The world appears to have entered (dating perhaps as far back as the Pakistani coup in 1999) a period of "democratic recession," in which setbacks to democracy are offsetting, and at this writing even outnumbering, advances (Diamond 2008). Not only has democracy broken down in Pakistan and Thailand, but it has been slowly strangled in Russia and Venezuela, and it is stalled and performing poorly in a number of African and Latin American countries. The rapid and seemingly confident rise of China suggests that authoritarian regimes remain formidable competitors for legitimacy, if they themselves can continue to deliver.

Yet, our findings also provide reasons to be hopeful. East Asian publics do anticipate democratic improvement, and they should know better than we do the likely trajectories of their regimes. They expect democratic deepening, not backsliding, and presumably are prepared to reward parties and politicians who deliver it. The Hong Kong survey shows that people who do not live under a democratic regime would like to have one, for all its flaws. The China survey shows that residents in the world's largest authoritarian system share a concept of democracy that overlaps considerably with those of neighboring democracies and that they value it highly.

Democracy in Korea and Taiwan has shown resilience despite hard challenges. In the face of scandals and political deadlock under each of Korea's four presidents of the democratic era, spanning a twenty-year period from Roh Tae Woo to Roh Moo Hyun, Korea's democratic system has endured and in many respects has become more democratic. Taiwan has gone through an even deeper political trauma, involving debilitating conflict between president and assembly, intense polarization over the twin issues of state and national identity, a bitterly disputed presidential election in 2004 that led the opposition to challenge the legitimacy of the incumbent president, Chen Shui-bian, and grave charges of corruption in the presidential family that generated calls for President Chen's resignation. Yet here, too, the future of democracy as a system of government does not appear to be in serious doubt.

Our data affirm that in each political system, high levels of authoritarian detachment make any overthrow of the formal structures of democracy improbable. While contending elites in Korea and Taiwan have not shown a steadfast commitment to the rules and spirit of democracy, neither do they challenge its desirability. The case of Japan shows that democracy can survive over a long period of time with low levels of public enthusiasm, in part due to the lack of support for nondemocratic alternatives. This point, however, does not apply uniformly throughout the region. In the Philippines and, as events have shown, in Thailand, military intervention remains a plausible alternative partly because of the stated preferences of a significant minority of the public and partly because of elites' willingness to consider authoritarian options.

Democracy in East Asia thus stands in a twilight zone. Citizens do not want authoritarian rule, but in the crucial domain of public attitudes democracy has not yet earned consistently strong support. Those who interpreted the third wave as a decisive historic victory for democracy spoke too soon. The easy optimism of the end of history was premature. Yet we should also let go of the pessimistic view that democratic values are only Western and have no appeal in the East (Sen 1999). If democracy is in trouble in Asia, it is not in worse shape than in other developing regions. And, most encouraging and discouraging at the same time, its troubles are not undeserved; ambivalent support is a response to mixed performance. Democracy in Asia has yet to earn its way.

NOTES

1. The number 59% was for the five new democracies; the change of one percentage point is attributable to the addition of Japan to the set of countries being described.

2. Unless otherwise stated, data from the most recent Afrobarometer (Round 3) are drawn from Afrobarometer 2006. Round 3 was conducted in 2005 and 2006; for brevity we refer to it as the 2005 survey. We appreciate the cooperation of Michael Bratton and Carolyn Logan of the Afrobarometer in providing us with selected additional data.

3. Those five countries were India, Sri Lanka, Bangladesh, Pakistan, and Nepal. Pakistan, of course, has not been a democracy since 1999, and Nepal was undergoing monarchical-dominated autocratic rule and Maoist insurgency at the time of the survey.

4. This mean figure is for the eight postcommunist democracies admitted in 2004 to the European Union—Hungary, Poland, the Czech Republic, Slovakia, Slovenia, Estonia, Latvia, and Lithuania—plus Bulgaria and Romania. With regard to the results for Latin America, a new and different regional survey, the Latin American Public Opinion Project (LAPOP), has recently found consistently higher levels of public support for democracy in the Americas. This may because of a more systematic effort to capture rural respondents in proportion to their actual share of the population, and perhaps to other differences in sampling and implementation. Rural respondents are less educated and less critical, and may tend to be more supportive of the current system. Overall, the thirteen-country mean for democratic preference in the 2006 LAPOP survey was 67%, versus 51% for the same thirteen countries in the 2005 Latinobarómetro. The Latinobarómetro figures may therefore be seen as low-end estimates, and quite possibly underestimates, of democratic

support. For further information on LAPOP, see http://sitemason.vanderbilt
.edu/lapop.

5. The Latinobarómetro question was worded slightly differently, however: "Some
people say democracy solves problems we have in [country name]. Others
say democracy does not solve these problems. Which statement is closer to
your view?" The proportion viewing the democratic system as capable in this
way has oscillated around half: 50% in 1995, 48% in 2002, 53% in 2005. See
Latinobarómetro 2005:49.

6. Throughout this chapter, the regional averages we provide represent the simple
means of all the country percentages within a region. None of these means is
weighted for country size, and therefore none represents an average of all people
in a region or set of countries. Rather, each regional average is the mean of the
different national response rates. When we say only half of Latin Americans, on
average, thought democracy could be effective, this indicates that the mean of
the country percentages on this item is about 50%.

7. Here again, however, the recent LAPOP survey finds a dramatically more positive
picture, with a mean level of democratic satisfaction of 48% in the thirteen
countries surveyed in 2006, compared with a Latinobarómetro mean of 28%
in the same thirteen countries. In seven of the thirteen countries, the LAPOP
survey found levels of democratic satisfaction more than twice as high as the
Latinobarómetro found (e.g., 54% vs. 24% in Bolivia, 49% vs. 24% in Mexico).

8. The higher level of openness to military rule than in Africa or East Asia may
have been prompted by the caveat, "if the situation got very bad."

9. About a quarter of Indians had no opinion, so the absolute level of opposition
was only 38%.

10. We noted in chapter 1 that authoritarian detachment and citizens' positive
orientations toward democracy are not always closely correlated.

11. "Explaining Trends in Popular Attitudes to Democracy in Africa: Formal or
Informal?" Michael Bratton, Afrobarometer presentation, October 2006.

12. The methodology for this survey was different from the others in that it provided
respondents with a 7-point scale from distrust to trust, and thus allowed a neutral,
midpoint answer.

13. Data from other EAB value batteries not discussed in this book show patterns
similar to those described in this paragraph.

14. Younger people in every society tend to be more prodemocratic, but Inglehart
argues and we agree that this is contingent on modernization; if younger
generations experienced harder rather than easier material lives their values
might change in the opposite direction.

15. These issues can be explored using questionnaire items on traditional social
values and democratic values that were included in the EAB survey but which
we have not analyzed in this volume.

APPENDIX 1

Sampling and Fieldwork Methods

The East Asia Barometer project was inaugurated in June 2000, with its head-quarters at the Department of Political Science at National Taiwan University. At the time of the first round of surveys (2001 through 2003), the project consisted of thirty-one collaborating scholars from eight East Asian countries and the United States, and five international consultants who were involved in similar projects in other regions. Coordination for the surveys was supported by grants from the Ministry of Education of the Republic of China, National Taiwan University, and the Academia Sinica. Local survey administration was supported by other funding, mostly local.

Leaders of the eight local teams and the international consultants collabora-tively drew up a 125-item core questionnaire designed for a forty- to forty-five-minute face-to-face interview. The survey was designed in English and translated into local languages by the national teams. Between July 2001 and February 2003, the collabo-rating national teams administered one or more waves of this survey in eight Asian countries or territories.

Further information on sampling and methodology is available on the project Web site at http://www.asianbarometer.org/newenglish/surveys/SurveyMethods.htm.

KOREA SURVEY

The South Korea survey was conducted in February 2003, by the Survey Research Center at Korea University. The survey population was defined as all Korean nation-als aged twenty and older with the right to vote residing in the territory of South Korea, except the island of Cheju-do, which has 1.2% of the population.

Sampling was conducted in four stages. At the first stage, the country was geo-graphically stratified into sixteen strata—seven metropolitan cities and nine provinc-es (*do*). Each province was further stratified into two substrata (urban and rural). At the second stage, the administrative subdivisions (*dong*) of the respective metropoli-tan cities and those (*dong* or *ri*) of the respective provincial substrata were identified. From these subdivisions preliminary sampling locations were randomly selected according to probability proportionate to their population size. At the third stage, urban districts (*ban*) and rural villages were randomly selected as primary sampling units from the respective preliminary sampling locations. Six to eight households from a district and twelve to fifteen from a village were randomly selected. Finally, at the household level, the interviewers were instructed to select for interview the person whose birthday came next.

If no one was at home at a household, or if the adult selected for interview was not at home, the interviewer was instructed to call back two times. A total of 3,224 addresses were selected. At 649 addresses, there was no one at home after two call-backs so that the household residents could not be enumerated and a respondent could not be selected. Of the 2,575 households where an individual name could be selected by the birthday method, thirty-two individuals were not interviewed be-cause they were too old or infirm or were absent from the household; 630 refused; and 413 were not completed because of the respondent's impatience, a common problem in surveys in Korea. Of 2,575 voters sampled, we completed face-to-face interviews with 1,500, registering a response rate of 58%.

Fieldwork was undertaken by regularly employed interviewers of the Garam Re-search Institute. Each interviewer participated in a one-day orientation session and completed three trial interviews. Twenty percent of the completed interviews were randomly selected for independent validation.

The EAB core questionnaire for the project was the main part of the South Korea survey. Interviews were conducted in Korean. The mean length of interviews was sixty minutes, with a range from fifty to ninety minutes.

SPSS chi-squared tests were performed to determine the comparability of sub-samples defined by gender, age, and region with the corresponding segments of the survey population, as defined in the 2000 report of the Population and Housing Census of the National Statistical Office. The subsamples matched the population segments with respect to gender, age, and region of residence, so no weighting vari-able was constructed.

PHILIPPINES SURVEY

The Philippines survey was conducted in March 2002 by Social Weather Stations, an independent, nonstock, nonprofit social research organization. It yielded 1,200 valid cases out of 3,059 sampled cases for a response rate of 39.2%.

In the conduct of the survey, the Philippines was divided into four study areas: the National Capital Region (NCR), Balance Luzon, Visayas, and Mindanao. The targeted sample size of each study area was set at three-hundred voting-age adults (aged eighteen and older), for a total sample size of 1,200. Within each of the four study areas, multistage sampling with probability proportional to population size (PPS) was used in the selection of sample spots. In the NCR, sixty precincts were sampled from among the seventeen cities and municipalities in such a way that each city or municipality was assigned a number of precincts that was roughly proportional to its population size. An additional provision was that at least one precinct must be chosen within each municipality. Precincts were then selected at random from within each municipality by PPS. In the other three study areas, each study area was divided into regions. Sample provinces for each region were selected by PPS, with the additional provision that each region must have at least one sampled province. Within each study area, fifteen municipalities were allocated among the sample provinces, and selected from within each sample province with PPS, again with the provision that each province must include at least one municipality. Sixty sample spots for each of the major areas were allocated among the sample municipalities. The spots were distributed in such a way that each municipality was assigned a number of spots roughly proportional to its population size. Sample precincts (urban) or sample barangays (rural) within each sample municipality were selected using simple random sampling.

Within each sampled unit, interval sampling from a randomly chosen starting point was used to draw five households. In each selected household, a respondent was randomly chosen among the household members of a given sex (to assure a fifty-fifty stratification by sex) who were eighteen years of age and older, using a Kish grid. A respondent not contacted during the first attempt was visited a second time. If the respondent remained unavailable, a substitute was interviewed who possessed the same attributes as the original respondent in terms of sex, age bracket, socio-economic class, and work status. The substitute respondent was taken from another household beyond the covered intervals in the sample precinct or barangay.

The questionnaire was incorporated within an omnibus survey, in which the EAB module was asked first, followed by a number of items comparing foreign and domestic companies and seeking opinions on the General Agreement on Tariffs and Trade (GATT).Interviews were conducted face to face. The EAB module was translated from English into Tagalog, Cebuano, Ilonggo, Ilocano, and Bicolano; Philippine-specific questionnaire items were translated from a Tagalog master version into the other four local languages (as well as into English to serve as a check on the meaning of the Tagalog original). All five Philippine languages (i.e., excluding English) were used in administering the questionnaire, depending on the language spoken by the respondent.

Interviewers were professional interviewers of NFO-Trends, a private market research survey group. In addition to general training, they underwent a minimum of three days of specific training on this questionnaire before going into the field. Supervisors observed at least 10% of field interviews. Spot checks were undertaken after 30% of interviews were completed, after 60% completion, and after 90% completion of interviewing. During spot checking, about 20% of the unsupervised interviews were reviewed with respondents or conducted again.

Since the sample contained three hundred individuals from each of four unequally-sized major areas of the country, weighting variables were constructed to weight each case proportionately to the population size of the area where the individual was interviewed.

TAIWAN SURVEY

The Taiwan survey was conducted in June and July 2001 by the Comparative Study of Democratization and Value Changes Project Office, National Taiwan University. The target population was defined as ROC citizens aged twenty and over who had the right to vote. This population was sampled according to the Probabilities Proportionate to Size (PPS) method in three stages: counties and towns, villages and precincts (li), and individual voters. Taiwan was divided into eight statistically distinct divisions. Within each division, four, six, or eight counties or towns were selected; from each of these two villages or precincts were selected; and in each of these between thirteen and sixteen individuals (not households) were sampled. In the municipalities of Taipei and Kaohsiung, only precincts and individuals were sampled.

The sampling design called for 1,416 valid interviews. In order to replace respondents who could not be contacted or who refused to be interviewed, a supplementary pool of fifteen times the size of the original sample was taken. If a respondent could not be interviewed, he or she was replaced by a person from the supplementary pool of the same gender and age. Of the original sample, 714 of 1,416 were successfully interviewed for a success rate of 50.4%. To produce the other 701 successful cases, a total of 1,727 supplementary respondents were contacted. Overall, we attempted to interview a total of 3,143 people and successfully completed 1,415 interviews for a response rate of 45.0%.

A chi-squared test showed that the procedure oversampled citizens between the ages of thirty and fifty, and those with educational levels of senior high school and above. Although the sample passed the chi-squared test for gender, it contained about 4% fewer males and 4% more females than expected. Weighting variables for the sample were therefore calculated along the three dimensions of gender, age, and educational level using the method of raking.

The questionnaire used in Taiwan was composed of the core questionnaire used in all participating countries and a supplementary module employed in the three predominantly Chinese societies of China, Taiwan, and Hong Kong.

The interviews were conducted by 140 university students. Over three hundred students interviewed for these jobs; we chose among the applicants based on their ability to communicate in both Mandarin and Taiwanese, previous interviewing experience, and our geographic needs. The interviewers were overseen by fifteen supervisors, most of whom had previously served as interviewers in a survey on the 2000 presidential election. All interviewers attended a day-long training session.

Of the interviews, 64.8% were conducted predominantly or exclusively in Mandarin, 14.1% were conducted predominantly or exclusively in Taiwanese, and 20.5% used a mixture of Mandarin and Taiwanese. The remaining 0.6% were conducted in other languages.

To check the quality of the data collected, we conducted post-tests of all 1,415 cases. Fifteen percent of these were done in person and the other 85% were conducted by telephone. Kappa values for all eight of the variables retested ranged between .328 (fair) and .860 (almost perfect). None of the kappa values fell in the "poor" or "slight" ranges, evidence that the data possess a fairly high degree of reliability.

THAILAND SURVEY

The Thailand survey was conducted in October and November 2001 by King Prajadhipok's Institute, an independent, publicly-funded research institute chartered by the Thai Parliament.[1]

The sampling procedure had three stages. In the first stage, fifty legislative constituencies were randomly selected from among four hundred across the nation. In the second stage, one hundred voting districts (precincts) were randomly selected from within the fifty constituencies. Because Thai constituencies and districts are of relatively equal population size, it was not necessary to use probability proportionate to size (PPS) methods. Finally, respondents' names were randomly sampled from voting lists from these districts. All persons aged eighteen and over are named on these voting lists, with the exception of a few small categories disenfranchised under the voting law. If selected respondents were unavailable, substitutes of the same gender were obtained from names on either side of the chosen respondent on the voting list. Such substitutions occurred in 116 cases. The procedure yielded 1,546 cases. After disqualifying fifteen for noncompletion of the questionnaire, the sample was reduced to 1,531.

The sample was consistent with census data with respect to gender and region, but failed the chi-squared test with respect to age. A weighting variable was constructed using gender and age statistics.

The questionnaire included all of the questions in the core survey, with about a dozen additional Thailand-specific questions. The interviews were conducted under the supervision of regional coordinators who accompanied teams of field workers, distributed and collected questionnaires, and checked to see that returned questionnaires had been completed. The coordinators were university professors who were paid to coordinate the study. The interviewers, who were students at regional universities, were paid for each interview. The interviews were conducted in the local dialects, including Malay in the southern provinces, except when the respondent preferred to speak in Central Thai. The language of each interview is coded in the data.

MONGOLIA SURVEY

The Mongolia survey was conducted from October through December 2002 by the Academy of Political Education, in cooperation with the Institute of Philosophy, Sociology, and Law of the Mongolian Academy of Sciences. The Academy of Political Education is a nongovernmental, nonprofit, nonpartisan institution established in 1993, to support and strengthen democratization and civil society in Mongolia.[2]

A one-stage probability sample was constructed of Mongolian citizens aged eighteen and older. We selected 1,150 from Mongolia's six provinces (*aimag*) and two cities with a probability proportional to size, based upon population data in the *Mongolian Statistical Yearbook* (National Statistical Office of Mongolia 2001). As a supplement, two thousand parliamentary election voter registration lists from the General Election Commission of Mongolia were used to check the number of citizens aged eighteen and older in selected provinces and cities.

A selection table was used to select the individual respondent within the sampled household. A sampled respondent who was not available was replaced by another respondent from the original sample. At initial contact, respondents were asked to agree to an interview and the interview was scheduled for a later time. The survey yielded 1,144 valid cases out of 1,200 sampled cases for a response rate of 95.3%.

The interviewers were twenty-four staff of the academy (twenty-two researchers and two technical staff) and twenty volunteer students of sociology from the Mongolian National University. Interviewers underwent one week of training in September 2002. The survey administered the project's core questionnaire, as translated from English to Mongolian, with a number of adjustments to accommodate Mongolian election dates and political party names. Questionnaires were administered face to face, in the Mongolian language.

Compared to national population statistics from the 2000 census, the sample overrepresented respondents aged forty through sixty-four, females, and those from certain regions. The sample is therefore weighted using the method of raking to correct for these three biases.

JAPAN SURVEY

The Japan survey was conducted by the Department of Social Psychology, University of Tokyo, in January and February 2003. It yielded 1,418 valid cases out of 2,000 sampled cases for a response rate of 70.9%. The target population was the voting age population in all forty-seven prefectures. The method was a two-stage random sample from the population of individual males and females twenty years and older throughout Japan.

The first-stage sampling units were districts established in the 2000 national census. The number of units was calculated so that the sample size in each unit would be about thirteen. This led to a first-stage sample of 157 districts, consisting of 122 cities or wards and thirty-five towns or villages. In the second stage of sampling, respondents were selected from voter lists, or in some districts complete residence registries, using an equal interval selection method. Voter lists and residence registries are substitutable because the proportion of residents disqualified from voting is small.

Fieldwork was undertaken by regularly employed interviewers of Central Research Services, a marketing and public opinion research firm. The interviewers were trained survey fieldworkers, who received an additional orientation session for this survey.

The EAB core questionnaire formed the main part of the survey. Interviews were conducted in Japanese. The mean length of interviews was 40.8 minutes, with a range from fifteen to 107 minutes. The survey also included some additional variables, among them evaluation of the current cabinet, Inglehart's values scale, a daily life political intolerance scale, a private life orientation scale, a local politics conversation scale, a local area attachment scale, a generalized trust scale, and a portion of the values scale developed in Taiwan by Fu Hu.

The sample was weighted for gender, age, and education using the method of raking.

HONG KONG SURVEY

The Hong Kong survey was conducted from September through December 2001 by Kuan Hsin-chi and Lau Siu-kai under the auspices of the Hong Kong Institute of Asia-Pacific Studies, Chinese University of Hong Kong. It yielded 811 valid cases out of 1,651 sampled cases for a response rate of 49.12%. The target population was defined as Hong Kong people aged twenty to seventy-five residing in permanent residential living quarters in built-up areas.

The sampling method involved a multistage design. First, a sample of two thousand residential addresses from the computerized Sub-Frame of Living Quarters maintained by the Census and Statistics Department was selected. In selecting the sample, living quarters were first stratified with respect to area and type of housing. The sample of quarters selected was of the EPSEM (equal probability of selection method) type and was random in the statistical sense. Where a selected address had more than one household with persons aged twenty to seventy-five, or was a group household (such as a hostel), a random numbers table preattached to each address was used to select one household or one person. If the drawn household had more than one person aged twenty to seventy-five, a random selection grid, i.e., a modified Kish grid, was employed to select one interviewee. A face-to-face interview was conducted to complete the questionnaire. The interviewers were recruited from the student body of the Chinese University. Apart from the core items, the questionnaire contained questions unique to the local context of Hong Kong.

SPSS nonparametric chi-squared tests were conducted to compare the gender, age, and educational attainment of the sample with the attributes of the target population as reported in the Hong Kong 2001 population census. The gender and educational attainment distributions of the sample did not differ significantly from those of the target population. Raking was used to generate a weighting variable to correct for the underrepresentation of the younger age group (aged from twenty to thirty-nine) in the sample.

CHINA SURVEY

The China survey was conducted from March through June 2002, in cooperation with the Institute of Sociology of Chinese Academy of Social Sciences. It yielded 3,183 valid cases out of 3,752 sampled cases for a response rate of 84.1%. The sample represents the adult population over eighteen years of age residing in family households at the time of the survey, excluding those living in the Tibetan Autonomous Region. A stratified multistage area sampling procedure with probabilities proportional to size measures (PPS) was employed to select the sample.

The Primary Sampling Units (PSUs) employed in the sample design are counties (xian) in rural areas and cities (shi) in urban areas. In province-level municipalities, districts (qu) were used as the PSU. Before selection, counties were stratified by region and geographical characteristic and cities or districts by region and size. A total of sixty-seven cities or districts and sixty-two counties were selected as the primary sampling units, distributed among all province-level administrative units except Tibet. The secondary sampling units (SSUs) were townships (xiang) and districts (qu) or streets (jiedao). The third stage of selection was geared to administrative villages in rural areas and neighborhood committees (juweihui) or community committees (shequ weiyuanhui) in urban areas. We selected 249 administrative villages and 247 neighborhood or community committees in the third stage of the sampling process. A total of 496 sampling units were selected. Households were used at the fourth stage of sampling.

In the selection of PSUs, the National Statistical Bureau's 1999 volume of population statistics (Guojia tongjiju renkou tongjisi 1999) was used as the basic source for constructing the sampling frame. The number of family households for each county or city was taken as the measure of size (MOS) in the PPS selection process.

For the successive stages of sampling, population data were obtained from the All China Women's Association (ACWA), using data collected by that organization for a 2000 survey on women's status in China. For areas not covered in the ACWA survey, we asked local ACWA chapters to collect sampling data for us. For all village and neighborhood committee levels, household registration (*hukou*) lists were obtained. The lists were used as the sampling frame for the fourth stage of the sampling process.

The response rate for urban areas was lower than that for the rural areas. For urban area, the response rate was 82.5%, and rural areas it was 86.5%. Weighting variables for the sample were calculated along the three dimensions of gender, age, and educational level using the method of raking.[3]

The questionnaire used in mainland China varied from the core questionnaire used in the other societies in two ways. First, for all the questions in the core questionnaire asking respondents to compare the current situation in their society to that of the authoritarian past, we asked respondents to compare the current situation with that in Mao's period. Second, the questionnaire repeated some questions used in our 1993 mainland China survey, to facilitate possible cross-time comparison.

Retired middle-school teachers were employed as interviewers for the survey. Before interviews started, our collaborators in China contacted the association of retired middle-school teachers in the Dongcheng and Haidian districts in Beijing to ask their help in identifying newly retired teachers. We invited retired teachers aged fifty-five to sixty-two to apply for jobs as interviewers. About 150 retired teachers applied, and we chose sixty-seven as interviewers. The interviewers went through an intensive training program, which introduced basic concepts of social science research, survey sampling, and interview techniques, and familiarized them with the questionnaire to be used in the survey. After a course of lectures, the interviewers practiced among themselves and then conducted practice interviews with residents of a rural village near Beijing. At the end of the training course, interviewers were subjected to a rigorous test.

The mainland China team adopted two measures of quality control. First, we sent letters to prospective respondents, stating that an interviewer would come to his or her home to conduct an interview within a month. The letter included a self-addressed envelope and an evaluation form asking the respondent to report 1) whether the interviewer arrived as promised, and 2) the respondent's evaluation of the interviewer's attitude toward his or her job. Second, field supervisors randomly checked 5% of respondents to evaluate the quality of the interview. We informed interviewers about the control mechanisms to deter them from cheating.

Mandarin was used for most interviews. Interviewers were authorized to hire interpreters to deal with respondents unable to understand Mandarin.

APPENDIX 2

Research Protocol

The eight teams who administered the surveys adopted the following standards.

- *National probability samples* that give every citizen an equal chance of being selected for an interview. Whether using census household lists or a multistage area approach, the method for selecting sampling units is always randomized. The samples can be stratified, or weights can be applied, to ensure coverage of rural areas and minority populations in their correct proportions. As a result, samples represent the adult, voting-age population in each political system surveyed.
- A *standard questionnaire instrument* which contains a core module of identical or functionally equivalent questions across countries. Wherever possible, theoretical concepts are measured with multiple items in order to enable testing for construct validity. Item wording is determined by balancing various criteria, including the research themes emphasized in the survey, the comprehensibility of the item to lay respondents, and the demonstrated effectiveness of the item in previous surveys.
- *Intensive training of fieldworkers*, including supervisors and fieldwork managers. We recruit interviewers from among university graduates, senior social science undergraduates, or professional survey interviewers. All managers and supervisors have extensive field experience. Field teams pass through intensive, week-long training programs to become familiarized with our research instrument, sampling methods, and the cultural and ethical contexts of the interview. Guidelines are codified in instruction manuals that spell out procedures for the selection and replacement of samples, the validation of interview records, and the etiquette of conducting interviews.
- *Face-to-face interviews* in respondents' homes or workplaces in the language of the respondent's choice. In multilingual countries, local-language translations are prepared with the goal of accommodating every language group whose members

constitute at least 5% of the population. To check for accuracy, the local-language versions are screened through blind back-translation by a different translator and any discrepancies are corrected. Interviewers are required to record contextual information on any situations encountered during the interview.

• *Adherence to ethical codes with respect to studying human subjects.* Respondents are asked for voluntary consent to participate in the interview. Researchers are to pay due attention to any potential political, physical, or other risk to the respondent before, during, or after the interview. The privacy of the respondents is protected. The individual questionnaires and survey data are archived in such a manner that they cannot be linked to the individual respondent.

• *Quality control* by means of strict protocols for fieldwork supervision. To ensure data quality, all interview teams travel together under the direction of a field supervisor. Interviewers are debriefed each evening and instructed to return to the sampled household to finish any incomplete returns. Supervisors undertake random back-checks with respondents to ensure that sampling and interviews were conducted correctly.

• *Quality checks* are enforced at every stage of data conversion to ensure that information from paper returns is edited, coded, and entered correctly for purposes of computer analysis. Machine-readable data are generated by trained data entry operators and a minimum of 10% of the data is entered twice by independent teams for purposes of cross-checking. Data cleaning involves checks for illegal and logically inconsistent values.

APPENDIX 3

Coding Scheme for Open-Ended Question on Understanding of Democracy

The Three-Digit Codes for Popular Understanding of Democracy

100 *Interpreting democracy in generic (populist) terms*
110 **Popular sovereignty**
111 Government of the people

120 **Government by the people**
121 People as their own master
122 Power of the people

130 **Government for the people**
131 Putting people's interest first
132 Care for people
133 Responsive to people's need
134 Governing in the interest of general welfare

140 **Absence of nondemocratic arrangements**
141 No dictator
142 No repression

200 *Interpreting a democracy in terms of some key elements of liberal democracy*
210 **Freedom and civil liberty**
211 Freedom in general
212 Freedom of speech/press/expression
213 Freedom of association
214 Political liberty
215 Protection of individual/human rights
216 Freedom from government repression

217 Freedom of participation
218 Freedom of belief
219 Freedom of individual choice

220 Political equality
221 One person, one vote
222 Equality before the law/justice
223 Nondiscrimination

230 Democratic institutions and process
231 Election, popular vote, or electoral choice
232 Parliament
233 Separation of power or check-and-balance
234 Competitive party system
235 Power rotation
236 Rule of law
237 Independent judicial
238 Majority rule
239 Respect for minority rights

250 Participation and citizen empowerment
251 Ability to change government
252 Voting
253 Direct participation
254 Demonstration
255 Voice one's concern

260 Social pluralism
261 Open society
262 Pluralist society

300 *Interpreting democracy in terms of social and economic system*
310 Free economy
311 Free market
312 Private properties/ownership
313 Free and fair competition
314 Personal economic opportunities
315 No central planning

320 Equality, justice, or fraternity
321 Social equality
322 Social justice
323 Fraternity
324 Equality of opportunities
325 Social rights or social entitlements
326 Welfare state
327 Socialism

328 Worker participation

330 Socioeconomic performance
331 Solve unemployment
332 Find anyone a job
333 Providing social welfare
334 Taking good care of the weak

400 Interpreting democracy in terms of good government
410 Good governance
411 Honesty
412 Responsible
413 Openness or transparent government
414 Fair treatment
415 Efficiency
416 No corruption
417 Law-abiding government (rule by law)
418 Social stability
419 Law and order

420 Reform in general
421 Political reform
422 Economic reform

500 Interpreting democracy in term of individual behaviors
510 Democratic style
511 Communication
512 Compromise
513 Rational
514 Tolerance
515 Taking into account all parties concerned
516 Freedom within legal limits
517 Respect for others' rights
518 No extremism

520 Duties
521 Citizen duties
522 Action within the limits of law
523 Bound by law

530 Individualism
531 Respect for individual privacy
532 Independence
533 Self-reliance
534 Having one's own views
535 Self-responsibility
536 Responsibility for one's own action/decision

540 Trust

600 *Interpreting democracy in other broad and abstract terms*

610 Political system

611 Governmental institution

612 Decentralization (local self-government)

620 Nationalism and statism

621 Better country

622 Wealthy state

623 National independence

624 Development of elite

625 Individual less important than nation

630 Stable and cohesive society

631 Patriotism

632 Solidarity

633 Harmony

634 No chaos, anarchy, or disorder

640 Other lofty elements

641 World peace

642 The commonwealth of the world

700 *Conditions or prerequisites for democracy*

710 Gradualism

711 Incremental

712 It takes time

713 No radicalism

720 Prerequisites

721 Democratic aptitude of citizens

722 Economic condition

723 Level of education

724 Fit our country's own conditions

800 *Evaluation of democracy or democratic regime*

810 Positive appraisal of democracy in general

811 The best or the better

812 Progressive

813 Universal acceptance

814 Global trend

820 Negative appraisal of democracy in general

821 Corrupt

822 Inefficient

823 Unstable, chaotic, anarchy

824 Conflict

825   Lead to injustice
826   Obstruct economic development
827   Focuses too much on individual interests, the worst system
828   Does not exist
829   We cannot have democracy

840   Positive appraisal of one's own country's (e.g., Taiwan's) democracy

850   Negative appraisal of one's own country's (e.g., Taiwan's) democracy

900   Reference or cognitive association
910   Country reference
911   Like United States, United Kingdom, Japan, etc.
912   Not like North Korea, etc.

920   Political figures (e.g., Sun Yat-sen, Lee Teng-hui, Abraham Lincoln, etc.)
921   Political parties or groups (e.g., DPP, KMT, etc.)
922   Other associations (state, politics, society)

097   No substance in answer
098   Don't know
099   No answer

TABLE 16.1   **DATA TRANSFORMATION FOR TEN CONDENSED CATEGORIES FOR PRODUCING A TABLE OF CUMULATIVE FREQUENCY DISTRIBUTION**

UNDERSTANDING DEMOCRACY AS:	CODES
1. Freedom and liberty	210–219
2. Political rights, institutions, and process	220–262
3. Market economy	310–315
4. Social equality and justice	320–334
5. Good government	400–422
6. In generic and/or populist terms	100–199
7. In other abstract and positive terms	500–642; 810–814
8. In negative terms	820–829
9. Others	Not listed

APPENDIX 4

Question Wording

POPULAR UNDERSTANDING OF DEMOCRACY

The meaning of democracy:

What does democracy mean to you? What else?

Or

What for you is the meaning of the word *democracy*? What else? (OPEN-ENDED; ALLOW UP TO THREE RESPONSES)

EVALUATION OF REGIME TRANSITION

Evaluate the old regime:

Where would you place our country on this scale during the period of [name of the most recent government under authoritarian rule]? (RATING BOARD)

Evaluate the current regime:

Where would you place our country under the present government? (RATING BOARD)

APPRAISING DEMOCRATIC INSTITUTIONS

Democratic Citizenship:

I have here other statements. For each statement, would you say you STRONGLY AGREE, SOMEWHAT AGREE, SOMEWHAT DISAGREE, or STRONGLY DISAGREE?

1. I think I have the ability to participate in politics.
2. Sometimes politics and government seem so complicated that a person like me can't really understand what is going on.
3. The nation is run by a powerful few and ordinary citizens cannot do much about it.
4. People like me don't have any influence over what the government does.

Perceptions of Corruption:

How widespread do you think corruption and bribe-taking are in your local/municipal government? Would you say...(SHOWCARD)?

1. Hardly anyone is involved
2. Not a lot of officials are corrupt
3. Most officials are corrupt
4. Almost everyone is corrupt

How widespread do you think corruption and bribe-taking are in the national government [in capital city]? Would you say...(SHOWCARD)?

1. Hardly anyone is involved
2. Not a lot of officials are corrupt
3. Most officials are corrupt
4. Almost everyone is corrupt

Have you or anyone you know personally witnessed an act of corruption or bribe-taking by a politician or government official in the past year? IF WITNESSED: Did you personally witness it or were you told about it by a family member or friend who personally witnessed it?

1. Personally witnessed
2. Told about it by a family member who personally witnessed
3. Told about it by a friend who personally witnessed

Institutional Trust:

I am going to name a number of institutions. For each one, please tell me how much trust you have in it. Is it: a great deal of trust, quite a lot of trust, not very much trust, or none at all?

The courts
The national government [in the capital city]
Political parties [not any specific party]
Parliament
Civil service
The military
The police
Local government
Newspapers
Television
The electoral commission [specify institution by name]
Nongovernmental organizations or NGOs

SUPPORT FOR DEMOCRACY

Desirability:

Here is a scale: 1 means complete dictatorship and 10 means complete democracy. To what extent would you want our country to be democratic now? (RATING BOARD)

Suitability:

Here is a similar scale of 1 to 10 measuring the extent to which people think democracy is suitable for our country. If "1" means that democracy is completely unsuitable for [name of country] today and "10" means that it is completely suitable, where would you place our country today? (RATING BOARD)

Efficacy:

Which of the following statements comes closer to your own view? (STATEMENT CARD)

1. Democracy cannot solve our society's problems.
2. Democracy is capable of solving the problems of our society.

Preferability:

Which of the following statements comes closest to your own opinion? (STATEMENT CARD)

1. Democracy is always preferable to any other kind of government.
2. Under some circumstances, an authoritarian government can be preferable to a democratic one.

3. For people like me, it does not matter whether we have a democratic or a nondemocratic regime.

Priority:

If you had to choose between democracy and economic development, which would you say is more important? (STATEMENT CARD)

1. Economic development is definitely more important.
2. Economic development is somewhat more important.
3. Democracy is somewhat more important.
4. Democracy is definitely more important.
5. They are both equally important.

DETACHMENT FROM AUTHORITARIANISM

Reject "strong leader":

We should get rid of parliament and elections and have a strong leader decide things.

1. Strongly agree.
2. Somewhat agree.
3. Somewhat disagree.
4. Strongly disagree.

Reject "military rule":

The military should come in to govern the country.

1. Strongly agree.
2. Somewhat agree.
3. Somewhat disagree.
4. Strongly disagree.

Reject "no opposition party":

No opposition party should be allowed to compete for power.

1. Strongly agree.
2. Somewhat agree.
3. Somewhat disagree.
4. Strongly disagree.

Reject "experts decide everything":

> We should get rid of parliament and elections and have the experts decide everything.

> 1. Strongly agree.
> 2. Somewhat agree.
> 3. Somewhat disagree.
> 4. Strongly disagree.

SATISFACTION WITH THE WAY DEMOCRACY WORKS

> On the whole, how satisfied or dissatisfied are you with the way democracy works in our country. Are you … (SHOWCARD)?

> 1. Very satisfied
> 2. Fairly satisfied.
> 3. Not very satisfied.
> 4. Not at all satisfied.

COMMITMENT TO THE RULE OF LAW*

> We often talk about the character and style of political leaders. Please tell me how you feel about the following statements. Do you STRONGLY AGREE, SOMEWHAT AGREE, SOMEWHAT DISAGREE, or STRONGLY DIS-AGREE?

> 1. "When the country is facing a difficult situation, it is OK for the government to disregard the law in order to deal with the situation."
> 2. "The most important thing for a political leader is to accomplish his goals even if he has to ignore the established procedure."
> 3. "When judges decide important cases, they should accept the view of the executive branch."
> 4. "If the government is constantly checked [i.e., monitored and supervised] by the legislature, it cannot possibly accomplish great things."

* Disagreement with a statement is coded as showing commitment to rule of law.

WORKS CITED

Abinales, Patricio N., and Donna J. Amoroso. 2005. *State and Society in the Philippines*. Oxford: Rowman & Littlefield.

Afrobarometer. 2006a. "Citizens and the State in Africa: New Results from Afrobarometer Round 3." Afrobarometer Working Paper no. 61, Afrobarometer, East Lansing, MI. http://www.afrobarometer.org/papers/AfropaperNo61.pdf.

——. 2006b. "The Status of Democracy 2005–2006: Findings from Afrobarometer Round 3 for 18 Countries." Afrobarometer Briefing Paper no. 40, Afrobarometer, East Lansing, MI. http://www.afrobarometer.org/papers/AfrobriefNo40_revised16nov06.pdf.

Albritton, Robert B., and Thawilwadee Bureekul. 2001. "Developing Democracy Under a New Constitution in Thailand." Paper presented at the annual meeting of the Midwest Political Science Association, Chicago, April 18–22, 2001.

——. 2002. "Support for Democracy in Thailand." Paper presented at the annual meeting of the Association of Asian Studies, Washington, D.C., April 4–7, 2002.

——. 2004. "Impacts of Asian Values on Support for Democracy in Thailand." Paper presented at the annual meeting of the Association of Asian Studies, San Diego, March 4–7, 2004.

Albritton, Robert B., Phan-ngam Gothamasan, Noree Jaisai, Manop Jitpoosa, Sunandpattira Nilchang, and Arin Sa-Idi. 1996. "Electoral Participation by Southern Thai Buddhists and Muslims." *South East Asia Research* 4 (2): 127–156.

Albritton, Robert B., and Sidthinat Prabudhanitisarn. 1997. "Culture, Region, and Thai Political Diversity." *Asian Studies Review* 21 (1): 61–82.

Alexander, Gerard. 2002. *The Sources of Democratic Consolidation*. Ithaca, NY: Cornell University Press.

Almond, Gabriel A., and Sidney Verba. 1963. *The Civic Culture: Political Attitudes and Democracy in Five Nations*. Princeton: Princeton University Press.

Ayal, Eliezer B. 1963. "Value Systems and Economic Development in Japan and Thailand." *Journal of Social Issues* 19 (1): 35–51.

Balch, George I. 1974. "Multiple Indicators in Survey Research: The Concept 'Sense of Political Efficacy.'" *Political Methodology* 1 (1): 1–43.

Batbayar, Tsedendamba. 2003. "Foreign Policy and Domestic Reform in Mongolia." *Central Asian Survey* 22 (1): 45–59.

Bauer, Joanne, and Daniel Bell, eds. 1999. *The East Asian Challenge for Human Rights*. New York: Cambridge University Press.

Bermeo, Nancy. 2003. *Ordinary People in Extraordinary Times: The Citizenry and the Breakdown of Democracy*. Princeton: Princeton University Press.

Boix, Carles, and Susan C. Stokes. 2003. "Endogenous Democratization." *World Politics* 55 (July): 517–549.

Boone, Peter. 1994. "Grassroots Macroeconomic Reform in Mongolia." *Journal of Comparative Economics* 18 (3): 329–356.

Bowie, Katherine. 1996. "The State, Capitalism, and the Struggle for Agrarian Democracy: A Local Election in Northern Thailand." Paper presented at the Sixth International Conference on Thai Studies, Chiang Mai, Thailand, October 14–17, 1996.

Bratton, Michael. 2004. "The 'Alternation Effect' in Africa." *Journal of Democracy* 15 (October): 147–158.

Bratton, Michael, Robert Mattes, and Emmanuel Gyimah-Boadi. 2005. *Public Opinion, Democracy, and Market Reform in Africa*. London: Cambridge University Press.

Bratton, Michael, and Wonbin Cho. 2006. "Where Is Africa Going? View from Below: A Compendium of Trends from 12 African Countries, 1999–2006." Afrobarometer Working Paper no. 60, Afrobarometer, East Lansing, MI. http://www.afrobarometer.org/papers/AfropaperNo60-trends.pdf.

Bremner, Brian, and Ihlwan Moon. 2002. "Cool Korea." *Business Week*, June 10: 54–58.

Brooks, Douglas H. 1998. "The Kyrgyz Republic and Mongolia." In *Social Sector Issues in Transitional Economies of Asia*, ed. Douglas Brooks and Myo Thand, 337–366. Oxford: Oxford University Press.

Bunbongkarn, Suchit. 1996. "Elections and Democratization in Thailand." In *The Politics of Elections in Southeast Asia*, ed. Robert H. Taylor, 184–200. New York: Cambridge University Press.

Carothers, Thomas. 2002. "The End of the Transition Paradigm." *Journal of Democracy* 13 (January): 5–21.

Census and Statistics Department. 2003. *Hong Kong Annual Digest of Statistics 2003*. Hong Kong: Government Logistics Department.

——. 2004. *Hong Kong Annual Digest of Statistics 2004*. Hong Kong: Government Logistics Department.

Cheng, Tun-jen. 1989. "Democratizing the Quasi-Leninist Regime in Taiwan." *World Politics* 41 (4): 471–499.

Chotiya, Parichart. 1998. "Beyond Transition in Thailand" In *Democracy in East Asia*, ed. Larry Diamond and Marc Plattner, 147–70. Baltimore: Johns Hopkins University Press.

Chu, Yun-han. 2001. "Taiwan's Unique Path to Democracy." In *Transitional Societies in Comparison: East Central Europe vs. Taiwan*, ed. National Science Council, 89–108. Frankfurt: Peter Lang.

——. 2006. "Third-Wave Democratization in East Asia: Challenges and Prospect." *ASIEN* 100 (July): 11–17.

Chu, Yun-han, Larry Diamond, and Doh Chull Shin. 2001. "Halting Progress in Korea and Taiwan." *Journal of Democracy* 12 (January): 122–136.

Chu, Yun-han, and Fu Hu. 1996. "Neo-Authoritarianism, Polarized Conflict and Populism in a Newly Democratizing Regime: Taiwan's Emerging Mass Politics." *Journal of Contemporary China* 5 (March): 23–41.

Chu, Yun-han, and Doh Chull Shin. 2005. "South Korea and Taiwan." In *Assessing the Quality of Democracy*, ed. Larry Diamond and Leonardo Morlino, 188–212. Baltimore: Johns Hopkins University Press.

CIA. 2002. *The World Factbook*. https://www.cia.gov/cia/publications/the-world -factbook/.

Citrin, Jack. 1974. "Comment: The Political Relevance of Trust in Government." *American Political Science Review* 68 (3): 973–988.

Cleary, Seamus. 1995. "Enhancing People's Participation." In *Poverty and the Transition to a Market Economy in Mongolia*, ed. Keith Griffin, 144–153. New York: St. Martin's Press.

Colton, Timothy. 2000. *Transitional Citizens: Voters and What Influences Them in the New Russia*. Cambridge, MA: Harvard University Press.

Cooter, Robert. 1997. "The Role of State Law Versus the Rule of Law: Economic Analysis of the Legal Foundations of Development." *Macroeconomics and Growth* 5 (4): 92–97.

Craig, Stephen C., Richard G. Niemi, and Glenn E. Silver. 1990. "Political Efficacy and Trust: A Report on the NES Pilot Study Items." *Political Behavior* 12 (3): 289–314.

Dahl, Robert A. 1971. *Polyarchy: Participation and Opposition*. New Haven: Yale University Press.

Dalton, Russell J. 1988. *Citizen Politics in Western Democracies: Public Opinion and Political Parties in the United States, Great Britain, West Germany, and France*. Chatham, NJ: Chatham House.

——. 1999. "Political Support in Advanced Industrial Democracies." In *Critical Citizens: Global Support for Democratic Government*, ed. Pippa Norris, 57–77. Oxford: Oxford University Press.

——. 2002. *Citizen Politics: Public Opinion and Political Parties in Advanced Industrial Democracies*. 3rd Edition. New York: Chatham House.

Danguilan-Vitug, Marites. 1990. *Kudeta: The Challenge to Philippine Democracy*. Makati, the Philippines: Philippine Center for Investigative Journalism.

De Bary, William Theodore. 1989. *The Message of the Mind in Neo-Confucianism*. New York: Columbia University Press.

——. 2004. *Nobility and Civility: Asian Ideals of Leadership and the Common Good*. Cambridge, MA: Harvard University Press.

Diamond, Larry. 1992. "Economic Development and Democracy Reconsidered." In *Reexamining Democracy: Essays in Honor of Seymour Martin Lipset*, ed. Gary Marks and Larry Diamond, 93–139. Newbury Park, CA: Sage Publications.

——. 1999. *Developing Democracy: Toward Consolidation*. Baltimore: Johns Hopkins University Press.

——. 2008. *The Spirit of Democracy: The Challenge of Building Free Societies Throughout the World*. New York: Times Books.

Diamond, Larry, and Byung-Kook Kim, eds. 2000. *Consolidating Democracy in South Korea*. Boulder, CO: Lynne Rienner Publishers.

Diamond, Larry, and Leonardo Morlino. 2004. "The Quality of Democracy: An Overview." *Journal of Democracy* 15 (October): 20–31.

Doronila, Amando. 1992. *The State, Economic Transformation, and Political Change in the Philippines 1946–1972*. Singapore: Oxford University Press.

Easton, David. 1975. "A Re-Assessment of the Concept of Political Support." *British Journal of Political Science* 5 (4): 435–457.

Easton, David, and Jack Dennis. 1967. "The Child's Acquisition of Regime Norms: Political Efficacy." *American Political Science Review* 61 (1): 25–38.

Embree, John F. 1950. "Thailand—A Loosely Structured Social System." *American Anthropologist* 52 (2): 191–193.

Finch, Christopher. 2002. "Mongolia in 2001: Political Consolidation and Continued Economic Reform." *Asian Survey* 42 (1): 39–45.

Finifter, Ada W., and Ellen Mickiewicz. 1992. "Redefining the Political System of the USSR: Mass Support for Political Change." *American Political Science Review* 86 (4): 857–874.

Fish, M. Steven. 1998. "Mongolia: Democracy without Prerequisites." *Journal of Democracy* 9, no. 3: 127–141.

Flanagan, Scott, Shinsaku Kohei, Ichiro Miyake, Bradley M. Richardson, and Joji Watanuki. 1991. *The Japanese Voter*. New Haven: Yale University Press.

Freedom House, 1978–. *Freedom in the World: The Annual Survey of Political Rights and Civil Liberties*. Annual. New York: Freedom House. Some issues are available at www.freedomhouse.org.

Freedom House. N.d. "*Freedom in the World* Country Ratings 1972–2006." http://www.freedomhouse.org/uploads/FIWrank7305.xls.

Fritz, Verena. 2002. "Mongolia: Dependent Democratization." *Journal of Communist Studies and Transition Politics* 18 (4): 75–100.

Fukuyama, Francis. 1995. "The Primacy of Culture." *Journal of Democracy* 6 (January): 7–14.

———. 1998. "The Illusion of Asian Exceptionalism." In *Democracy in East Asia*, ed. Larry Diamond and Marc F. Plattner, 224–227. Baltimore: Johns Hopkins University Press.

Garam Research Institute. 2003. *2003 Korea Democracy Barometer: A Codebook*. Seoul: Garam Research Institute.

Ginsburg, Tom. 1998. "Mongolia in 1997: Deepening Democracy." *Asian Survey* 38 (1): 64–68.

Goldman, Merle. 1994. *Sowing the Seeds of Democracy in China: Political Reform in the Deng Xiaoping Era*. Cambridge, MA: Harvard University Press.

———. 2005. *From Comrade to Citizen: The Struggle for Political Rights in China*. Cambridge, MA: Harvard University Press.

Goldman, Merle, and Elizabeth J. Perry. 2002. *Changing Meanings of Citizenship in Modern China*. Cambridge, MA: Harvard University Press.

Grossholtz, Jean. 1973. "Philippines 1973: Whither Marcos?" *Asian Survey* 14 (1): 101–112.

Gunther, Richard, Hans-Jurgen Puhle, and Nikiforos P. Diamandouros. 1995. "Introduction." In *The Politics of Democratic Consolidation: Southern Europe in Comparative Perspective*, ed. Richard Gunther, Nikiforos P. Diamandouros, and Hans-Jurgen Puhle, 1–32. Baltimore: Johns Hopkins University Press.

Guojia tongjiju renkou tongjisi [National Statistical Bureau, Department of Population Statistics]. 1999. *Zhongguo renkou tongji nianjian* [Population Statistics of the People's Republic of China]. Beijing: Guojia tongji chubanshe.

Haggard, Stephen. 2000. *The Political Economy of the Asian Financial Crisis*. Washington, D.C.: Institute for International Economics.

Håvard, Hegre. 2001. "Toward a Democratic Civil Peace? Democracy, Political Change, and Civil War, 1816–1992." *American Political Science Review* 95 (1): 33–48.

Hawes, Gary. 1987. *The Philippine State and the Marcos Regime: The Politics of Export*. Ithaca, NY: Cornell University Press.

Hedman, Eva-Lotta E., and John T. Sidel. 2000. *Philippine Politics and Society in the Twentieth Century: Colonial Legacies, Post-Colonial Trajectories*. New York: Routledge.

Hernandez, Carolina. 1985. "Constitutional Authoritarianism and the Prospects of Democracy in the Philippines." *Journal of International Affairs* 38 (2): 243–258.

Hill, Kim Quaile. 1982. "Retest Reliability for Trust in Government and Governmental Responsiveness Measures: A Research Note." *Political Methodology* 8:33–46.

Hong Kong Council of Social Service. 2001. *Submissions to the Panel on Welfare Services, the Legislative Council of the HKSAR*. Hong Kong: Hong Kong Council of Social Service.

Huntington, Samuel P. 1968. *Political Order in Changing Societies*. New Haven: Yale University Press.

———. 1991. *The Third Wave: Democratization in the Late Twentieth Century*. Norman: University of Oklahoma Press.

Huntington, Samuel P., and Joan M. Nelson. 1976. *No Easy Choice: Political Participation in Developing Countries*. Cambridge, MA: Harvard University Press.

Hutchcroft, Paul D. 1991. "Oligarchs and Cronies in the Philippine State: The Politics of Patrimonial Plunder." *World Politics* 43 (April): 414–450.

Inglehart, Ronald. 1988. "The Renaissance of Political Culture." *The American Political Science Review* 82 (December): 1203–1230.

———. 1990. *Culture Shift: In Advanced Industrial Society*. Princeton: Princeton University Press.

———. 1997. *Modernization and Post-Modernization: Cultural, Economic, and Social Change in 43 Societies*. Princeton: Princeton University Press.

———. 2000. "Culture and Democracy." In *Culture Matters: How Values Shape Human Progress*, ed. Lawrence E. Harrison and Samuel P. Huntington, 80–97. New York: Basic Books.

Inglehart, Ronald, and Christian Welzel. 2005. *Modernization, Cultural Change, and Democracy: The Human Development Sequence*. New York: Cambridge University Press.

Inkeles, Alex. 1969. "Making Men Modern: On the Causes and Consequences of Individual Change in Six Developing Countries." *The American Journal of Sociology* 75 (September): 208–225.

Inkeles, Alex, and Larry Diamond. 1980. "Personal Qualities as a Reflection of Level of National Development." In *The Quality of Life: Comparative Studies*, ed. Frank M. Andrews and Alexander Szalai, 73–109. London: Sage.

Inkeles, Alex, and David Smith. 1974. *Becoming Modern: Individual Change in Six Developing Countries*. Cambridge, MA: Harvard University Press.

Jang, Soo Chan. 2000. "Driving Engine or Rent-Seeking Super-Cartel." Ph.D. diss., Michigan State University.

Jaung, Hoon. 2000. "Electoral Politics and Political Parties." In *Institutional Reform and Democratic Consolidation in Korea*, ed. Larry Diamond and Doh Chull Shin, 43–71. Stanford: Hoover Institution Press.

Kabashima, Ikuo, Jōji Watanuki, Ichirō Miyake, Yoshiaki Kobayashi, and Ken'ichi Ikeda. 1998. *JES II Kōdobukku* [Japanese Electoral Study 2 Codebook]. Vol. 6. of *Hendō suru Nihonjin no senkyo kōdō* [Changing Japanese Voting Behavior]. Tokyo: Bokutakusha.

Kang, David C. 2002. *Crony Capitalism: Corruption and Development in South Korea and the Philippines*. Cambridge: Cambridge University Press.

Karnow, Stanley. 1989. *In Our Image: America's Empire in the Philippines.* New York: Random House.

Kerkvliet, Benedict J., and Resil B. Mojares, eds. 1992. *From Marcos to Aquino: Local Perspectives on Political Transition in the Philippines.* Honolulu: University of Hawaii Press.

Kil, Soong Hoom. 2001. "Development of Korean Politics." In *Understanding Korean Politics*, ed. Soong Hoom Kil and Chung-In Moon, 33–69. Albany: State University of New York Press.

Kim, Byung-Kook. 2000. "Party Politics in South Korea's Democracy." In *Consolidating Democracy in South Korea*, ed. Larry Diamond and Byung-kook Kim, 53–85. Boulder, CO: Lynne Rienner.

Kim, Jae Han, and Arend Lijphart. 1997. "Consensus Democracy and Power Structure in Korea." *Korean Political Science Review* 31 (1): 99–120.

Kim, Kwang Suk, and Sung Duk Hong. 1997. *Accounting for Rapid Economic Growth in Korea, 1963–95.* Seoul: Korea Development Institute.

Kim, Samuel, ed. 2003. *Korea's Democratization.* New York: Cambridge University Press.

Kim, Sunhyuk. 2000. *The Politics of Democratization in Korea.* Pittsburgh: University of Pittsburgh Press.

King, Gary. Christopher J. L. Murray, Joshua A. Salomon, and Ajay Tandon. 2004. "Enhancing the Validity and Cross-Cultural Comparability of Survey Research." *American Political Science Review* 98 (1): 191–207.

Klingemann. Hans-Dieter. 1999. "Mapping Political Support in the 1990s: A Global Analysis." In *Critical Citizens: Global Support for Democratic Government*, ed. Pippa Norris, 31–56. Oxford: Oxford University Press.

Korea National Statistical Office. 2001. *Annual Reports on Urban Households.* Daejun, South Korea: Korea National Statistical Office. http://www.nso.go.kr.

———. 2003. *World Development Indicators 2002.* Daejun, South Korea: Korea National Statistical Office. http://www.nso.go.kr.

Kuan, Hsin-chi. 1991. "Power Dependence and Democratic Transition: The Case of Hong Kong." *China Quarterly* 128 (December): 774–793.

Kuan, Hsin-chi, and Siu-kai Lau. 1988. *Mass Media and Politics in Hong Kong.* Hong Kong: Centre for Hong Kong Studies, Chinese University of Hong Kong.

———. 2002. "Between Liberal Autocracy and Democracy: Democratic Legitimacy in Hong Kong." *Democratization* 9 (4): 58–76.

La Mont, Robert. 2002. "Some Means of Addressing Judicial Corruption in Mongolia." http://www.forum.mn/res_mat/Judicial%20Corruption%20in%20Mongolia.pdf.

Lam, Wai-man. 2003. "An Alternative Understanding of Political Participation: Challenging the Myth of Political Indifference in Hong Kong." *International Journal of Public Administration* 26 (5): 473–496.

———. 2004. *Understanding the Political Culture of Hong Kong: The Paradox of Activism and Depoliticization.* Armonk, NY: M.E. Sharpe.

Landé, Carl. 1965. *Leaders, Factions, and Parties: The Structure of Philippine Politics*. New Haven: Yale University Press.

Laothamatas, Anek. 1996. "A Tale of Two Democracies: Conflicting Perception of Elections and Democracy in Thailand." In *The Politics of Elections in Southeast Asia*, ed. Robert H. Taylor, 201–223. New York: Cambridge University Press.

———. 1997. "Development and Democratization: A Theoretical Introduction with Reference to the Southeast Asia and East Asian Cases." In *Democratization in Southeast and East Asia*, ed. Anek Laothamatas, 1–20. Singapore: ISEAS.

Lapitan, A. E. 1989. "The Re-Democratization of the Philippines: Old Wine in a New Bottle." *Asian Profile* 17 (3): 235–242.

Larkin, John. 2001. "Kim Dae Jung Comes Up Short." *Far Eastern Economic Review* 24 (May): 18–24.

Latinobarómetro. 2005. *Latinobarómetro Report 2005: 1995–2005, A Decade of Public Opinion*. Santiago: Corporación Latinobarómetro.

Lau, Siu-kai. 1998. *Democratization, Poverty of Political Leaders, and Political Inefficacy in Hong Kong*. Hong Kong: Hong Kong Institute of Asia-Pacific Studies, Chinese University of Hong Kong.

Lau, Siu-kai, and Hsin-chi Kuan. 1988. *The Ethos of the Hong Kong Chinese*. Hong Kong: Chinese University Press.

———. 1995. "The Attentive Spectators: Political Participation of the Hong Kong Chinese." *Journal of Northeast Asian Studies* 14 (1): 3–24.

Lee Teng-hui. 1997. "Taiwan jingji fazhan de chenggong yuanyu xianzheng gaige de shunli tuixing." [Taiwan's success in economic development was based on the smooth promotion of constitutional reform]. In *Yangxin luntan: cong Li Denghui zongtong de shengming gongtongti tanqi*, eds. Chen Shenghong and Nian Mingchang, 7–25. Taipei: Yangxin wenjiao jijinhui.

Lemco, Jonathan. 2002. "Korea: Still the Best Comeback Story in Asia." *Asia Times*, October 9.

Li, Lianjiang, and Kevin J. O'Brien. 1999. "The Struggle over Village Elections." In *The Paradox of China's Post-Mao Reforms*, ed. Roderick MacFarquhar and Merle Goldman, 129–144. Cambridge, MA: Harvard University Press.

Li, Pang-kwong. 2000. *Hong Kong from Britain to China: Political Cleavages, Electoral Dynamics and Institutional Changes*. Aldershot, U.K.: Ashgate.

Lim, Hy-Sop. 2000. "Historical Development of Civil Social Movements in Korea." *Korea Journal* 40 (5): 5–25.

Lim, Seong-Ho. 1998. "A Paradox of Korean Democracy." *Korea and World Affairs* 22 (4): 522–538.

———. 2002. "Divided Government and Legislative Politics in South Korea." Presented at the annual meeting of the American Political Science Association held in Boston, August 29–September 1, 2002.

Ling, L. H. M., and Chih-yu Shih. 1998. "Confucianism with a Liberal Face: The Meaning of Democratic Politics in Postcolonial Taiwan." *The Review of Politics* 60 (1): 55–82.

Linz, Juan. 1990. "Transition to Democracy". *The Washington Quarterly* 13 (3): 143–163.

Linz, Juan, and Alfred Stepan. 1978. *The Breakdown of Democratic Regimes*. Baltimore: Johns Hopkins University Press.

——. 1996a. *Problems of Democratic Transition and Consolidation: Southern Europe, South America, and Post-Communist Europe*. Baltimore: Johns Hopkins University Press.

——.1996b. "Toward Consolidated Democracies." *Journal of Democracy* 7 (April): 14–33.

——. 2001. "Toward Consolidated Democracies." In *The Global Divergence of Democracies*, ed. Larry Diamond and Marc F. Plattner, 93–112. Baltimore: Johns Hopkins University Press.

Lipset, Seymour Martin. 1959. "Some Social Requisites of Democracy: Economic Development and Political Legitimacy." *American Political Science Review* 53 (March): 69–105.

——. 1981. *Political Man: The Social Bases of Politics*. Baltimore: Johns Hopkins University Press.

Lo, Shiu-hing. 1995. *The Politics of Democratization in Hong Kong*. Ann Arbor: University of Michigan.

Logerfo, Jim. 1996. "Attitudes Toward Democracy among Rural Northern Thais." *Asian Survey* 36 (9): 904–923.

Lu, Xiaobo. 2000. *Cadres and Corruption the Organizational Involution of the Chinese Communist Party*. Stanford: Stanford University Press.

Madsen, Douglas. 1987. "Political Self-Efficacy Tested." *American Political Science Review* 81 (2): 571–581.

Magno, Alexander. 1992. "The Altered Terrain of Electoral Politics in the Philippines." Paper presented at the East West Center, University of Hawaii.

Manapat, Ricardo.1991. *Some are Smarter than Others: The History of Marcos' Crony Capitalism*. New York: Aletheia Publications.

Mao Zedong. 1949. "On People's Democratic Dictatorship." In *Selected Works of Mao Tse-tung*. Vol. 4, 411–424. Beijing: Foreign Languages Press, 1961.

May, Ronald James, and Francisco Nemenzo. 1987. *The Philippines after Marcos*. New York: St. Martin's Press.

McCargo, Duncan. 2001. *Politics and the Press in Thailand*. London: Routledge.

McCoy, Alfred W., and Ed C. de Jesus. 1982. *Philippine Social History*. Sydney: Allen & Unwin.

McDonough, Peter, Samuel Barnes, and Antonio Lopez Pina. 1994. "The Nature of Political Support and Legitimacy in Spain." *Comparative Political Studies* 7 (3): 349–380.

Miller, Arthur H., Vicki L. Hesli, and William M. Reisinger. 1997. "Conceptions of Democracy across Mass and Elites in Post-Soviet Russia." *British Journal of Political Science* 27 (April): 157–190.

Miners, Norman. 1975. *The Government and Politics of Hong Kong*. Hong Kong: Oxford University Press.

Mo, Jongryn. 1998. "Political Culture, Democracy, and the Economic Crisis in Korea." *International Studies Review* 2 (1): 85–100.

——. 2001. "Political Culture and Legislative Gridlock: Politics of Economic Reform in Precrisis Korea." *Comparative Political Studies* 34 (5): 467–492.

Mongolian Chamber of Commerce and Industry. 2000. *Corruption in the Business Sector, Mongolia*. Ulaanbaatar: Mongolian Chamber of Commerce and Industry.

National Statistical Office of Mongolia. 2001. *Mongolian Statistical Yearbook*. Ulaanbaatar: National Statistical Office of Mongolia.

Montero, Jose Ramon, Richard Gunther, and Mariano Torcal. 1997. "Democracy in Spain: Legitimacy, Discontent, and Disaffection." *Studies in Comparative International Development* 32 (3):124–160.

Moon, Chung-In. 1994. "Changing State-Business Relations in South Korea since 1980." In *Business and Government in Industrializing Asia*, ed. Andrew MacIntyre, 142–166. Ithaca, NY: Cornell University Press.

Moon, Chung-In, and Yong-Cheol Kim. 1996. "A Circle of Paradox: Development, Politics and Democracy in South Korea." In *Democracy and Development*, ed. Adrian Leftwich, 139–167. Oxford: Polity Press.

Morlino, Lenardo, and Jeso Ramon Montero. 1995. "Legitimacy and Democracy in Southern Europe." In *The Politics of Democratic Consolidation: Southern Europe in Comparative Perspective*, ed. Richard Gunther, Nikiforos P Diamandouros, Hans-Jürgen Puhle, 231–260. Baltimore: Johns Hopkins Press.

Narthsupha, Chatthip. 1970. *Foreign Trade, Foreign Finance, and the Economic Development of Thailand, 1956–65*. Bangkok: Prae Pittaya.

Nathan, Andrew J. 1985. *Chinese Democracy*. New York: Knopf.

——. 2003. "China's Changing of the Guard: Authoritarian Resilience." *Journal of Democracy* 14, no. 1 (January): 6–17.

Nathan, Andrew J., and Bruce Gilley. 2003. *China's New Rulers: The Secret Files*. New York: New York Review of Books.

Nathan, Andrew J., and Tianjian Shi. 1993. "Cultural Requisites for Democracy in China: Findings from a Survey." *Daedalus* 122:95–124.

National Statistical Office. 2003. *Summary of Survey: Public Opinion on Corruption*. Bangkok: National Statistical Office.

Neher, Clark D. 1996. "The Transition to Democracy in Thailand." *Asian Perspective* 20 (2): 301–321.

Niemi, Richard G., Stephen C. Craig, and Franco Mattei. 1991. "Measuring Internal Political Efficacy in the 1988 National Election Study." *American Political Science Review* 85 (December): 1407–1413.

Nixson, Frederick, Bat Suvd, and Bernard Walters, eds. 2000. "Poverty in Mongolia." In *The Mongolian Economy: A Manual of Applied Economics for a Country in Transition*, 189–204. Cheltenham, U.K.: Edward Elgar.

Noble, Lela Garner. 1976. "The Moro National Liberation Front in the Philippines." *Pacific Affairs* 49 (3): 405–424.

O'Brien, Kevin J. 1990. *Reform without Liberalization: China's National People's Congress and the Politics of Institutional Change*. New York: Cambridge University Press.

——. 1994a. "Agents and Remonstrators: Role Accumulation by Chinese People's Congress Deputies." *China Quarterly* 138: 359–379.

——. 1994b. "Chinese People's Congresses and Legislative Embeddedness: Understanding Early Organizational Development." *Comparative Political Studies* 27 (1): 80–109.

O'Brien, Kevin J., and Lianjiang Li. 2000. "Accommodating 'Democracy' in a One-Party State: Introducing Village Elections in China." *China Quarterly* 162: 465–489.

O'Donnell, Guillermo A. 1973. *Modernization and Bureaucratic Authoritarianism: Studies in South American Politics*. Berkeley: Institution of International Studies, University of California.

——. 1994. "Delegative Democracy." *Journal of Democracy* 5, no. 1 (January): 55–69.

——. 1996. "Illusions about Consolidation." *Journal of Democracy* 7, no. 2 (April): 34–51.

——. 1998. "Horizontal Accountability in New Democracies." *Journal of Democracy* 9, no. 3 (July): 112–126.

O'Donnell, Guillermo, and Philippe C. Schmitter, eds. 1986a. *Transitions from Authoritarian Rule: Southern Europe*. Baltimore: Johns Hopkins University Press.

——, eds. 1986b. *Transitions from Authoritarian Rule: Tentative Conclusions about Uncertain Democracies*. Baltimore: Johns Hopkins University Press.

O'Donnell, Guillermo, Philippe C. Schmitter, and Laurence Whitehead, eds. 1986. *Transitions from Authoritarian Rule: Comparative Perspectives*. Baltimore: Johns Hopkins University Press.

OECD. 1997. *Income Distribution and Poverty in Selected OECD Countries: Annex 4. Main Trends in Income Distribution and Poverty: Evidence from Recent Studies*. (Working Party on social policy. DEELSA/ELSA/WP1(97)1/ANN4). Paris: OECD.

Overholt, William. 1986. "The Rise and Fall of Ferdinand Marcos." *Asian Survey* 26 (11): 1137–1163.

Park, Chong-Min. 1998. "The Executive Branch's Dominance over the Legislature." *Legislative Studies* 4 (2): 6–29.

Park, Jae Chang. 2002. "Political Stability and the National Assembly: An Empirical Analysis." *Review of Korean Administration* 11 (3): 32–52.

Pereira, Luiz Carlos Bresser, José María Maravall, and Adam Przeworski. 1993. *Economic Reforms in New Democracies: A Social Democratic Approach*. Cambridge: Cambridge University Press.

Perlas, Nicanor. 2000. *Shaping Globalization: Civil Society, Cultural Power, and Threefolding*. Pasig City, the Philippines: The Center for Alternative Development Initiatives.

Pharr, Susan J. 2000. "Officials' Misconduct and Public Distrust: Japan and the Trilateral Democracies." In *Disaffected Democracies: What's Troubling the Trilateral Countries?* ed. Susan J. Pharr and Robert D. Putnam, 173–201. Princeton, NJ: Princeton University Press.

Pharr, Susan J., and Robert Putnam, eds. 2000. *Disaffected Democracies: What's Troubling the Trilateral Countries?* Princeton: Princeton University Press.

Phatharathanunth, Somchai. 2002. "Civil Society and Democratization in Thailand: A Critique of Elite Democracy." In *Reforming Thai Politics*, ed. Duncan McCargo, 125–142. Copenhagen: Nordic Institute of Asian Studies.

Phongpaichit, Pasuk, and Chris Baker. 2000. *Thailand's Crisis*. Chiang Mai, Thailand: Silkworm Books.

Phongpaichit, Pasuk, Nualnoi Treerat, Youngyuth Chaiyapong, and Chris Baker. 2000. *Corruption in the Public Sector in Thailand: Perceptions and Experience of Households*. Bangkok: Chulalongkorn Political Economy Center.

Przeworski, Adam. 1991. *Democracy and the Market: Political and Economic Reform in Eastern Europe and Latin American*. Cambridge: Cambridge University Press.

Przeworski, Adam, Michael E. Alvarez, Jose Antonio Cheibub, and Fernando Limongi. 2000. *Democracy and Development*. New York: Cambridge University Press.

Putnam, Robert D. 2000. *Bowling Alone: The Collapse and Revival of American Community*. New York: Simon & Schuster.

Putnam, Robert D., Robert Leonardi, and Raffaella Y. Nanetti. 1993. *Making Democracy Work: Civic Traditions in Modern Italy*. Princeton: Princeton University Press.

Putnam, Robert D., Susan J. Pharr, and Russell J. Dalton. 2000. "Introduction: What's Troubling the Trilateral Democracies." In *Disaffected Democracies: What's Troubling the Trilateral Countries?* ed. Susan J. Pharr and Robert D. Putnam, 3–30. Princeton: Princeton University Press.

Putzel, James. 1995. "Democratization and Clan Politics: The 1992 Philippine Elections." *South East Asia Research* 3 (1): 18–45.

Pye, Lucian W. 1991. "Political Culture Revisited." *Political Psychology* 12 (33):487–508.

———. 1992. *The Spirit of Chinese Politics*. Cambridge, MA: Harvard University Press.

———. 1995. "Factions and the Politics of Guanxi: Paradoxes in Chinese Administrative and Political Behaviour." *The China Journal* 34 (January): 35–53.

Rocamora, Joel. 1999. "Philippine Political Parties, Electoral System and Political Reform." A paper presented on UNPAN (United Nations Online Network in Public Administration and Finance), http://unpan1.un.org/intradoc/groups/public/documents/APCITY/UNPAN006915.pdf.

Rose, Richard. 2005. "Insiders and Outsiders: New Europe Barometer 2004." *Studies in Public Policy 404*. Glasgow: Centre for the Study of Public Policy, University of Strathclyde.

Rose, Richard, and Christian Haerpfer. 2006. "New Democracies Barometer IV: A 10-Nation Survey." *Studies in Public Policy 262*. Glasgow: Center for the Study of Public Policy, University of Strathclyde.

Rose, Richard, and Doh Chull Shin. 2001. "Democratization Backwards: The Problem of Third Wave Democracies." *British Journal of Political Science* 31 (2): 331–354.

Rose, Richard, and William Mishler. 1994. "Mass Reactions to Regime Change in Eastern Europe." *British Journal of Political Science* 24 (2): 159–182.

Rose, Richard, William Mishler, and Christian Haerpfer. 1998. *Democracy and Its Alternatives. Understanding Post-Communist Societies*. Baltimore: Johns Hopkins University Press.

Rose-Ackerman, Susan. 1999. *Corruption and Government*. Cambridge: Cambridge University Press.

Rustow, Dankwart A. 1970. "Transitions to Democracy: Toward a Dynamic Model." *Comparative Politics* 2, no. 3 (April): 337–363.

Sabloff, Paula L. W. 2001. "Genghis Khan, Father of Mongolian Democracy." In *Modern Mongolia: Reclaiming Genghis Khan*, ed. Paula L. W. Sabloff, 91–119. Philadelphia: Museum of Archeology and Anthropology, University of Pennsylvania.

———. 2002. "Why Mongolia? The Political Culture of an Emerging Democracy." *Central Asian Survey* 21 (1): 19–36.

Samudavanija, Chai-Anan. 1995. "Thailand: A Stable Semidemocracy." In *Democracy in Developing Countries*, ed. Larry Diamond, Juan Linz, and Seymour Martin Lipset, 305–346. Boulder, CO: Lynne Rienner.

Samudavanija, Chai-Anan, and Parichart Chotiya. 1998. "Beyond Transition in Thailand." In *Democracy in East Asia*, ed. Larry Diamond and Marc Plattner, 147–170. Baltimore: Johns Hopkins University Press.

Schmitter, Philippe C. and Terry Lynn Karl. 1991. "What Democracy Is and Is Not." *Journal of Democracy* 2 (July): 75–88.

Sen, Amartya. 1999. *Development as Freedom*. New York: Alfred Knopf.

Severinghaus, Sheldon. 1995. "Mongolia in 1994: Strengthening Democracy." *Asian Survey* 35 (1): 70–75.

——. 2000. "Mongolia in 1998 and 1999: Past, Present, and Future at the New Millennium." *Asian Survey* 40 (1): 130–139.

Shi, Tianjian. 1990. "The Democratic Movement in China in 1989: Dynamics and Failure." *Asian Survey* 30 (12): 1186–1205.

——. 1996. "Survey Research in China." In *Research in Micropolitics*, ed. Michael X. Delli Carpini, Huddy Leonie, and Robert Y. Shapiro, 213–250. Greenwich, CN: JAL Press.

——. 1997. *Political Participation in Beijing*. Cambridge, MA: Harvard University Press.

——. 1999a. "Mass Political Behavior in Beijing." In *The Paradox of China's Post-Mao Reform*, ed. Roderick MacFarquhar and Merle Goldman, 145–169. Cambridge, MA: Harvard University Press.

——. 1999b. "Village Committee Elections in China: Institutionalist Tactics for Democracy." *World Politics* 51 (3): 385–412.

——. 1999c. "Voting and Nonvoting in China: Voting Behavior in Plebiscitary and Limited Choice Elections." *Journal of Politics* 61 (4): 1115–1138.

——. 2001. "Cultural Impacts on Political Trust: A Comparison of Mainland China and Taiwan." *Comparative Politics* 33 (4): 401–419.

Shin, Doh Chull. 1999. *Mass Politics and Culture in Democratizing Korea*. New York: Cambridge University Press

——. 2003a. "Mass Politics, Public Opinion, and Democracy in Korea." In *Korea's Democratization*, ed. Samuel Kim, 47–77. New York: Cambridge University Press.

——. 2003b. "The Korea Democracy Barometer Surveys." Paper presented at an international conference on Asiabarometer and Social Science Research, University of Tokyo, Japan, May 6–7.

——. 2007. "Democratization: Perspectives from Global Citizenries." In *The Oxford Handbook of Political Behaviour*, ed. Russell Dalton and Hans Klingemann, 259–282. Oxford: Oxford University Press.

Shin, Doh Chull, and Huo-yan Shyu. 1997. "Political Ambivalence in South Korea and Taiwan." *Journal of Democracy* 8 (July): 109–124.

Shin, Doh Chull, and Jaechul Lee. 2006. "The Korea Democracy Barometer Surveys, 1997–2004." *Studies in Public Policy* 411. Aberdeen: Centre for the Study of Public Policy, University of Aberdeen.

Shin, Doh Chull, and Junhan Lee. 2003. Democratization and its Consequences." In *The Quality of Life in Korea*, ed. Doh Chull Shin, Conrad Rutkowski, and Chong-Min Park, 71–92. Dordrecht, the Netherlands: Kluwer Academic Publishers.

Shin, Doh Chull, and Chong-Min Park. 2003. "The Mass Public and Democratic Politics in South Korea: Exploring the Subjective World of Democratization in Flux." Asian Barometer Working Paper Series no. 15, Asian Barometer Survey, Taipei. http://www.asianbarometer.org/newenglish/publications/workingpapers/no.15.pdf.

Shin, Doh Chull, Chong-Min Park, and Jiho Jang. 2002. "The Growth of Sophistication in Democratic Politics among the Korean Mass Public." Paper presented at the annual meeting of the American Political Science Association, Boston, August 29–September 1.

Shin, Doh Chull, Chong-Min Park, Ah-Ran Hwang, Hyeon-Woo Lee, and Jiho Jang. 2003. "The Democratization of Mass Political Orientations in South Korea." *International Journal of Public Opinion Research* 15 (3): 265–284.

Shin, Doh Chull, and Jason Wells. 2005. "Is Democracy the Only Game in Town?" *Journal of Democracy* 16 (April): 88–101.

Silliman, Sidney, and Lela Garner Noble, eds. 1998. *Organizing for Democracy: NGOs, Civil Society, and the Philippine State.* Honolulu: University of Hawaii Press.

Tachibanaki, Toshiaki. 1998. *Nihon no keizai-kakusa* [Economic Inequality in Japan]. Tokyo: Iwanami.

Tanaka, Aiji. 2002. "System Support in Japan (II): How Democratic Values Have Been Fostered and Changed in Japan's Postwar and Post-Industrial Periods." *Waseda Political Studies* XXXIII: 1–20.

———. 2003. "Does Social Capital Generate System Support in Japan?: An Empirical Study of System Support." *Waseda Political Studies* XXXIV: 51–72.

Thompson, Mark R. 1995. *The Anti-Marcos Struggle: Personalistic Rule and Democratic Transition in the Philippines.* New Haven: Yale University Press.

———. 1996. "Off the Endangered List: Philippine Democratization in Comparative Perspective." *Comparative Politics* 28 (2): 179–205.

Thompson, W. Scott. 1992. *The Philippines in Crisis: Development and Security in the Aquino Era 1986–1992.* New York: St. Martin's Press.

Tien, Hung-mao, and Yun-han Chu. 1998. "Building Democracy in Taiwan." In *Contemporary Taiwan*, ed. David Shambaugh, 97–126. New York: Oxford University Press.

Tu, Weiming. 1998. "Epilogue: Human Rights as a Confucian Moral Discourse." In *Confucianism and Human Rights*, ed. William Theodore de Bary and Weiming Tu, 297–307. New York: Columbia University Press.

Unger, Danny. 1998. *Building Social Capital in Thailand.* New York: Cambridge University Press.

United Nations Development Program. 2002. *Human Development Report 2002. Deepening Democracy in a Fragmented World.* New York: Oxford University Press.

Villegas, Bernardo M. 1987. "The Philippines in 1986: Democratic Reconstruction in the Post-Marcos Era." *Asian Survey* 27 (2): 194–205.

Wang, Zhengxu. 2005. "Political Trust in China: Forms and Causes." In *Legitimacy: Ambiguities of Political Success or Failure in East and Southeast Asia*, ed. Lynn T. White, 113–140. Singapore: World Scientific Press.

Watanuki, Joji, Ichiro Miyake, Takashi Inoguchi, and Ikuo Kabashima. 1986. *Nihonjin no senkyo kōdō* [Japanese voting behavior]. Tokyo: University of Tokyo Press.

Watanuki, Joji, and Ichiro Miyake. 1997. *Kankyo hendō to taido henyō* [Environmental changes and attitudinal transformation]. Volume 2 of *Hendō suru Nihonjin no senkyo kōdō* [Changing Japanese voting behavior]. Tokyo: Bokutaku-sha.

Winckler, Edwin A. 1984. "Institutionalization and Participation on Taiwan: From Hard to Soft Authoritarianism?" *The China Quarterly* 99 (September): 481–499.

——. 1992. "Taiwan Transition?" In *Political Change in Taiwan*, ed. Tun-jen Cheng and Stephan Haggard, 221–259. Boulder, CO: Lynne Rienner.

World Bank. 2001. *2001 World Development Indicators*. Washington, D.C.: The World Bank.

——. 2003a. *Philippines Development Policy Update*. Washington, D.C.: The World Bank. http://www.worldbank.org.ph/downloads/DevUpdate2003.pdf.

——. 2003b. *Combating Corruption in the Philippines*. Washington, D.C.: The World Bank. http://wwww.worldbank.org/servlet/WDS_IBank_Servlet?pcont=details&eid =000094946_0006020538276.

Youngblood, Robert L. 1987. "The Corazon Aquino 'Miracle' and the Philippine Churches." *Asian Survey* 27 (12): 1240–1255.

Zakaria, Fareed. 1997. "The Rise of Illiberal Democracy." *Foreign Affairs* 76 (November/December): 22–43.

Zhang, Baohui. 1994. "Corporatism, Totalitarianism, and Transitions to Democracy." *Comparative Political Studies* 27 (1): 108–136.

Zhang, Liang, comp.; Andrew J. Nathan and Perry Link, eds. 2002. *The Tiananmen Papers*. New York: Public Affairs.

CONTRIBUTORS

ROBERT ALBRITTON is professor of political science at the University of Mississippi. His current research focuses on Thai political behavior. His publications are primarily in the areas of public policy analysis, political methodology, and Thai politics and behavior.

THAWILWADEE BUREEKUL is the director of the Research and Development Department, King Prajadhipok's Institute. Her areas of specialization include public policy analysis, public participation, good governance, environmental policy management, and election behavior.

YU-TZUNG CHANG is associate professor of political science at National Taiwan University. He has published articles examining democratization, traditionalism, democratic and authoritarian values, election studies, and identity politics in mainland China, Taiwan, and Hong Kong.

YUN-HAN CHU is distinguished research fellow at the Institute of Political Science, Academia Sinica, and professor of political science at National Taiwan University. His recent publications include *Crafting Democracy in Taiwan* (1992), *Consolidating Third-Wave Democracies* (1997), *China Under Jiang Zemin* (2000), and *The New Chinese Leadership: Challenges and Opportunities after the 16th Party Congress* (2004).

LARRY DIAMOND is a senior fellow at the Hoover Institution and coeditor of the *Journal of Democracy*. Among his books are *Developing Democracy* (1999) and *The Spirit of Democracy* (2007), as well as numerous edited and coedited works on democratic development.

DAMBA GANBAT is the executive director of the Academy of Political Education in Ulaanbaatar, Mongolia. His research interests include democratic transition, human rights, reform of social structure, and elections. He has been project director of the Asian Barometer Survey in Mongolia since 2002.

LINDA LUZ GUERRERO is the vice president/COO and manager, Surveys and Training Group, of Social Weather Stations (SWS). She is project director of all SWS crossnational surveys, including the World Values Survey (since 1995), the Comparative Study of Electoral Systems (since 1998), and the Asian Barometer (since 1999).

KEN'ICHI IKEDA is professor in the Department of Social Psychology, University of Tokyo, and the author or editor of works in Japanese including *Changing Reality of Politics* (1997), *Networking Community* (1997), *Communication* (2000), *Internet Community and Daily Social World* (2005), and *Political Reality and Social Psychology: The Dynamics of the Koizumi Years* (2007).

MASARU KOHNO is professor of political science at Waseda University in Tokyo. He has published numerous books and articles in Japanese on Japanese politics, Japanese foreign policy, and social science theories and methods, including *Japan's Postwar Party Politics* (1997), *Institutions* (2002), and *Experimental Approaches in the Social Sciences* (2007).

HSIN-CHI KUAN is academician, Pontifical Academy of Social Sciences, Vatican, emeritus professor of government and public administration at the Chinese University of Hong Kong, and director of its Universities Service Centre for China Studies. He is an editorial board member of several journals in the China field including the *Journal of Contemporary China*. He has published in *Asian Survey*, *The China Quarterly*, *Democratization*, *Electoral Studies*, and elsewhere.

WAI-MAN LAM is assistant professor at the University of Hong Kong. She is the author of *Understanding the Political Culture of Hong Kong: The Paradox of Activism and Depoliticization* (2004), and coeditor of *Contemporary Hong Kong Politics: Governance in Post-1997 Era* (2007).

ANDREW J. NATHAN is Class of 1919 Professor of Political Science at Columbia University and author or coauthor of *Chinese Democracy* (1985), *The Great Wall and the Empty Fortress: China's Search for Security* (1997), *The Tiananmen Papers* (2001), and *China's New Rulers: The Secret Files* (2003), among other books.

CHONG-MIN PARK is professor of public administration and director of the Survey Research Center, Institute of Governmental Studies, Korea University. He has published articles examining Asian values, social capital, institutional trust, and local governance.

TIANJIAN SHI is associate professor of political science at Duke University and author of *Political Participation in Beijing* (1997). His research has appeared in *World Politics*, *Journal of Politics*, *Comparative Politics*, *Daedalus*, *Asian Survey*, and *China Quarterly*.

DOH CHULL SHIN is professor of political science at the University of Missouri. His recent publications include *Mass Politics and Culture in Democratizing Korea*

(1999), *The Quality of Life in Korea* (2003), and *Economic Transition and Dual Transition in Korea* (2004).

ROLLIN F. TUSALEM is a doctoral student in political science at the University of Missouri at Columbia. He has published articles on consequences of social capital and partisanship for democratization in the *International Political Science Review* and the *Journal of East Asian Studies*.

DAVID DAHUE YANG is an associate political scientist at the RAND Corporation, Washington, D.C. He has contributed articles to various scholarly journals including *World Politics* and *China Economic Review* as well as to edited volumes. He is completing a book entitled *The Social Basis of the Third Wave: Class, Development, and the Making of the Democratic State in East Asia.*

INDEX